W9-BAR-337

THE NICHOLAS EFFECT

A Boy's Gift to the World

Reg Green

O'REILLY®

Beijing · Cambridge · Farnham · Köln · Paris · Sebastopol · Taipei · Tokyo

The Nicholas Effect: A Boy's Gift to the World
by Reg Green

Copyright © 1999 O'Reilly & Associates, Inc. All rights reserved.
Printed in the United States of America. Cover photograph of Nicholas
Green taken by Maggie Green. Photograph of the Green family taken by
Larry Watson.

Published by O'Reilly & Associates, Inc.,
101 Morris Street, Sebastopol, CA 95472.

Editor: Linda Lamb

Production Editor: Claire Cloutier LeBlanc

Cover Art Direction and Design: Kathryn Heflin and Paula Romich

Interior Design: Alicia Cech and Edie Freedman

Photo Gallery: Alicia Cech, Edie Freedman, and Hanna Dyer

The O'Reilly logo is a registered trademark of O'Reilly & Associates, Inc.
Many of the designations used by manufacturers and sellers to distinguish
their products are claimed as trademarks. Where those designations appear in
this book, and O'Reilly & Associates, Inc., was aware of a trademark claim,
the designations have been printed in caps or initial caps.

Library of Congress Cataloging-in-Publication Data

Green, Reg, 1929– .
    The Nicholas effect : a boy's gift to the world / Reg Green.
        p. cm.
    ISBN 1-56592-597-1 (hc: acid-free paper)
    ISBN 1-56592-860-1 (pbk.)
    1. Donation of organs, tissues, etc.—Social aspects. 2. Organ
donors—United States—Biography. 3. Organ donors—Italy—Biography.
I. Title.
RD129.5 .G74 1999
362.1'783—dc21
                            99-22558
                            CIP

To Nicholas

for all that he was,
all that he might have become,
and all that he still is
to his family and friends.

CONTENTS

Once Upon a Time...

"Now let's get this straight," I said to myself. "He was a hero, he was a real person, and we've been in places where he lived. But he wasn't American, he wasn't British, not French, not Roman, not Greek. We've read about him but never met him." Out loud I said what I always regretted. "I give up."

"Bonnie Prince Charlie," said Nicholas, my son, with quiet satisfaction.

"You said he wasn't British."

"No, I said he wasn't English." It was true, that's what he had said. I could have kicked myself. It was the last game he ever played. Two hours later he was shot in the head by car robbers on the road to Sicily and never regained consciousness.

This last win was typical of him. He chose well, answered carefully, and had a lot of fun doing it. He never cheated. He was a joy to play games with.

It seems fitting that this radiant little creature, just seven years old, should have touched the hearts of millions of people all over the world.

Chapter One

A Long Journey Starts

The four-week vacation, the longest we'd ever taken, had been planned for months, a combination of hikes in the Swiss Alps and the color and history of southern Italy. Switzerland was my responsibility and I had a few routes marked out in the guide books. But there's a limit to how much you can anticipate a hike by letting your eyes do the walking.

Not so for the Italian part. Just about every night that summer either Maggie, my wife, or I read stories to Nicholas about the classical world, the other parent going through *The Tales of Amanda Pig* and such with his four-year-old sister, Eleanor. Greek gods, Roman soldiers and ancient buildings, what clothes they wore in Pompeii, how quickly the legions could move, how they kept food cool in hot weather, where they fought, this was the staple fare of those quiet summer nights.

Nicholas thrilled to stories of heroes risking their lives for the common good, was puzzled by the cheap tricks of gods who ought to have known better, and laughed at Cupid's mischief. He was pained by the story of Persephone, imprisoned all winter in the underworld. When the blinded Cyclops ran his hands over the sheep Ulysses and his men were clinging to, I thought he'd burst. He seemed to grasp the meaning underneath the stories: the fatal flaw, the good and bad in us all, life's fragility, but its higher purposes too.

All this was his way of life. His core games were dressing up and doing great deeds as St. George of England, a pioneer on the Oregon Trail, or his most enduring role, Robin Hood. All were supported by the props that imagination and needle and thread could supply. The broom handle was the quarterstaff, the sign of Ye Olde Blue Boar Inn was tacked to the bedroom door, the longbow came from Kmart. Then Robin and Maid Marian—sometimes two Maids Marian—and a pickup group of merry men would set off to conquer evil, often squabbling among themselves about what they would do with it when they met it.

At parties we held, he would put on his best clothes—blue blazer, light-colored shirt, clip-on bow tie—and with a small pad of paper and stumpy pencil take drink orders in illegible writing. On hikes near our home in Bodega Bay, California, we would keep one eye open for sneak attacks by the enemy army or, on the beach, their navy.

Our local library allows thirty books for each card and we had three cards. My memory of the first days of the summer of 1994 is of Maggie bumping up against the borrowing limit with every possible variation on the Italian scene. I was allowed one novel and she got one of those pulp love stories. (Doesn't she get enough romance at home?) For Nicholas and Eleanor, there were a few books like *Cloudy With a Chance of Meatballs*, a story about a town whose food comes with the weather—overcooked broccoli one day, a record-breaking fall of pasta another. But the rest of them were Greek myths for children, Roman history for children, maps of the ancient world for children, junior versions of the *Odyssey* and the *Aeneid*, stories of travels in Sicily, archaeological digs, famous buildings, and picture books of modern Rome.

Maggie found a Roman cookbook and we planned a banquet, but none us could stomach the fish with honey dish. Nicholas only consented to eat at all that night when we told him spaghetti was Julius Caesar's favorite meal. My main concern was overdue fines: think of ninety times twenty-five cents a day. The reading itself was a delight. We read to the children, read to ourselves, swapped tales over meals. On one long car journey we took that year, Nicholas wanted so many stories read to him from *D'Aulaire's Book of Greek Myths* that my spells as a passenger in the back seat with him are a complete haze. But not, as it happens, to him. Weeks afterward he would remind me, for example, that the echo we heard was a girl who had talked too much and been punished by only being able to repeat other people's words.

We all loved traveling. I've done a lot on my own, and as a family we'd walked on volcanic craters in California and the Icefields Parkway in Alberta, seen waterfalls as different as Niagara and Frank Lloyd Wright's Fallingwater, canoed in Canada and rafted in Idaho, seen Indian rain dances in New Mexico and immigrants' toys on Ellis Island, and spent long, sticky days in both Disney World and Disneyland. In Europe, Nicholas had stormed the invasion beaches in Normandy, hiked on the shoulder of the Matterhorn, visited Sleeping Beauty's Castle in the Loire Valley, and climbed with us (when no one was looking) to the top of the lighthouse on the extreme northwest tip of Scotland, the area where my mother's ancestors, the McKays, have lived since the Middle Ages.

But of all places abroad, he liked Italy best—the theatricality of the settings, its exuberance, and its uninhibited love of children. For his age, he'd seen a lot of it. He'd splashed in the sea at Portofino, taken walks around the melodramatic peaks of the Dolomites, and got his socks wet in Lake Maggiore. He'd tramped around Pisa and Florence and Verona. We'd all been together in Asolo, the hill town where Browning wrote "God's in his Heaven, all's right with the world," and I'd say that for us, sitting under the awning of a restaurant on that hot, still day, and chatting quietly amongst ourselves, it was the literal truth. He'd marched around the giant chessboard in the town square at Marostica, where people dress sumptuously as knights and castles and pawns to reenact classic games. At six years old, he was silenced by the power of the mosaics in Ravenna. He always said his favorite city was Venice—after Bodega Bay. But this was the first time he had been as far south as Rome, and with a mind crammed with gods and heroes, he was on edge to see it all.

This pint-sized classical education didn't have some of the practical results I'd hoped for. His room remained messier than the Aegean stable. He continued to watch far more television than we'd have liked, was frequently exasperated by his sister, and wouldn't eat his crusts. To the end, he resolutely refused to widen his diet beyond his basic likes—bread and butter, plain spaghetti with Parmesan cheese, carrots, water, and vanilla ice cream, with salami and pâté thrown in for balance, and very, very little else.

The learning, however, went deep. Nicholas loved the thought of striding along Roman roads, bringing back the Golden Fleece, and playing with the idea that thunder and lightning were Zeus getting mad at somebody. Staying high up in the Alps on the first part of the vacation and walking through the early snows, we were mountain folk, never conquered by Rome, proud of our traditions, such as—my idea—not whining when it rained. On visits to the valley, in the once-Roman town of Martigny, with its ruined walls and reconstructed amphitheater, we reverted to being Roman soldiers due to return to Italy in a few days at the end of our military service.

That return was one of the high spots of the vacation, a sleeping car from Geneva to Rome, rushing through Italy overnight. At one point, I awoke to find the train in a station and, peering through the window, made out the name: Domodossola. The Frontier! "We're in Italy," I whispered in case anyone was awake. In the darkness, I fancied I heard a sleepy, contented sigh from Nicholas' bunk.

It's true the reality did not put us immediately into Elysian fields. On the first and only day he spent in Rome, there were the usual tired feet, elusive bathrooms, and a long search for Super Mario ice cream. But the paved roads at the very start of their journey to the ends of the earth, the triumphal arches with tales of victories in mysterious lands, and the soaring columns, looking vulnerable to a strong wind yet standing through centuries, all worked their spell on an imagination eager to be spellbound.

The next day, we picked up the little rental car at the railroad station, filling in forms we couldn't understand, including two insurance policies, one for damage, the other for theft. We got off to an early start and spent the afternoon among the ghosts of Pompeii, Nicholas serving us with a make-believe meal at the counter of an ancient fast-food store decorated with a picture of his favorite Mercury. If there was a sign that the next night the messenger of the gods would carry his story to the four corners of the world, I missed it.

We stayed overnight in a small hotel in Positano, which hung from the cliff (333 steps up that interminable flight of steps, wasn't it?) above the Mediterranean. We had a wonderfully happy meal by the quayside, local seafood, local wine, local fruit for us, some of the same for Eleanor, plain spaghetti and Parmesan cheese for him. He loved it. Then a quick bet: how many steps did we come down? His guess, wildly inaccurate, meant we had to count each one going back up and no mistakes allowed. Maggie, naturally, had come closest. I, as usual, tried to cheat, changing my guess when it became clear how far off I was and being scolded by everyone. I cried when the winner was announced. Even an endless flight of stairs was fun. I really regret being unsure of that number now: he would be disappointed by such sloppiness.

On the last day of his life, I had just eaten breakfast on the small balcony when he came out of the bedroom, dressed in pajama pants, hair ruffled, sleep in his eyes. "Hello, Daddy," he said drowsily. "Hello, little boy. Close your eyes and come and have a look at this." He screwed his eyes extravagantly shut and I guided him onto the balcony. "Now look." We'd arrived in the dark the night before, so this was his first clear view of the cliff we were on, dropping sheer to the sea, the mountains behind stretching high above us. "There's the restaurant we went to last night—let's see, what did you have for dinner? It wasn't the octopus, was it? Or the fishhead stew? Oh, now I remember, spaghetti and Parmesan cheese." Later, Maggie took the children to the beach and they came back with the exact tally of the stairs, happy to prove yet again that my estimate was hopelessly wrong. "But Daddy, I have something to tell you," Nicholas added eagerly. "When I was in the water, some of the sea splashed on my face. When I licked it off, it tasted really good. So, there's another thing I like." We added the Mediterranean to the meager list of foods he would eat and decided he was well on the way to becoming an epicure.

Late in the morning, we set off for Paestum, site of some of the best-preserved Greek temples anywhere, a place, fittingly, at the intersection of heaven and earth. The journey was a series of improvisations, detours to avoid bottlenecks, lunch by the side of the road at one of scores of possible pull-ins, a last-minute decision not to visit a view we'd read about, dozens and dozens of apparently random choices. When Maggie and Nicholas were on their own for a few minutes at Paestum, they saw four white doves, symbols in that place of message carriers from the gods. When two of them flew away, she told him it reminded her of children leaving home and, thinking of that far-off day, gave him a special hug.

He gave us one last example of the lessons he'd learned that summer, the dual names, Greek and Roman, of the classical gods. Inside the biggest temple, the core of the pantheon, he announced, "Look, I'm Zeus." Then running outside, onto Italian soil, "Now, I'm Jupiter." Even then it was a memorable moment. Now it has a touch of divinity about it.

CHAPTER TWO

ATTACK ON THE ROAD

Over the previous weeks, we'd discussed the next stage of the journey, the choices being to travel a few hours and stay overnight or to go right through to Palermo in Sicily, where we would be staying for the next ten days. It wasn't much of a decision. We had habitually traveled long distances at night in both the United States and Europe since the children were born so as not to eat into vacation time. They slept comfortably and were generally well rested when we reached our destination, and we avoided the drag of a long journey through the daylight hours, everyone awake and impatient to be there. We were on the Salerno-Reggio di Calabria autostrada, the only main route south from northern Europe to Sicily, a limited-access divided highway, well engineered and well used day and night.

Did I know there was anything to worry about? Like everyone, I had heard stories of the Mafia in Sicily, pickpockets in Naples, elaborately planned thefts of anything from wallets to cars. I had spoken to friends who knew the south, asked at the Italian tourist office, told hotel keepers what we planned to do. The response, whoever gave it, and whatever language they used, generally amounted to the same advice: petty crime is rife and tourists are vulnerable. Be as careful as you can and, if you are robbed, be philosophical about it. None of this added up to murderous attacks on innocent travelers. As far as I knew, the most dangerous feature of the road we were on was the possibility of an accident and, by driving carefully, I thought I could minimize that.

Leaving Paestum, as usual the last visitors to go, we repacked the car, clearing the back seat and stuffing clothes into the pillowcases we'd brought for the children. We drove along, playing a few car games, talking about what we'd seen that day and what lay ahead. It was a perfectly normal scene, something I'd done dozens of times: cars overtaking or being overtaken, trucks laboring up steep hills or crowding the rearview mirror on the downslopes, bunches of traffic in places, quiet patches in between.

By now we were in Calabria, the toe of Italy. The children were fast asleep, their small heads resting peacefully on their makeshift pillows at both ends of the back seat. We decided to pull into a rest area so we could close our eyes too, but immediately saw it wouldn't do. There were several trucks and lots of cars, one with the radio playing loudly, and people lounging around in the warm air. "We can't get any sleep here," I said. "Let's go on. I'm not tired, really."

As we set off, Maggie closed her eyes and was soon asleep. I took it easy so as not to waken anyone. A few miles farther, I noticed something in the rearview mirror that looked quite ordinary at first glance, a car coming up behind us. It came closer and closer and for the first time I felt a quiver of uneasiness. Cars overtaking in Italy move out a long way behind and come by fast. This one was getting too close. It came nearer still, and I remember saying quietly to myself, "There's something wrong here."

At that moment, it pulled out into the overtaking lane and I breathed a sigh of relief. Nothing wrong after all. Then, a split second later, instead of pulling away it was running alongside us. Now I spoke aloud: "Something's happening." Maggie woke immediately, just as from the other car came the sound of loud, angry voices, a deep-throated menacing roar, the words indistinguishable, but clearly ordering us to stop. Maggie leaned forward, looked across at them, and then sat back in her seat. That may have saved her life.

In the next sliver of time, all the things I'd thought about violent crime came rushing into my mind. "Don't resist, they just want your money." "Keep calm. It'll all pass soon." "They can't mean it: they're just trying to frighten you." But overriding everything was the sound of those savage threatening voices and the conclusion: "Once we are in their power they can do anything they like—kill us all, kidnap the children, take Maggie." Out of the corner of my eye, I saw the hood of their car, next to ours, and noticed what appeared to be spots of rust or dirt. A thought ran through my mind, "It looks like an older car than ours. We can probably outdistance them." I held the wheel tight, in case they tried to force us off the road, and fixed my eyes on the road ahead.

"We can't stop," I said to Maggie. "We have to get away." As usual, she didn't try to second-guess. I was at the wheel and she left the decision to me. I pressed the accelerator and the voices roared out again. By now we were picking up speed. I saw the speedometer crawl up. Come on, come on, maybe we can do it.

A moment later, all hopes of an easy way out disappeared. An explosion blew out the side window by the back seat. Until then, I didn't know they had guns. Now I did and there were another few seconds to change the decision. Even as the thought came, I dismissed it: "People as reckless as this aren't going to stop at anything. We've got to outrun them." By now we were traveling fast and still accelerating.

At that moment there was another explosion, and the side window where I was driving disintegrated. The bullet must have missed Maggie and me by an inch or two. There was no question any more. These weren't warning shots. Now, however, we were definitely pulling away, and to an onset of relief I saw them falling farther and farther behind until, from being next to us, I saw their lights in my driving mirror. "They've dropped back," I said. I felt safer, but who knew if they might not come again. Maggie looked back at the children, both apparently fast asleep, while I kept my foot on the floor. We sped through the night, on our own again.

In all this time, I had never looked at the attackers. All my concentration had been on getting the last ounce of speed out of that strong-hearted little car. It's difficult to sort out the flood of emotions at that stage. I wasn't shaking, for example, and my hands had been steady on the wheel throughout. Frightened, certainly, but not terrified. Perhaps it was all too unreal, another of Italy's theatrical displays. Astounded perhaps comes closest and now, of course, mightily relieved. Neither of us, I think, was even angry. Perhaps we were just in shock. Maggie wryly summed up the mood of the moment, "Now I suppose the two insurance companies will be arguing for the next six months whether this is car damage or theft."

Just about then Eleanor, on the back seat, woke up for a moment, saying she was cold: the wind was rushing in through the blown-out windows and we were still traveling full out. Maggie put some clothes around her and glanced again at Nicholas, sound asleep as usual. We drove on, looking for a filling station, somewhere with bright lights and people, and a telephone to call the police. As it happened, before we reached one, we came across a serious accident, with police already there and an ambulance at the side of the road. I stopped despite the loud protests of a young policeman controlling traffic, intending to show him the blown-out windows. As I opened the car door and the light came on, we both looked at Nicholas. He didn't move. His tongue was sticking out a little, and he had a trace of vomit on his chin. Maggie cried out in horror and called to the policeman. He looked casually inside the car for a moment, then, horrified too, he ran distractedly, shouting, shouting continuously, to the police car twenty yards back along the road.

Eleanor, frightened and confused, wanted to know what was happening. Maggie picked her up and held her tight. "Nicholas has been shot," she replied, quiet again. "We're going to get him to the hospital." In all the time since then, I can't remember an occasion when she has raised her voice about any aspect of this affair. The ambulance men didn't ask any questions. "Wait a minute," I called and found the little shred of sheepskin Nicholas had taken to bed almost every night of his life. "He won't feel comfortable if he wakes up and doesn't find this," I told an attendant. There was no common language, but he understood and placed it gently on the stretcher next to the little pale face. The ambulance took off at high speed, and we were told to wait to tell the police what had happened.

A driver who had stopped at the accident to see if he could help offered to take us to the hospital. "Your car has to stay here," he explained. We climbed in, numb with anxiety, and turning off the autostrada drove ten, twenty miles on dark, winding, slow roads. With only a few words of English, this quiet pious man tried to quiet our fears, repeating over and over, "It's all right. You'll see." Then, searching for some more tangible reassurance, he said, "You aren't Catholic, I know, but this will help," and handed us his rosary. His name was

Giuseppe Ioppolo, but to Maggie he was the Good Samaritan and that is what we have called him ever since. On the back seat of the car, and sitting close together, Maggie explained to Eleanor as simply as possible what had happened. In a tiny voice, Eleanor asked if Nicholas would get better. It was a question that could neither be ducked nor answered, and we said only that the doctors would do everything they could.

At last we drove into the parking lot of a small hospital. All the floodlights were turned on, and in their glare what looked like the entire medical staff was grouped in total silence in a semicircle around the open back of an ambulance. I looked in, hoping against hope they were waiting for some other patient. But inside, his face newly washed, looking just as he did when he went to bed, was Nicholas. The one hope I'd clung to was that he'd been hit by a glancing blow that had knocked him out. Seeing now that they hadn't treated him, I knew it must be as bad as I'd feared. The head doctor explained gently that they were sending him to the nearest big hospital, in Messina, Sicily, because he was too seriously wounded for them to deal with. I've never known such bleakness.

We were driven to a police station filled with large strong men, apparently as stunned as the doctors. We pieced together the shocked whispers. "A child has been shot...He's badly hurt...He's being taken to Messina." And when the head of the police unit took our statements, it was with a quiet solicitousness that belied his military bearing. It was now after 11:00 p.m., and he had with him a professor from the local college who had been telephoned at home to come in and help with the language. He spoke English fluently, removing that terrible feeling of helplessness when trying to describe something precisely in a foreign language. But it took a long, long time, trying to remember every detail that might prove useful, anxious not to be too definite about what was hazy, but not too vague either or to leave out something important. Everything had to be translated, read back to us and signed, while all the time Nicholas was being taken farther and farther away.

The Good Samaritan had applied the spiritual comfort. Now the police officers in that little Calabrian town, whose names we didn't bother to ask—what did it matter?—searched for practical ways to help, bringing cup after cup of water and, when we left, pressing on us half a loaf, a knife, and some homemade marmalade.

A police car took us back to the still-busy autostrada—it was a shock to see everything looking so normal—and onto the ferry for the short crossing to Sicily. Only a handful of passengers were onboard, but it was clear from the hushed tones everyone knew something dreadful had happened. Every now and then someone would come in from another part of the boat, look at us for a moment or two, and then leave. Maggie sat with Eleanor on her lap, and I lay down on the hard bench, feeling cold and empty. We'd all looked forward to this crossing, its history full of wars and wrecks and monsters. Now one half of me wanted just to get it over with as quickly as possible, the other half for it to go on and on, to push away whatever news was waiting for us on the other side. The police had assured us a car would be waiting on the quay. I was surprised to find it there, but that was the last time I doubted their word. The police in Italy are widely criticized, but with us they were models of attentiveness and efficiency.

As we docked, a flutter of hope started up. Suppose the decision of the small hospital was just precautionary. Suppose the much bigger hospital had facilities that would reveal a less serious situation. Children can have recoveries that seem miraculous: their little bodies are so adaptable. "Do you know children Nicholas' age have been known to grow a new finger?" Maggie said as we docked. "Even if he's very badly hurt, he could recover." Please, please, someone, let it be.

The signs were against it. The police car drove us to the hospital, the Policlinico, and stopped at a door marked *Rianimazione*, literally, reanimation. The waiting room hushed as we entered. We were taken immediately into a bare room with perhaps a dozen doctors and nurses, all waiting for us, all absolutely still. Maggie was offered a chair, a bad sign, she felt. Eleanor, tired and bewildered, but proud and straight-backed, sat on her lap. The chief surgeon introduced himself. Without preamble he said simply, "The situation is very dramatic." The small shoots of hope withered away.

The bullet had lodged at the stem of the brain, the base from which all the main functions are controlled. It was too deep to operate on. The only hope was that his condition would stabilize and that in time they might be able to do something. The only thing for us to do, they said, was to go to bed, keep as strong as possible, and check back the next day.

The police had reserved a room at a nearby hotel, and as we were driven there I don't think I have ever felt I was in a more alien environment. I wanted only to go home, take Nicholas with us, however badly damaged, help nurse him through whatever he faced, hold his hand again, put my arms around him. I knew without asking that Maggie felt the same way. It was the worst night of my life. Overriding everything was the dullness of a terrible loss to come, a void that could never be filled. But underneath was a nagging, recurrent accusation. "You led him into this danger. You should have known better. He trusted you and you let him down."

CHAPTER THREE

DEATH AND A DECISION

The next morning, we caught a bus to the hospital. There had been no change, no improvement, but no deterioration either. With a shock, we saw him through the glass of a special room, tubes and monitors all over his pale face. "You know, there are miracles," said the man who had been appointed to act as an interpreter. They wouldn't let us go in to him, however. He needed rest, they said. Maggie found this hard to take, and asked firmly but quietly to speak to someone who could give permission for her to sit with him. Nothing could be done that day, they told us. Perhaps tomorrow. The visit, far from easing our minds, had only made us feel worse.

The police were shocked to find we had come by bus. A high-level officer, told of our arrival at the hospital, rushed out there to say that as long as we were there a police car would be on twenty-four-hour-a-day duty to take us anywhere. We began to see we were not alone. We filled in forms—in Italian, but with everyone's help we managed—and were asked about his medical history. That was easy. He didn't have any. Until a few hours before, he was in perfect health. Now, even if he lived, his life was shattered.

Back at the hotel it was clear something had changed: there were police officers in the lobby, reporters and cameramen outside. First one journalist, then another, came up to express sorrow and ask for details.

All seemed baffled by our account. "On the autostrada itself? A private car? You really were moving at the time, not stopped somewhere? Your child was with you in the car when you were attacked?" By now the plainclothes police had arrived. They said they knew what we had been through and would wait as long as they could for us to feel better, but they must talk to us sometime to discuss the police report sent from Calabria. I told them I'd do it right away. They said I was very brave. I said—to myself, how could I explain to them?—that what was happening to that little boy was so overwhelmingly more important than anything else that nothing anyone could do could make it worse.

We went through the details again, with the help of a fluent interpreter, and they said things I remembered being asked when we made our statements the night before. Did I do business with anyone in Italy? One of my jobs was editing a newsletter. Did it ever cover Italian affairs? Did anyone know we were on that road last night? I became aware that, like the Calabrian police, these people could not comprehend an unprovoked attack on a small private car. They were groping for some other explanation. In the following days, this pattern of questions was repeated over and over: Was I sure I hadn't written about Italy? Did no one know of our movements? Had we gone into one of the cafés on the autostrada and shown our American money?

I took a deep breath and asked, "Is this kind of incident rare?" The reaction was absolute. "In my entire experience, I have never known anything like this," the ranking detective replied. "Please ask again?" I said through the interpreter. "Have I understood you? Does this sort of thing happen from time to time?" "I know of no similar case to yours," the answer came back emphatically.

As a newspaper reporter, I'd learned people characteristically give at least two kinds of misleading answers to hard questions: first, the one they want you to believe about them and, second, the one they think you want to hear. In this case, there would be an obvious temptation for them to downplay the dangers and no one, I guessed, would willingly tell a grief-stricken father he should have known better. So I did what I would have done as a reporter. From then on, I asked every knowledgeable person I met if the road we took was dangerous: our police interpreters, the detectives who arrived from Rome, the doctors in the intensive care unit, journalists, businessmen, traveling salespeople. Every one of them seemed flabbergasted.

It's true, they said, this is a crime-ridden area. It's professional crime, however. Trucks are regularly hijacked, the merchandise disappears, but the truck drivers are not normally hurt. "It's a lucrative business: organized crime is not going to risk a public backlash by unnecessary violence," they explained. Still not content, I read everything I could in the newspapers with the help of our interpreters. The media know better than anyone what is unusual. This was a front-page story from the start, not in just the local papers, but the nationals too. Searching for a precedent, *La Sicilia* found nothing that came close. Its top-of-the-page headline on page one read, "Calabria Wild West."

Since then, I have driven on that section of the autostrada a score of times, day and night. Anyone traveling any distance on the west coast of Italy has to use it. In the end, the only theory the police took seriously was that our car was mistaken for one thought to be delivering a cargo of jewelry, a case of mistaken identity that raised what happened to Nicholas to a new level of tragic absurdity.

I had made another decision that night, to drive on when told to stop. Again I asked everyone what I should have done. Here the answers were more ambivalent. Many shrugged their shoulders: how can you tell? When pressed to say what they would do, almost all said, "I'd have done what you did." Clearly, however, their views were colored by wanting to shield me from self-reproach. So here I have been thrown back on my own thoughts.

Every moment of it remains perfectly vivid. The car coming up and puzzlingly keeping pace instead of overtaking, then the shock of those voices filling the night. What would have happened if we'd stopped? They might have taken everything we had and left us stranded: it would have been terrible at the time, but soon we'd have been over it and probably found something in it to laugh about. But what instead if they had been vicious? Once we stopped, we would be completely at their mercy. What happened from then on would be what they decided. They could be easygoing with us or brutal, but we would have no say. Michele Iannello, one of the men later accused of the killing, admitted to murdering four other people. Whoever fired the shots that night, it shows the kind of values we might have had to deal with. If, worst of all, we'd stopped after the first shot and together found Nicholas hit in the head, I find it hard to believe that men who hold life so cheaply would have left any witnesses.

Long before any arrests had been made, Tony, one of our many police interpreters, told me, "The people who did this are loners. They are probably on drugs. They are completely unpredictable. You may just say the wrong thing or they may think you'll recognize them again. Then they can do whatever they want with you." It's the kind of informed response that helped me, then and since. But, of course, it will trouble me to my dying day.

That night, a man called the hotel and falteringly said he was an American born in Italy on a visit to his birthplace. "We've been watching the television, Mr. Green. I'm so sorry, so very sorry. My wife and I can't sleep for thinking about you and your family." His voice choked into a sob. Deflated too, I forgot to make a proper note of his name. If he reads this, I want him to know how often I've thought of him: he was the first person who let me see that all over Italy people were praying for the little American boy to make it.

After that, however, the signs were unmistakable. When Eleanor looked out of our bedroom window, she was immediately photographed. A crowd of reporters followed when we went to the hospital. Almost always, they asked in such a restrained manner if we'd mind being interviewed that I could see what pitiful figures we had become. This turned out to be an important moment. We had the option of saying no, and I think everyone would have understood. From the start, however, we had taken the view that the more that came out about the story, the better it would be for everyone. If that road was dangerous, it should be known. If any of the details of our story helped catch the attackers, how could we hold back? Those interviews in the hospital parking lot, on the steps of the police station or in the crowded lobby of the Hotel Europa set the pattern for all that followed: it was the genesis of "the Nicholas effect."

So from the beginning, besides giving the press all the details of the attack we could remember, we dredged our memories to think of stories to tell about Nicholas, things he'd said, the books he liked, the songs he sang. A photographer asked if we had a photo of Nicholas with us. We didn't, but Maggie remembered we had taken some pictures in Switzerland which were still in the camera. "Can I take them, develop them, and bring you the negatives back?" he asked. He flashed a soiled ID which meant nothing to me. "You know how important they are to us," I said. I didn't need to labor the point: these were the last pictures we'd taken. We might never get another chance. "You can trust me, Mr. Green," he said with a quiet certainty. I fetched the undeveloped film. One of the police escort joined us. "Are you sure you want to do this?" he asked. "He knows how important they are," I replied. I squeezed the roll, as I might have squeezed a child's hand before he went off with a stranger, and handed it over.

Later that night, he came back with the negatives, half a dozen prints, and a handshake that said, "You see, I didn't let you down." That night too the photographs that accompanied Nicholas' story went around the world, putting a face and a personality on an otherwise anonymous tragedy. None of this added up to the complete Nicholas, of course, but it was a thumbnail sketch and it made readers and viewers feel they knew a little more about him, reminding them too of their own children. Nor was it all fanciful. We received scores of letters that spoke of the level gaze and quizzical smile, the gentle nature and honesty we knew so well.

In one of these curbside press conferences, we answered a few routine questions, then Maggie was asked something out of the blue that proved to be seminal. "What would you say to the men who shot your child?" True to herself, as always, she said, "When they see what they have done, I hope they will turn away from this kind of life." It was done with such simplicity and conviction that tears sprang to my eyes. The effect on the press was electrifying. I don't think I have ever seen a group of reporters so moved.

We were driven to the hospital where the news was what we'd been dreading. His condition had worsened during the night. His body was still strong, but his brain was beginning to give up the struggle. We took turns to sit with him for a few minutes while the other one stayed with Eleanor, but it was a grim business. In those days I had not yet become a U.S. citizen, and Richard Brown, the thoughtful and attentive British honorary consul, met us at the hotel. He was immediately thrown into translating questions from the press, who were out in greater force than ever, and we were asked again to go over every detail of the shooting as though some vital piece might have been left out.

While we were there, the hotel clerk approached softly, "There's a lady here who says she would like just to say something to you. She doesn't want to bother you, but she's been waiting quite a long time." I turned to see the tear-stained face of a beautiful, youthful woman and her young daughter. "I'm nobody," she said. "Just a mother. But I wanted to say how sorry we are, Mr. Green." I put my arms around her and we wept together. Then, still crying, she asked her daughter to hand me a stuffed animal and a huge box of chocolates for Eleanor.

That was the first of a series of presents, dozens of hugs, and some thousands of shared tears over the next few days. The hallways of the hotel always seemed to be filled with people, some of whom just smiled sadly at us from a distance or shook hands without a word. The Profumo family, whose apartment we had planned to take over for our vacation, came in all the way from Palermo, not once but twice. They didn't speak English, they just wanted to sit with us. Italy was beginning to enfold us in its arms.

The end came dully. We were called to the hospital, and the chief neurologist said in a flat voice, "I have bad news. We can find no sign of brain activity." What does this mean? "He is brain dead." Is there any hope? "I don't believe there is any hope at all. However, we will do another test to be sure." A half hour or so passed while we sat and held hands in that sunny room, silent and oppressed. Then the result of the scan was brought in: there was still no activity. He had died, like one of his classical heroes, on the shores of the straits of Messina, and I knew I would never be really happy again.

A few more moments passed as we struggled to come to grips with what had happened. Then one of us—we don't remember which, though, knowing her, I'd guess Maggie—looked at the other and asked, "Now that he's gone, shouldn't we give his organs?" "Yes," said the other and that's all there was to it. We told the doctors and they explained the procedure, which seemed clear and simple. We signed the forms and left. It was the least difficult major decision either of us has ever had to make: the boy we knew was not in that body any more.

Italy, however, saw it differently and a second electric charge seemed to go through our still-growing band of press contacts. We had thought it was a purely private decision, but when we arrived back at the hotel from the hospital, the press already knew. Until then, the questions had been about the attack. Now, in public, organ donation dominated everything else.

Not in private, however. Early the next morning, one of the hotel staff pushed a telegram under the door. It was a message of condolence and offer of help from a charitable association in Italy with ties to the United States. The name caught at my heart: the Robin Hood

Foundation. The words on the paper made official what last night's dreams had feared but shied away from. It was true after all. We had lost our own Robin Hood forever.

We switched on the television set in our little hotel room in Messina to find out if there was any news about the killing and saw a strange sight, hospital staff loading ice coolers onto ambulances. "It's Nicholas," said Maggie quietly, and so it was. His pure heart and the rest of his organs were going off into the night to bring relief to seven people and their families. It was another wrenching moment, but it wasn't horrifying. To us Nicholas was not a collection of organs, but what he had always been, a generous, loving, and intelligent boy, and now deeper inside us, in our hearts, our memories, in everything we do, than ever before. A day or two later, I even managed to say to Maggie, "I thought they were carrying the drinks for the hospital picnic." "So did I," she smiled. But even then we had no idea of the human results those little boxes would bring.

Within a few hours we received a message from the mayor of Rome, expressing his sympathy and gratitude. From this we learned the heart had gone to a Roman boy, Andrea Mongiardo, who had spent half his life in the hospital. At age fifteen he was scarcely bigger than Nicholas at seven. The liver was for Maria Pia Pedalà, a nineteen-year-old from Sicily, who was in her final coma when Nicholas died. "We'd given up on her," one of her doctors said when we met him later. "You really did save her life." The kidneys went to Anna Maria Di Ceglie, fourteen years old, a tiny bright-eyed vivacious girl, and Tino Motta, age ten, the youngest of the seven, a manly little boy, whose lives had been ruled by dialysis machines and whose families lived in a state of suppressed fear. "Think of something nice," the doctors said when Tino was wheeled into the operating room. "I am," he said. "I'm thinking of Nicholas." The pancreas cells went to Silvia Ciampi, from Rome, whose long fight with diabetes had ravaged her health and happiness. The corneas were for two Sicilians: Domenica Galletta, who had been waiting for five years for a transplant and had never seen her baby's face clearly, and Francesco Mondello, once a keen rugby player and father of a young active family, whose world was gradually darkening.

That night, these people were still just statistics to us. But knowing what we do now of the agony they had gone through, it's clear to me that if we had made a different decision, nursed our grief and shrugged off their troubles as none of our concern, we could never have looked back without a deep sense of shame.

From the start, and quite instinctively, both Maggie and I wanted to minimize the horror of it for Eleanor, but not its seriousness. As it happened, we had little choice about the seriousness: she saw Nicholas through glass in a hospital bed, his face covered with tubes. The stream of people who came to the hotel all looked solemn or tearful. In visits to the hospital, even the tone of the clinical talk must have made its meaning clear.

At all times, whenever she asked, we tried to tell her exactly what was happening. "Is Nicholas going to die?" she asked once in a break-ing voice. It was a question I'd been asking myself from the beginning, and I knew I had to answer it for her the way I was answering it for myself, "We don't know, dear. Those doctors we saw today are giving him all the help they can. And all those nurses are helping too. We must just keep hoping." I tried not to dramatize it or cling to her too closely, but I put my arm around her, hoping she wouldn't see my tears.

More and more visitors arrived—the police, political leaders, the media, sympathizers—a generous procession, but an additional source of confusion for her. Among them, however, was someone Maggie had asked the hospital to assign to us, a doctor who spoke English well enough to act as an interpreter, but who was fluent in medicine too. She turned out to be Alessandra Barraco, who had an understanding that inspired confidence from the start. Better still, she won over Eleanor as instantly as she had won us and when she suggested a trip to the beach, Eleanor beamed with pleasure. As it happened, they were away when Nicholas died, and we were glad to be on our own to take the blow.

When Eleanor came home that day, she jumped into Maggie's arms, but smiled happily at her memories of the swimming and ice cream and the games she played at Alessandra's apartment. We took her up to the room and sat on the bed with her and told her Nicholas had died. The happiness drained from her face. "Won't I ever see him again?" she asked quickly. "Nicholas is an angel now. He'll always be with us, all of us," Maggie told her. "He'll always love you and you'll always love him. You can think about him any time you want to."

We went to the hospital and they asked if we would like to see him. "Can I come to say good-bye?" Eleanor asked. "I wonder if we should?" I said to Maggie. "It might frighten her." "You know, the unknown is so much more difficult to deal with than the known. I think she should come if she wants to," Maggie replied. I saw at once that she was right. It was a chilling experience, another blow to steel ourselves against, but now more than ever I'm sure it was the correct decision.

That afternoon, as the three of us huddled close together in the back of a police car, Eleanor asked in a barely audible voice, "Can I have another brother?" It pierced the heart. "I don't know," I told her. "It's too early to think about, but…" and a new thought formed…"but I do know we can have a kitten." It was something she and Nicholas had been talking about for months, but which I'd resisted because of the traveling we always seemed to be doing. Her eyes opened wide. "Can we? Oh, yes. What color is it? What's its name? What does it eat? Where will it sleep?" As we talked about this kitten and everything it would do, sunshine came back for a while into that little face that had gone through so much.

Back at the hotel was a message from the owner of the Syracusan, a large department store in Messina, offering to supply the clothes Nicholas would be buried in. She is known, appropriately, as Lady Syracusan for her good works and, with Eleanor helping, we found what we needed. So Nicholas is dressed for eternity in a blue blazer and slacks, just as he dressed at home when he wanted to look his best. There was no tie like the grown-up ones he wore, but there was one with Goofy on it and that seemed right too. On our final visit to the hospital, I slipped a 500 lira coin in his pocket so he could pay the ferryman to cross the River Styx, the final curtain of the game we'd been playing those past few months.

We gave away the clothes he'd taken on vacation to the Little Sisters of the Poor, where we met Mother Imelda, an Irish nun, bursting with vitality and high spirits, despite working with some of the poorest people in Sicily. Their home is next door to the Messina brewery and she pressed a beer on me, just about the first break from the bread and marmalade we'd lived on for three days. It somehow reminded me that life would go on.

The diversion with Alessandra was the only time I can remember one of us not being with Eleanor until we got back home: we felt we had to convey at all times a feeling of safety and love so that not a moment's doubt would come to her that she could depend on us. She was with us when we met the president and prime minister of Italy and the mayor of Rome. She was there for presentations and press conferences and speeches, quiet but receptive, as her memories later showed. A few weeks afterward, an acquaintance told me, "Your wife must have a very strong back. I've never seen a picture of her without your daughter in her arms."

That's Maggie's style. She listened attentively to all that was said to us from the first moments of the tragedy, through police statements and heartbreaking doctors' reports and affecting meetings with some of the most influential men in Italy. She was interviewed by the world's press, made a decision about Nicholas' body that was to influence millions of people, and said good-bye to her only son. But in that time she had never stopped thinking about Eleanor's needs. It's the daily miracle of motherhood.

Even at times of great turbulence, we all go on making decisions, both mundane and far-reaching. When death comes, there are other family members to inform, funeral arrangements to make. Mothers may have to find someone to drive the children to school, fathers change business schedules. You can be emptied by these preoccupations, but they have to be done. For the 15,000 American families every year with a loved one who suffers brain death, one of those decisions is whether to give the organs to someone else. For some it is an easy choice, for others heart-wrenching, but each year 5,000 families in lonely hospital rooms do decide in favor. Many more donate tissues—corneas, bone, skin, ligaments, and so on—which can be done in cases other than brain death.

Most of them, I suppose, feel much as we did. We would have done anything to have kept Nicholas alive. But he was no longer in a coma: he was dead. That beautiful body was of no further use to him, and nothing we did to it could hurt him in any way conceivable to us. It could still help others, however, and far from disfiguring him, that gift, like that of all donors, transformed his earthly self into a symbol of sharing life rather than hoarding it. As I went into the room to say good-bye, the first thing I saw on his pale face were his freckles. "I wish they could have used those," I thought.

Nor was it really a spur-of-the-moment decision. When I think back to what came to mind when I saw we had this option, I don't think of the shudder that went through me when I realized his calm regular breathing, which for a moment had seemed so hopeful, was dependent on a clever machine. Nor of the brain scans showing that his mind, once filled with brightly colored fancies and high ideals, was now quite empty.

I suppose you could say the choice had been made for me twenty years before he was born. It was then that Dr. Christiaan Barnard was conducting his tenuous operations on heart patients in South Africa. I remember talking about them to a doctor friend who was concerned that the sensational effect would divert attention from mass killers like cancer or tuberculosis. I thought the objection prosaic. "Those things are on a different level," I remember saying. "This is like going to the moon."

Although I can never remember discussing it with Maggie or paying anything more than casual attention to the subject over the intervening years, nothing changed my views either. Transplantation was a leap of the human spirit that transcended mere numbers. Death we know has a necessary purpose, replacing the old and infirm with fresh life. But in its clumsy way death gathers up spring flowers too. Transplantation meant we were no longer at the mercy of this arbitrariness. We had a say in the outcome.

Chapter Four

A Nation Grieves

Although we know much more now than we did then about the low rates of organ and tissue donation in Italy, we are still astonished by the effect of our decision. It seemed to take the whole country by storm. When we got back to the hotel on the afternoon of our last day in Messina, the desk clerk had a sheaf of messages in his hand from people all over Italy.

The president's office had called to ask if we had time (!) to receive a medal before we went home. The prime minister had suggested a meeting. The mayor of Rome wanted to make a presentation and asked if we could think of something Nicholas would have liked. The clerk reeled off the invitations, one by one. "We don't know how we can do any of these. We're flying home tomorrow morning," we told him. He shrugged his shoulders in a "you know best" gesture. If we couldn't meet Italy's leaders, that was our affair. But at the last message, he paused and said firmly, "But this one, Mr. Green, you really must accept. It's for tonight and it's from the most important talk show host in Italy."

In the end, we said yes to everything and crossed our fingers. Keeping these appointments meant catching a plane from Catania on an excruciatingly tight schedule, and we still had to pack our clothes—characteristically, spread in every corner of the hotel room—telephone the police to let them know we wanted to leave at once, and check out of the hotel. Ten minutes later, we were ready. As we stepped outside, a police car drew up. "Don't worry," said the codriver as I handed him a paper on which I'd written the time of the plane. I'd used the twenty-four-hour clock system so there'd be no confusion. "16.40 hours. We'll get you there." I knew they would. They breathed an air of relaxed self-confidence. Still, it was a hairy ride. We shot past everything on the road, lights flashing, warning siren going. At the edge of Catania, another police car was waiting to guide us through the tumultuous city center.

At that point our codriver, who had been on the telephone with the airport, handed back my note and asked, "16.40?" I checked my notes and got a sinking feeling. 16.10, not 16.40. I hung my head in shame. "Oh, you turkey," said Maggie softly. The codriver said something even more quietly to the driver, and the car, already traveling at its limit, suddenly went even faster. Neither man uttered a word of reproach. By now we were racing through the heart of Catania, the wrong way down one-way streets, careering round corners, continuously sounding the familiar "Mommy, mommy" siren. Since that day, Steve McQueen's chase through San Francisco has looked like child's play.

On and on we hurtled, the minutes dragging by, and since it was now already 16.10, Toad's Wild Ride was clearly a lost cause. At last we turned into the airport and there already on the runway was the 16. 10 plane to Rome. We had missed it, and there was no other flight that would get us there in time. "I'm sorry," I said to our policemen. "It was my fault." "Oh, don't worry about it," one of them said. "They're bringing it back for you." And they did. As we watched, that big aircraft turned back and trundled to where we were waiting. Handshakes all round. Smiles on sad faces, "Good luck, lady. Good luck, mister. Good-bye, little miss," and we were climbing a temporary staircase that had been dragged out to the plane. As we entered the cabin and shrank shamefaced into our seats, the passengers broke into applause, warm and prolonged.

In Rome, we were ushered off the plane first and into the arms of the staff of the mayor of Rome. All six misshapen pieces of luggage magically appeared, and the Alitalia agent thrust first-class tickets into our hands for the next day's flight home. Radio and press reporters were there in force, the mayor's staff in silent agony at the hold-up. But being silent isn't the best way to deal with journalists, so I added to their misery by not only answering questions, but also placing a call to the Rome correspondent of the *New York Times*, Alan Cowell, who had called just as we left Messina.

At last, however, we were on the way, the police escort slicing through the dense traffic. At city hall, Francesco Rutelli, the charismatic mayor, met us explaining that because we were due at the television station, time was pressing. "But at least," he said, "I can show you the most beautiful balcony in Rome." And there it was, an aerial view over the classical ruins that less than a week earlier the four of us had wandered around so happily. We could even see the fountain where Nicholas, his face running with perspiration, had drunk three cups of what we told him was Julius Caesar's private water supply. It seemed an age away.

We were taken into a large room filled with officials and the press. Mr. Rutelli gave a speech, short but moving, with the sort of restraint I came to recognize in our dealings with Italians at all levels, and gave us what we had said on the telephone Nicholas would have wanted most, a medal from Rome. It was beautiful, large and gold and breathing tradition. It was easy to respond. I said what I knew to be true, that Nicholas would have regarded it as his finest possession. There occurred to me also a phrase from Roman history that people all over the civilized world once said proudly, "*Civis Romanus sum*. I am a citizen of Rome." Now, I said, it applied to Nicholas. He would have liked that.

Before leaving, we were taken into the council chamber, a magnificent hall where the elected officials, filling the benches, stood and applauded on all sides. For a moment we had united the city government of Rome—and that probably does count as a miracle. Outside, a crowd of people standing in the rain applauded as we got into the car. It was becoming clearer by the minute that something very big was happening.

The Maurizio Costanzo show, broadcast nightly, is less of a television program than an institution. "Everybody watches it, everybody,"

everybody told us. We had reason later on to believe them. The interviews are held on the stage of a theater in front of a large audience. Having traveled without a moment's break, we were still in the clothes we were wearing for the walk we'd planned to the harbor wall at Messina. The mayor and council, and even the chauffeur, had courteously let pass Maggie's most shapeless dress and my worn sandals and even more worn bare feet. But this was national television and in fashion-conscious Italy too. However, there still was no time to spare and, introduced by a cheery tune on an organ from a musician dressed in a white suit, the host himself was seating us, the audience was standing, and twenty minutes of sympathetic but careful questions began. "You have given us a lesson in civility," he said at one point. Several times I noticed tears in his eyes.

Some days later in a newspaper article, he said he couldn't get us out of his mind. In many years of television, he wrote, he had never seen anything like it. It apparently affected audiences the same way. Three years afterward, we received a letter from Turin which said, "I will never forget the evening when you were invited at the Maurizio Costanzo show. Everyone present standed up when the three of you appeared. I was in front of the TV and I could not stop my tears." At the end of the show, we were asked to give an impromptu press conference, crammed into one of the dressing rooms. Show business reporters are hardened against the shallow emotions they come across daily, but as we told our story again I saw the tears welling up and the sniffles to hide them.

We were whisked to the Inter-Continental Hotel, where the hotel manager had come back from his home to show us to a suite of such dimensions that we had to shout to make ourselves heard across its spaces. The bathrooms looked as big as many of the hotel rooms we've stayed in. There were baskets of fruit and flowers. A huge patio looked across the roofs of Rome to a distant view of St. Peter's. In the plush dining room, we ate a late dinner, Eleanor curled up asleep on the thick carpet under the table.

To save carrying all our Swiss mountain clothes to Sicily, we'd left some pieces of luggage at the small hotel where we'd stayed on our way through Rome a few days earlier. I'd planned to collect them, but yielding to the pleas of so many people to "please let us do something for you," I asked someone to pick them up. As we went back into our hotel room after dinner, I glanced back along the long luxurious corridor, which until then had never seen anything less than a Gucci or an Armani, and saw the hotel porter, with an expression of distaste, carrying two overfilled backpacks that kept falling off their frames.

Knowing I couldn't sleep, I decided to go for a walk, drawn by the idea of visiting the sights we had planned to see on our vacation. It was a beautiful night, warm and increasingly calm as midnight passed into the small hours. I experienced a feeling I know well, wandering without a plan through a big city and coming across some of the world's masterpieces unexpectedly, though now with a leaden reminder at each one that Nicholas would never see any of them. I passed the Trevi fountain, the Pantheon, Piazza Navona.

As I crossed the almost empty Cavour bridge at around 2:00 a.m., I stood with my back against the parapet to savor the moment. A small car came out of nowhere and screeched to a halt. In it I could make out three burly men. "Oh no, not again," I thought. "This time they can have my wallet." The two windows facing me were rolled down fast and the driver leaned over, pointing a finger at my chest. I felt too weary to try to get away. Then he spoke, "Meester Green, Meester Green. I just seen you on television. Oh, Meester Green, I'm so sorry." I walked over to the car and we all shook hands, four fully grown men, all tearful, as I am now, just thinking about it. I walked on, into deserted St. Peter's Square, then across the river again and slowly back to the hotel, feeling—as I have felt in almost every city I've walked around late at night—no hint of menace in the silence.

The next morning, the American ambassador, Reginald Bartholomew, came to the hotel and took us to meet the Italian president, Luigi Scalfaro, at the Quirinale Palace, once the home of the popes, then the kings of Italy, now the president. As we drove by the colorful operatic uniforms and the saluting soldiers, all three of us had the same thought, "Wouldn't Nicholas have loved this?" We were shown the high-ceilinged rooms, the priceless tapestries, the longest corridor in Europe. But all this splendor turned out to be less memorable than the kindness and courtliness of the man we had come to see. In a simple ceremony, he presented us with the president's gold medal. "I am a father too," he told us. "You must be brave." The president's medal is a glorious ornament—given usually, we were told, only to heads of state, and even then not always in the gold version. "The king of Spain got one," someone said. "You're in good company."

We talked with Mr. Scalfaro for a while and, as we got up to go, I said something about dealing with the pain. "Let me tell you a story," he said. "A long time ago, an Italian man married a young woman he loved dearly. In time she had the child they both wanted, a lovely daughter. But the mother died. The man is now quite old, but he still thinks of her and the love they had. He never married again. That man is me." "I knew you understood," said Maggie quietly. It was like visiting a wise and loving member of the family.

We were taken to the office of the prime minister, Silvio Berlusconi, a controversial figure in Italian politics, but to us a model of simple compassion. There were no reporters, no camerapeople, no breast-beating or lamentation. This was a private visit. He talked gently in fluent English. "He rarely does that," we were told afterward. "He prides himself on his command of Italian and doesn't like to miss the subtleties when he speaks in a foreign language. He was obviously very moved." He walked down the stairs with us and into a courtyard where a car was waiting, said good-bye to Maggie and Eleanor, and turned to me. "May I embrace you?" he asked. "Of course," I said, impressed again by the correctness of everyone's behavior. But as he put his face to mine, I felt a tear run down his cheek and realized that all this time he had held his emotions in check so as not to upset us.

In Messina and again at the Rome airport, the weight of the state had been brought into play to change our flight reservations so we could go home as soon as our appointments were over. This effort turned out to have been unnecessary. The president offered instead to have us flown home in one of his military jets. This changed our procession, formerly one police car ahead, one behind, into a cavalcade. Led by a godlike figure on a motorcycle, graceful and commanding, our fleet of cars sped across Rome, lights flashing, horns blaring, and the little stick with the circle on it that police cars use to ward off other cars—the American ambassador calls it "the magic wand"—repelling anyone who threatened to get in the way. All along the route, policemen jumped to hold back the traffic. We drove round the Piazza Barberini without one other car to share it with. "I'll never see it like this again," I thought. At every street leading into the square we could see the traffic backed up. You could almost feel the pent-up fury. But the god ahead cut his way past all this human debris, dragging us along behind him.

At the military airfield, we clambered aboard the plane and found the three of us were outnumbered by the crew. A meal, simple but elegant, was already prepared, and there was a choice of wines. We had the cabin to ourselves, the two stewards out of sight in their own quarters. There was space to lie down and move around and watch from the windows on both sides. The military markings on the wings were a thrill. "If only Nicholas could have seen this," we said again.

At Gander in Newfoundland, where we refueled, I telephoned home. Dee Wickham, my secretary, who had handled everything at her end single-handedly, said a large press contingent was planning to meet the plane at the airport. The phone had never stopped ringing. As we approached San Francisco, we ran into a huge storm, sheets of rain and high winds. "It must be Zeus," smiled Maggie sadly. "He knows it's a big occasion."

The crowded press conference at an uncomfortably late hour for deadlines didn't add much information, but it confirmed this was not just an Italian but a worldwide story. We were asked again how we felt about the killers. "I know this sounds strange, but the men who did this are probably shocked," Maggie replied. "I hope they get caught, but I hope it changes their lives." The Italian consul general in San Francisco, Giulio Prigioni, and his wife, Esther, were there. The assistant of a Hollywood movie producer introduced herself and said she'd be in touch, and we said no to a request for an exclusive interview with a talk show. Then Dee drove us home to Bodega Bay with a rapid fire of details about the arrangements she'd been making: the funeral, press calls, movie company calls, letters from all over the country. She had risen to the occasion nobly, as I'd expected.

We took a deep breath and went in the house. This, we thought, was going to be one of the worst ordeals, all those memories underlining the emptiness. Surprisingly, it wasn't that way. The kitchen was filled with food and flowers, cider was being kept warm in an urn someone had brought, the whole house was warm and welcoming. It was the first example of the well-thought-out help the people of our little town have given us from that day to this.

Maggie took Eleanor into the bedroom she had shared with Nicholas, undressed her, put her to bed, and kissed her good night. She went to sleep without a murmur. Maggie avoided looking at the other bed where a tousled head usually lay. It was a wrenching moment. But we were learning something: Eleanor had made a crucial step on the path she would take to deal with a blow that could have crushed her. She wasn't afraid. She was the spunky little person we'd always known, and the next day she went to school as usual.

That day too Nicholas' body was flown home in a second presidential plane, in a manner befitting a national hero and the sensibilities of a proud nation. The plane arrived in the middle of the night, and in the silence of San Francisco's almost deserted airport, the guard, who had traveled all the way with him, performed the full ceremony to which military tradition, and a small boy's dreams of honor, entitled him.

A hurricane of meetings, arrangements, and media interviews followed. All three major network morning talk shows came to the house on our second day home and, after that, the television magazine programs. A procession of reporters, photographers, and feature writers came too. The telephone rang incessantly, with calls from friends and strangers, and Dee's "things to do" notices, which already covered the office walls, began taking over the kitchen.

Every day, the mail brought stacks of letters. It threatened to overwhelm us, but I can't remember ever wanting to damp it down. Quite the reverse: if, as seemed likely, we'd been handed a life's work and if people were that interested, it seemed clear we had to expand our efforts, not contract them.

CHAPTER FIVE

FUNERAL IN A COUNTRY CHURCHYARD

St. Teresa of Avila's in Bodega, four miles inland from Bodega Bay, is famous in our part of the world. Built in 1860, its first parishioners were mainly immigrant Irish farmers, soon followed by Italians. It has been beautifully photographed by Ansel Adams, a shapely splash of white among the green rolling hills. Maggie and I are not Catholic, but when Nicholas died, we each thought independently how much we would like him to be buried in the cemetery there. While we were still in Rome, we had asked if it was possible. The church's reply was immediate: "Of course." I remember the relief I felt. It was something to hold on to at a terrible time, a vision of soothing visits on quiet afternoons.

Now it was time to attend to the details. Father Dan Whelton, who arranged to meet us at the cemetery, is the very spirit of an Irish priest, warm, generous, and studious too, who spent several years in Rome and is visibly pained by man's cruelty to man. He was with Tom Chapman, a kind and gentle man, who at that time looked after the graveyard and had steadfastly refused to raise the price for gravesites set decades before. We chose a site almost at the top of the hill, in a section where almost all the names are Italian, the Gonnella and Maretti families, Mazzonis and Ponzas, Piazzas and Mantuas. I thought of Nicholas dwelling on a little Italian street among friendly neighbors.

Our own neighbors in Bodega Bay took the rest of the work out of our hands. As Maggie's family arrived for the funeral from across the United States, my half-brother Grahame from England, and brother-in-law Laurent from Belgium, all were billeted in nearby houses, fed and tucked into bed at night. The owners of one house moved out entirely. Susan and Cyrus Griffin, proprietors of the beautiful Sonoma Coast Villa, a Californian dream of the Mediterranean, offered their extensive grounds for the reception. All around town, homemakers chopped, buttered, and baked, and every restaurant donated one of its special dishes. For the next two weeks, neighbors took turns to make us a hot dinner every night, some with a bottle of wine or a rose in a vase, and all brought to the door without the slightest fuss.

Saturday, October 8, was one of those exquisite fall days on the California coast, blue and gold and green. By the ocean, the wind blew and the flag at the clubhouse crackled at half staff, and I smiled at this final tribute to Nicholas' staunch heart. But inland all was calm. Entry to the church was restricted because of the large numbers wanting to be there, the Sonoma County police volunteered to direct traffic without pay, and the road from Bodega village to the graveyard was lined with cars.

Many people had helped with the funeral arrangements, but we wanted the service to be ours. "Is there anything special you'd like?" Maggie had asked on our last night in Rome. As she said it, I remembered something vividly from my own childhood. It was a song called "Sonny Boy," about a small boy dying and his father's broken heart. My father had a scratchy record of it, by Al Jolson, and was always saddened by it. I have a memory as a six-year-old of putting my arms around his shoulders as he sat in a chair and telling him not to worry, I wasn't going to die, not for a long, long time. "We should ask my grandmother to sing it," Maggie said, without hesitation. We telephoned when we got back home, and Thelma found the music. "It's perfect," she said. But, although she has spent a lifetime performing and teaching singing, she added, "I couldn't sing it in church. I'd never get through it." Instead she recorded it and we played the tape, her strong maternal voice filling that old building.

"But the angels, they grew lonely
And they took you because they were lonely
And now I'm lonely, too, sonny boy."

For a moment four generations of our family came together as one.

Loretta Smith, Nicholas' teacher in kindergarten and first grade, whom he adored, gave the eulogy. "Nicholas was the most giving child I have ever met," she said. "He was very wise, and he taught me about love and patience and caring. He stood out as someone so well adjusted, so confident, and so full of love that he could afford to be giving. I always knew he was my teacher." "Mine too," I thought. "But I had no idea," she went on, "that this smiling little boy who walked into my class every morning would be a teacher to millions."

As the solemn service went on, Eleanor dabbed Maggie's eyes with the Sally Rabbit she had brought as her own comforter. It was photographed, and the world responded to the heartrending purity of it all. "I can never forget the picture of your little daughter," said a stranger from Chicago, one of dozens who wrote later. "That this little girl had the power to deal with her own grief and still be able to console her mother moved me beyond belief."

We walked the few hundred yards from the church, led by bagpipes played by Maggie's stepfather, Richard Sheridan, a former captain in the Marines. The sound filled the narrow valley, adding something from my own traditions. A few months before I'd read *Kidnapped* to Nicholas. Night after night we followed Stevenson's young hero, as principled and truthful as Nicholas was, and as brave as he wanted to be, dodging his way across the Scottish Highlands. What pleasures I'd looked forward to then as Nicholas grew in body and mind. Now, as we walked up the final hill, I heard on the bagpipes a tune that has conjured up poignant visions for me since childhood.

"The minstrel boy to the war is gone.
In the ranks of the dead you will find him."

The brief, choking ceremony at the graveside over, the local children watched in a mixture of awe and curiosity as the casket was lowered deeper and deeper into the ground, farther and farther from those he was leaving behind. It was a dreadful moment. Would it ever stop? I asked Eleanor to wave good-bye and we both did, for the very last time.

We drove to the reception, where Andy Harris, the father of Luis, a special friend of Nicholas, read a poem he'd just written, recalling how they never knew in what role Nicholas would lead the game that day, centurion or Mercury or a general on a silver saddle, but they could count infallibly on what he wanted to eat:

"Always spaghetti, spaghetti please,
No sauce, no sauce, just Parmesan cheese."

Susan, the preschool teacher, told how one day he'd put on the sailor's peaked cap we'd bought in Venice, announced that he was a taxi driver, and offered to drive the other kids to the best restaurant in Paris. Even in death he was kind: the Paris he knew was covered on foot, searching for cheap restaurants.

Then it was my turn and this is what I said:

"He was a liability to any sports team he was on: he couldn't throw a ball, he couldn't catch a ball, and he was always falling over his own feet. He was one of the most finicky eaters I've ever met. And his room was a mess. But in his short life he was Robin Hood, George Washington, and St. George of England. In the Colosseum he was both a Christian and a lion. At his seventh birthday party a few weeks ago, he was Robinson Crusoe: prophetically, perhaps, because it was Daniel Defoe who said 'the good die early.'

"He had traveled so far that the airline still owes him a free trip to Europe. He won two gold medals in Rome, has had trees planted in his name, and will have parks named for him. He has already helped save the lives of other children and indirectly perhaps many more in the future. He could have lived to a hundred and done less. He has also struck a spark of love in the hearts of millions of parents and children around the world. If this isn't immortality, it must surely come close.

"But now, little boy, although your radiance is still with us, it's time for you to sleep. From all of us, good night and sweet dreams."

CHAPTER SIX

WHAT WAS NICHOLAS LIKE?

We went home from the burial to a house that on the outside was just as it was when our vacation started three weeks earlier. It had then belonged to a family of four, statistically unrepresentative in some obvious ways—a mother of thirty-three and a father of sixty-five, for example—but quite normal for the rest: a boy of seven, a girl of four, a house with a large view and a larger mortgage, decent but not lavish furniture, two cars past their prime, books spread around, a fair-sized collection of popular and jazz CDs ranging from Peter Rabbit to the Beatles (but no later) and classics to Delius (but no later). All the rooms had a slightly untidy look as though whoever lived there couldn't remember where things belonged.

The boy had just moved into second grade, the girl was still in pre-school. The husband worked from an office in the house, and the wife did the books, fixed the computers, looked after the children, and helped keep the house untidy. They lived next to a golf course, over-looking the ocean. They didn't eat out much, rarely went to the mov-ies, and none of them liked shopping. They all seemed to feel the house and the area around had all they needed for day-to-day living. They walked on the beaches and the nearby hills a lot, read a lot, talked a lot, and found plenty to argue about. When they broke out, they did so decisively. Every year for several years, generally in the fall, they had exchanged houses with people in Europe—Scotland, France, Switzerland—and at other times tacked days on to business trips to travel all over the western United States. The boy never learned there was any way to get to Colorado from California other than traveling twenty-four hours continuously in a station wagon.

Now only three people were living in the house. An idyllic period was over, and a new phase was beginning, full of uncertainty.

What was Nicholas like? It's important for me to get it right while the memory is still strong. There won't be any conversations between a father and a grown-up son to rekindle childhood incidents. Not that any two people ever remember things in the same way. ("That wasn't me, that was Eleanor.") But they are among the most satisfying parts of being a family, the intimacy of growing and changing together. Losing them is another casual sideswipe that death deals.

For one thing, he was like Maggie. Perhaps that's why I loved him so much. Straightforward, trusting, genuinely caring about others, and with a keen intelligence. He also had her mixture of good humor and gravitas: life, he seemed to feel, is a serious business but not solemn. On the way home from Italy, Maggie said, "You know, I never knew him to tell a lie." Neither did I, nor to do those sneaky things most of us do as children. I think his honesty was connected to his trusting nature: he felt the world was fair-minded enough not to punish him unduly for a genuine mistake. He also assumed everyone else was telling the truth. Nor did he seem to be good because he was afraid of the consequences. I mentioned this to Dererca, a friend who loved him. "He had a conscience," she said simply.

When the children in his school were asked to write what they remembered of him a few days after his death, they obviously reached for kindness. Even so, the unanimity of his peers is convincing. "He would play with kids when no one else would." "When you were upset, he'd make you laugh." "When a kid didn't know how to do something, he'd show him the way." One even said, "He never told a lie that I know of." And, perhaps most revealing of all, "He was nice to his sister." It's an epitaph a great man might envy.

David Tully-Smith, my doctor and the ablest I've ever had, told me he was struck by what he called the wisdom he saw in Nicholas when he was not much more than a year old. "It's remarkable that among the hundreds of patients I meet he should stand out so vividly almost ten years later. Most infants are inwardly focused, but he had a perceptiveness about the environment around him that was quite striking. He looked at me as if to say, 'I see, you're the man in the white coat and this is what you do.' Then, having understood it at the level he needed to, he turned to look at something else." I know that reflective gaze. It's dangerously pretentious to say so, but even at that age he did strike you as being wise.

"He doesn't talk nonsense, does he?" my daughter-in-law, Shan, said of him when he was about three. It was true. He didn't babble, didn't say a string of silly things without knowing what they meant. He didn't repeat parrotlike something he'd been told, as I did when I was a child, getting the words mixed up and failing to grasp the idea behind them. When something was explained to him that was beyond his years, he seemed to shelve it until he was ready to absorb it. Months after I'd told him something without evoking any obvious reaction, I'd hear him say it with enough understanding to have made it his own.

From time to time, someone in Italy tried to call it "the Green effect." We always resisted. It's true, Nicholas knew nothing about organ donation and it was our decision, not his. But when you were with him, you wanted to be worthy of his expectations, and I feel quite sure the donation is what his expectations would have been. He stamped his personality on the news stories and brought a fragrance of himself to the dullest organ donation meeting. No one who watched Jamie Lee Curtis on the Oprah Winfrey show can easily forget how profoundly she was moved when she was shown a video of him for the first time. Three years after he died, a man stopped me in the San Francisco airport. "That boy of yours was really going to do some wonderful things, wasn't he?" he said. It took me by surprise, and I asked if he'd known Nicholas. "No," he said, "but I could tell from the things people said about him in the paper."

Nicholas felt things keenly, good and bad, and his summing up of a transient disappointment was routine: "This is the worst day of my life." I think I maligned him in my eulogy, however. The room he shared with Eleanor, now hers, is messier than ever. I now believe he was simply powerless in the face of her relentless untidiness.

Sometimes I'd go out to meet him at the bus stop as he came home from school. Generally late, I'd hurry along the road, trying to spot his head bobbing up and down over the tops of the bushes. At last I'd see him and we'd both quicken our pace. "Nicholas, do you know what happened to me today...?" "Daddy, during recess this morning, a boy..." He'd slip his hand into mine—he loved that contact with other people—and we'd return home full of the day's events. Normally, I'd go straight to the room that's become my office and shut the door, and he'd head for the television room. The whole meeting would have taken less than ten minutes, but it left a glow that lasted all afternoon.

Once, when he was four, I went on a trip to Texas. At the airport check-in on the way back, the security belt with the carry-on luggage suddenly stopped, bells rang, and lights flashed. There to my horror I saw the x-ray machine was highlighting, among my socks and underwear, the cowboy pistol I'd bought for $1.79 at Kmart. Two policemen arrived and corralled me into a corner. If they felt their reactions were overdone when they discovered the gun was a toy still wrapped in its plastic, they didn't show it. "This incident will be reported to the Federal Aviation Authority. Under section de da de da de da of the Enemies of the People (or some such) Act, taking a simulated weapon aboard an aircraft is punishable by a fine not exceeding $10,000." I went home in a state of depression. No cap gun was worth $10,001.79. But when I gave it to Nicholas the next morning, he banished all the clouds. "It's the best present I've had in years," he said.

He joined the Cub Scouts and loved those Tuesday evenings. He'd wear his uniform at school, and all afternoon after he came home he'd ask, "How long will it be till we go?" Just before seven, we'd walk over to Mr. Halloran's house, where the blue and yellow uniforms were converging. At six years old, he wasn't ashamed to hold my hand in front of his pals. An hour or so later, I'd walk back and pick him up. No, he hadn't caught anyone out at softball. And yes, he'd lost every arm wrestling contest. But he didn't seem to mind. He'd had a good time with people he liked.

He never really cared about winning. He could have stepped straight out of a boy's book of Edwardian England. Playing the game by the rules was what made him feel good. Lording it over an opponent degraded the spirit of the contest. I knew at the time those Tuesday walks were precious. Now they are touched with gold.

When Eleanor started to take dancing lessons, Nicholas opted to go too. Dressed in black tights and tap dancing shoes, he never looked the part to me. He was the only boy among mostly younger girls, but he didn't seem to find that odd and went about his business, falling over his feet and coming in off the beat. But this year, four boys were in that class. He was also taking piano lessons, again at his choice and again, I felt, without any special talent. The green shoots, however, were beginning. One night after he had gone to bed, I was listening, quietly I thought, to Chopin's *Nocturnes*. I turned and Nicholas was standing by my chair. "You know, Daddy, I might be playing like that one day." That, at least, is something death has allowed us to keep unsullied, a dream of Nicholas as Horowitz.

We talked about what he'd do when he grew up. For a long time, he had set his heart on becoming a truck driver for Safeway supermarkets, and he stared hard into their cabs as we passed them on the highway—did they know their jobs were in jeopardy?—but as time passed he'd decided he wanted to try everything. On my first job as a reporter, I had worked with the son of the sheriff of Nottingham. Nicholas showed more interest in journalism when I told him that than at any other time. But he was too young to catch the news bug, so we took to finding more meaningful jobs for him: pâté taster, spaghetti grower, captain of the trash boat in Venice. We discussed the problems they'd have, the tools they'd want, the training they'd need.

One night, two years after he died, I stopped for gas on the autostrada in Calabria. There, outside the toilet, a man was sitting at a table with a few coins in a saucer. In some parts of Europe after World War II, the attendant who depended on tips was a common sight. In the poorest places he (or generally, she) handed you your two sheets of toilet paper. What a memory to describe to today's children. For a flicker of time the old excitement bubbled up, and the words rushed into my mind, "Nicholas, Nicholas, I've got another job for you," then just as quickly went out again.

Similarly, when asked what he liked to learn, he'd say he wanted to know about everything. He found it all exciting: fairy tales, comic strips, poems, songs, children's encyclopedias, maps, everything. Fairy tales had always bothered me as a child: I could never understand why the hero, having been told never to look back or eat an apple offered by a kind old lady, fell at the first test. Waywardness of that sort

forfeited my interest. But Nicholas listened with, I think, deeper understanding, seeing the underlying concept of human willpower pitted
against deep unconscious forces.

From an early age he'd started to read books for himself, and every
evening one of us would read to him also. "I'm bringing my bony bum
over there to sit on your lap," he'd say, picking up the expression I'd
used with him since he was tiny (Eleanor was "soft tush"). We were
progressing well right up to the end: by then we'd read the Robin
Hood tales in every version we could get our hands on, were getting on
well with Robert Louis Stevenson, and were in the middle of *The Swiss
Family Robinson* when we left for Switzerland.

But he was even more deeply touched by the C. S. Lewis *Narnia*
books Maggie read to him when he was just six. Those books had
what he loved most: the perilous conflict of good and bad in an imagined world. I can still feel, quite palpably, the intense silence that surrounded those bedtime readings. Maggie's voice low and serious,
Nicholas almost fearing to breathe, an occasional shocked intake of
breath at danger lurking and a long sigh of relief when it passed. If you
could sum up a view of life in one set of books, I'd guess that for
Nicholas this would have been it.

He loved the magic in life, and in Maggie found the perfect chore-
ographer. He would inch toward his next role, and in her battered
boxes they'd find ribbons and buttons and colored cloth that in a few
hours would turn into tunics and shields and suits of Lincoln green.
Both were hard to please. The breastplate had to have the red cross of
England on it, the Mountie pants the yellow stripe. "It's not right,"
he'd say tearfully. "This hat looks dumb." "Well, it's the best I can do.
Let's look at it in the morning and you may like it better." Another
two hours of late-night stitching and cutting followed, and there would
be a hat Richard the Lionheart would not have been ashamed to wear.

He thrilled to stories of honorable behavior, and I made a tape of
the 1930s Errol Flynn movie *The Charge of the Light Brigade*, which
had entranced me too as a boy. He saw it time and again, the quintessential battle of right (in tailored uniforms) against might (in ill-fitting
tunics). Sometimes in another room I'd hear the preparations for the
charge being made, and I'd drop what I was doing to sit on the sofa
with him as yet again the wounded standard-bearer bravely held up the
flag until another trooper swept alongside to keep it aloft. I'd just
started picking out some of the easier classic verses to read to him, and

after one of these television viewings I took Tennyson's poem from the bookshelf. The effect was enough to gladden a poet laureate's heart: his little body erect, and an imaginary steed under him, he rode undaunted into the jaws of death and the mouth of hell.

Maggie's sister, Isabel, remembered him like this in an article in the *Los Angeles Times*. "He organized and oversaw the games of childhood with authority, sweeping along the others in his powerful wake. Even my little Kathryn, ever strong and defiant, would willingly play Maid Marian to his Robin Hood." So too with music. My Frank Sinatra records have ruined many a dinner party. But they found a second home in Nicholas' heart. Quick to find the right costume, he'd appear dapper and cosmopolitan, hands resting lightly in his blazer pockets, for "I Love Paris" or in his Venetian sailor's peaked cap like an airline pilot for "Come Fly with Me." I bought the most booming recording of "The 1812 Overture" I could find so he could prance with Napoleon's cavalry outside Moscow and the Tsar's outside Paris, while Eleanor handed out flowers indiscriminately in both cities.

When he was only a few weeks old, we took him on his first hike, and he seemed happy to be on our backs as we climbed a steep mountain in mid-California. He came to many places after that and often it was just the two of us, going up slopes and over rocks I'd never have attempted with Maggie watching, and in the backpack or the car I talked to him long before he could reply. But a rapport grew up, and when he'd go to sleep as we journeyed on, I'd look forward to him waking up and continuing the one-sided conversation. Once speech did get started, however, it came strong and clear. One of his expressions was "Let's chat," and we often did. And so all the time I was teaching him about St. George and Robin Hood, he was teaching me about kindness and gentleness.

From an early age, he was good company. He looked around, taking things in and reacting to them. One evening, coming back through the woods in British Columbia when he was about four, we'd strayed from the trail, and up on my shoulders Nicholas realized it. I could feel the lack of confidence through that bony bum. At length, in deep twilight, I spied a light from the cottage where we were staying. What a relief. "Hey, little man, what can you see through the trees there?" He peered ahead. "A bear," he said, and there in shadows fifty feet ahead, sure enough, that's what he could see.

One night, I made up a bedtime story about a baby playing near a river that was rising swiftly. Nicholas and a friend were alerted to the danger but desperately late. As I talked, the bedroom was hushed, his breathing barely audible, until at last with the flood rushing toward them the heroes snatched up the baby. He breathed a long, happy sigh and put his slender arm around my neck in silent gratitude for having saved that baby. I think of it now as the first remembered example of the utter contentment Nicholas' love could bring.

By then he was walking part of the way on hikes, and we took on more and more—along the Continental Divide ("Shall we walk north toward Canada today, Nicholas, or south to Mexico? It's warmer in Mexico, remember"), through the snows of the Sierras, the long walk down from Gornergrat for the close-up view of the Matterhorn, solitary lakes in the Canadian Rockies. But ecstasy on even the best hike can fade fast and one of the treasures of memory is how by swinging Nicholas up on my shoulders I could instantly change dejection into happiness.

As he grew older and Eleanor joined us, something else was needed. I found it in telling stories. That's how Puffer was born, a locomotive who lived in Toys 'R' Us in Santa Rosa and could shrink children to his size and fly them to adventures and dream lands. Most of these stories started wherever we were and were sparked by some incident on the trail. A hot sun would become a desert or a patch of snow an avalanche, and only the children, with Puffer's help, could rescue families in danger. Puffer was also a bit of a clown: he'd suggest climbing to the very pineapple of the mountain (he pinched other people's jokes freely) or confuse obstacles with popsicles. The thought of Nicholas, footsore and dispirited one minute, helpless with laughter the next, still makes me smile.

None of these tales would stand up to literary examination—when she was there I always walked well ahead of Maggie to avoid hearing her snorts of disbelief—but they were astonishingly successful. "Tell us a Puffer story," became the standard demand from both children on a hike of any length and we journeyed miles under his spell. His fame spread a little too. As we came to the end of the crowded trail from the Nevada Falls in Yosemite National Park, a Japanese hiker who had overtaken us on the way was waiting. "And how did Puffer get away from the witch?" he asked with a smile.

Largely unconsciously then, Nicholas was learning geography by being involved in it: about glaciers by touching them, about the tides by scrambling over the rocky seashore, about vegetation by crossing the timberline. He was absorbing history in much the same way. Traveling to Colorado, we'd often stop at dusk at a place where the Pony Express trail crosses the road. I liked to take Nicholas along the trail, looking at the lonely way heading straight for the distant purple hills and feeling the emptiness of the desert and a departed world. He guarded the Roman frontier against the Scots on Hadrian's Wall and scrambled over the walls of Fort McHenry, sometimes a British attacker, sometimes an American defender, because he understood there are good people on both sides of any dispute. He'd been to the American and British forts disputing the entrance to the Niagara River, felt the touch of Iona's civilizing society at the very tip of the Old World, and had the best sight of his life when he saw the Edinburgh castle and the railroad station in one view.

He startled one of the mothers when he got into the pool car one day and announced this was the anniversary of the eruption of Vesuvius. He didn't carry the date in his head: one of us had read it to him from the Today in History paragraph in the paper. Still, he thought it important enough to share with the other five-year-olds.

He was more interested in museums than almost anyone else I've ever known. On our last vacation in Switzerland, high up in the Alps, but fogged in and wet, he complained, "All you guys want to do is go for walks." "Well, what would you like to do?" asked Maggie. "Go to a museum," he said. We found one in Martigny, which was probably as close to perfection as he could have imagined: one part the contents of a Roman garrison, the other a collection of vintage cars. His favorite: the one with three windshield wipers.

I think of him as a Renaissance boy. So, when we went touring, it was rarely a problem to include art galleries or famous buildings. He didn't just tolerate them, he yearned for them. In Italy we could spend fifteen minutes looking at a painting like the *Assumption of the Virgin* or a crowded scene by Veronese. Why were some people looking happy and some sad? What was that dwarf doing there? What was the dog waiting for? He was awed by St. Mark's and laughed aloud at the trick paintings at Maser.

On what proved to be his last Halloween, he was a Royal Canadian Mountie, correct in every detail to the casual eye, except for the cowboy boots and his mother's hat. Eleanor was a rose, her slim body the stem, all green, and her face surrounded by a red homemade ruff. They were two of Maggie's finest creations. Waiting at the end of driveways, I'd hear at door after door, "Hey, Nora (or Jim), come and look at this. A real live Mountie and he's brought a beautiful flower with him." No wonder he trusted people. He looked for kindness in them and found it.

In his last few days in Switzerland, we had a visit from one of my old friends from England, Roy Atherton, who, knowing his audience, brought his box of conjuring tricks. As on previous occasions, Nicholas treated a coin coming out of Eleanor's ear as a miracle. "One of these days he'll want to know what deception Roy used to palm that coin," I thought, but for now his innocence made me want to hug him.

That was how he had always been. Planning a trip to Europe in a previous year, I showed the children a map of the route which went over the land where Santa Claus lived. "You should drop your notes out of the plane when we pass over so he'll be sure to get them," I suggested. "How can we do that?" Nicholas asked scornfully. "The windows don't open." I was ready for this. "Haven't you noticed that when you flush the toilet in an aircraft a flap opens? We'll wait until we're right over Greenland, go for a pee, and send the letters down." They wrote the notes and on our first visit to the toilet we had a dummy run. They were mightily impressed as the trial pieces of paper disappeared in an explosive swoosh. They were both asleep when we flew over Greenland and I pocketed the notes. Some time ago I found in a drawer the one Nicholas wrote, but I could scarcely bear to read it.

Maggie worried at times that the world might crush him. It's possible. No doubt his gentleness would have been tested. But I like to think he would have gone through life believing unswervingly in something—God, man, goodness—that would have given him the strength to stay the course. Certainly his total honesty would have protected him against ordinary corrosion. It was part of his DNA. When I remember him on his last night, as he settled contentedly into a sleep from which he never woke, he fits Dante's picture as if it had been written for him, "Pure and ready to mount to the stars."

CHAPTER SEVEN

WHAT ARE WE LIKE?

I became Nicholas' father by a roundabout route. I was born in the small cotton-spinning town of Accrington in the north of England in 1929. At one time cotton led the industrial revolution, and spinners were among the working aristocrats. By the time I was growing up, foreign competition and a world slump had knocked it around badly, but the town still had a great deal of civic and individual pride. There were no rich people, but no wretchedly poor ones either, the houses were well kept up, and the schools, libraries, and local government offices were serious places. The whole area believed in self-help, but invariably rallied around anyone in need.

I had loving parents, a grandfather who was a boy's dream, firm friends, and a world to explore through books. Only occasionally in those early years did I sense the blight the Great Depression was causing among grown-ups. My father had a solid education by the standard of those days, but now worked in the office of the nearest cotton mill. It was a sad decline from the hopes he must once have entertained, though I never once heard him speak of them. I have a vivid memory of walking to the end of the street with him after he had been home for a midday meal, when I was about five, and looking down at the mill where he worked in the valley below. Even to me it looked grim. We'd been holding hands and now it was time for me to turn back. He seemed reluctant to break off, but, after a pause, he walked slowly away. Saddened, I turned round for one last look, and he had turned around too and was looking back at me. I ran all the way home, feeling the walls closing in on him.

I was an only child and, because of my mother, never had any difficulty understanding what unreserved love is. She encouraged me in everything, showing the way and always sure I'd get there in the end. She practiced the virtues of tolerance, kindness, and truthfulness as though she couldn't conceive of any other way to live decently. I had plenty of evidence that this wasn't just for home consumption—like the day an elderly woman stopped me in the street and demanded, "Aren't you Nellie McKay's son? Yes? Well, you're a very lucky little boy." I squirmed with embarrassment. Or the day a full-scale dinner was delivered from a local restaurant. It turned out that, without mentioning it at home, she'd scrubbed the floors for them the week before when they'd suddenly needed help and had refused all payment.

Best of all, she was enormous fun, seeing the amusing side of everything and instinctively finding ways to pull herself up from the blows life dealt her. On the twin pillars of good humor and belief in other people, she built a life that must have cheered almost everyone she met. To the end of her days, she was a legend for helping others in any kind of trouble.

The 1930s wore on, we moved from town to town, and I began to see more clearly the strain the chronic depression was casting over everything, numbing everyone into an acceptance of whatever was, for fear that it might get worse. But that was the adult world, and mine was still filled with undimmed possibilities. Eventually my father landed a job as a movie theater manager in Manchester, where he wore a tuxedo for the 6:00 and 8:00 shows. This was more like it. It meant a nicer house, with a cherry tree, friends I still have, and unlimited moviegoing.

The war came, dreary at first, then devastating as allies crumpled one by one. In 1940, soon after France fell, my father idealistically volunteered for the Royal Air Force. He was too old at the time to be conscripted, but he felt it was his duty and characteristically chose the RAF Regiment, the infantry arm and least glamorous and most arduous part of the service. In five years of war, which included numbing months of boredom on remote airfields and landing in France in the first few days after D day, he started as an aircraftsman second class and ended up as leading aircraftsman, achieving that minuscule promotion only because it depended solely on length of service. It must have been quixotic: he had the education, the physique, and the ability to get on with people that should have given him some place in the hierarchy other than the very bottom, but he steadfastly refused to take it.

My mother worked throughout the war, and almost every schoolday I came home to an empty house. For one prolonged spell, until the war moved east, there was an air raid nearly every night and we sat for hours on stiff-backed chairs in the unheated iron shelter in the backyard as the bombs fell and the guns went off. Two hundred yards away, half a row of houses was flattened one night. Two boys of my age at school were blown up playing with a metal object they'd picked up in a field. We celebrated madly on the best day of the war when the school was bombed during the night and we were given a week's holiday.

In those five years, my father came home perhaps twenty times and then only for a few days at a time. The long separation took its toll on the marriage and when the war was over, he found it hard to settle down. Before long there was a separation and then a divorce. Both parents married again, but I saw my father only once after that, at his mother's funeral, and my mother's new husband, Philip, an ideal partner for her, died a few years later.

In the meantime, I went to the university in Manchester, got a degree in economics at nineteen, and did my two years' compulsory military service in the RAF. There my father's example was useful: it produced an equal and opposite reaction, and I became an officer in the education branch in three months. My level of competence was a disgrace to Britain's military traditions, and I've been in favor of a volunteer army ever since. My only distinction was that as the youngest member of the officers' club I became its vice president and was known in the language of the time as Mr. Vice. I never knew if that helped or hindered at the local dances.

My adult life began to take shape. I met Jane, a nurse of great beauty, fell in love instantaneously, wooed her single-mindedly, and got my first job as a reporter on an evening paper in Blackburn, a nearby engineering and cotton town. One night I came home late to find my mother waiting up for me. At her Red Cross class she'd been paired with the wife of Bill Pilkington, the business editor of the (Manchester) *Guardian*, who was badly overworked because he couldn't find the assistant he wanted. "Reg could do that," my mother said firmly, as she wrapped a crepe bandage round Mrs. Pilkington's wrist. At the time it was a prize I could only dream of. But such is the power of a mother's belief that a couple of months later that's just what I was doing.

A few years later, this happy association with one of the best bosses I've ever had propelled me to Fleet Street, the peak of British newspapering, first to the *Birmingham Post*, then to *The (London) Times*, and then, still upwardly mobile, to a top writing position on the *Daily Telegraph*. Jane and I, now contentedly married, went through the struggles of most young families, worked hard, watched the world opening, and had two children, Michael and Annie.

I've always loved journalism and when I came to cover the biggest story of my life, it repaid that love in full. At one time or other I've written for almost every page of the daily paper, starting with stories about cats stuck in trees and petty crime. I wrote engagingly, I think, but ignorantly, about sports, pretentiously about jazz, and cockily reviewed history books written by some of the most famous historians of the time while I was still a history undergraduate at London University's night school. But my bread and butter was business writing and, although never a star, I had climbed the greasy pole sufficiently far to hear regularly on the BBC's *What the Papers Say* items starting, "R. F. D. Green of the *Daily Telegraph* says this morning…"

My days were filled with anything from the visit of a foreign head of state or an unending series of economic crises to tramping round London's Royal Group of docks and being derided as "a capitalist lick-spittle" by strike leaders—nothing personal, they said that of all the reporters except the man from *The Daily Worker*. Outside regular hours, I was as likely to interview Louis Armstrong as the captain of the English soccer team. I also did occasional commentaries on economics for the BBC and learned on my first attempt why British broadcasters pay such attention to their diction. "I want you to speak up strongly in this last sentence," the producer told me. "The Queen listens to this program."

It was a heady time for newspapers, with seven or eight national dailies in hot competition. The proprietors didn't really approve of paying their employees wages, but they could be quite foolhardy about spending money on travel. So, mixed in with the daily news, I also looked (in vain) for industrial development on the majestic west coast of Ireland, was stormbound on a Scottish island where the only place to stay was a whiskey distillery, and hiked overnight through mountains in Iceland. I rode on the roof of a bus through the Kabul gorge in a snowstorm because there was no room inside, and climbed a peak in Ethiopia, while one of Emperor Haile Selassie's chauffeurs in a peaked hat and knee-length boots waited at the bottom. I ate dinners on trains in India, where one course would last until the next station and the new course would be handed in at the windows, and drank furniture polish, or something very like it, with converted headhunters in Borneo.

I had a moment of reflected fame in Moscow where Mr. Krushchev, then isolated in enforced retirement, was due to vote for the first time since he had fallen from power. I was there for another reason, but this was too good to miss, so on the day before polling day, one of the Moscow-based newspaper correspondents took me to the little building where the votes would be cast. Not a soul was about, and, following instructions, I kept watch while he opened the back door, by some method I was glad not to have seen, and left it closed but unlocked.

The next day the little street in front, which had been deserted the day before, was crammed with journalists. Every media face stationed in Russia seemed to be there and some famed imports too. At length the street was abuzz. "He's left the house." "He's walking." "He's alone." "His wife's with him." "He's wearing a homburg." "He's wearing a fedora." As he appeared at the end of the street, a tiny figure with an even tinier wife and surrounded by massive guards, my mentor and I went to the still-deserted back of the building, walked through the door, and waited by the table where the votes were cast. The polling clerks looked up in surprise, but, being good Communists and used to accepting the inexplicable, continued to simulate work.

In a moment, Krushchev entered, and we stepped forward. We had spent hours the day before trying to work out the one question we thought we might get in. Discarding dozens of alternatives, we asked, "How are you, sir?" Not much inspiration, perhaps, but open-ended enough to make the front page around the world if he said anything remotely damaging to the Communist regime. He looked surprised to see these two visitors from Mars—as did everyone else—but, as we'd calculated, with the entire press corps invited by the authorities to watch him vote, this wasn't the time for any of the guards to start a row. He paused a moment and said, "In 1917 when..." He spoke longer and more volubly than we could ever have expected. But he told us nothing that was not fifty years old. All I now recall that appeared in the papers was a photograph with a small caption. Still, I will treasure forever the sight of the world's press over his shoulder, held back by the guards and out of earshot, eyes popping with indignation as we apparently got our world scoop.

These years in the trenches helped me tell Nicholas' story. I knew about deadlines. I knew you could interest even the grandest editors if you had something worthwhile. I knew there would be many rebuffs. Most of all, I knew it was a big story.

I'd always expected to stay in newspapers, but in time another possibility opened and I found myself applying for a job as head of public information for the British nationalized gas industry, a huge organization in those days, with more than 100,000 employees. It was one of the top jobs of its kind in Britain, had to be vigorously fought for—that was one of the attractions—and came with a feeling of considerable self-importance. A car and chauffeur were available at all times, and my first job was to take a viscountess to Paris.

Another bug was biting me, however, and he had been at it a long time. I had studied the United States since my early schooldays. I knew by heart not just the Gettysburg Address, but all the verses of the "Star-Spangled Banner" and what the capital of Michigan was. Once when one of the teachers at school was asked a question about America, he replied shortly, "I don't know. Ask him." So I was predisposed to like the real thing and when, on the morning of my first visit to this country, I flew down the coast from San Francisco to Los Angeles, I looked out of the plane window and said to myself, "This is where I want to live forever and ever." Years of effort followed—letter-writing, phone calls, and unnumbered revisions of my résumé to make it fit every job possibility. Jane liked the idea too, and when the American Gas Association needed someone to run its public relations, we didn't hesitate.

So in 1970 I got the famous green card, so-called because it was a blue-colored piece of plastic, that—with one exception—gave access to whatever you could make of this rich and generous land. Being foreign-born, I could never become President of the United States. The vice presidency was still a long shot, however, and as it was then held by Spiro T. Agnew, the odds weren't all that bad. I've always been grateful to the people who brought me here, but I have to say the job lacked the pizzazz of the one I'd left—as far as I know, there wasn't a single viscountess in any gas company in the United States—and after three years I moved to the Investment Company Institute, the trade association of mutual funds, an industry where I have found decades of intellectual stimulus, lifetime (I hope) friendships, and a niche where longevity has conferred a spurious guru status.

For more years, Jane and I had a happy and productive household. As the children grew up, however, we were moving apart, spending more time away from each other. I was developing different interests, meeting new people, and in the end the marriage couldn't stand the strain. In 1984, we separated. What can you say about someone you've loved half your life and then left? Only, I suppose, that while I don't believe the marriage itself was salvageable, the qualities that started it in the first place are as memorable today as they were then. I saw that again when Nicholas died and Jane exhibited all the goodness and generosity of heart that on the night we met made her seem the most beautiful person I'd ever seen.

Meanwhile, Michael had majored in physics at Yale, went on to get his Ph.D. at Stanford, and now does something impressive but incomprehensible in Silicon Valley, and Annie is vice president of a public relations agency in Washington—a fun-loving, intelligent, and loyal pair who now have families of their own.

Like so many others before me, when I arrived in the United States I didn't feel I could break the ties with my own country any time soon. Giving up all that heritage was too much. It turned out there was no compelling need. In more than twenty years of working and living here, only a handful of people ever thought it mattered enough to ask if I had become naturalized. In time, however, it became clear this was now my home, and further delays began to seem silly. In 1994, I started the process and the next year became a citizen. Like the organ recipients who write to us because, although not knowing who their donors are, they want to thank someone, I'm aware that you reading this book didn't personally frame the laws and create the tolerance that allows someone from any country in the world to come here and take his place at the table. But knowing no other way to do it, I want to seize this chance to say thank you for the beacon you hold to the world.

My mother came to live in the United States and it proved to be the happiest time of her life. But in her mid-eighties she developed cancer of the esophagus and quickly weakened. I was with her at the hospital when the doctor came to tell her they couldn't operate and she would have to be fed through a tube for the rest of her life. Effectively, it meant she would live only a few months more. Until then it was the hardest blow I'd ever had to take.

She knew too, but made light of it. As we sat there, I remembered a story Harold Sykes had told me at school. "Did I ever tell you about the man who had to be fed by a tube?" I asked her. "It was his first time and he was quite scared. He told them he'd like to start on something simple, like tea. The doctors got everything ready. 'Don't worry,' they said, 'We've done this a thousand times.' They began to pour, but after a moment he started to scream and yell. 'What's the matter?' they cried 'Is it too hot?' 'No, no,' he shouted, 'There's no sugar in it.' " She was already smiling as I writhed on the end of the bed, and when I'd finished she started to laugh. She rocked back and forth, tears were streaming down her face, and on mine too, as I mimed the agony. In the end we finished and I said good night, yelling in pain one last time as I left. Out in the corridor, I leaned against the wall for a moment, realizing that this formidable spirit would not be there to laugh with much longer. When she died a few months later, I knew I had lost my most constant friend.

I knew Maggie was remarkable from the start. She didn't seem to care about appearances. Rather, she was disconcertingly frank. When you asked for an opinion, she gave it to you unvarnished. She shared information about her life of the kind others hide forever. She didn't fake her emotions or change her way of thinking because it would be convenient. I called her Contraggy Maggie. Now, individuality is all very well, but if it is allied to a shallow mind or a self-centered personality, it can quickly lose its charm. Happily, Maggie has a penetrating intelligence and a gentle and generous disposition. She is witty, well-read, and imaginative.

When she first told her mother there was a Significant Other in her life—though she'd have given up the relationship before describing it that way—she put it this way: "He's older than I am, he's shorter than I am, he's an immigrant, and he likes Frank Sinatra. Now you know the worst." I was, it's true, more older, more shorter, and more of a Sinatra fan than even this description suggested. But at least, with a green card, I was legal.

Scholarship was integral to her heritage: one grandfather was dean of Princeton, the other was comptroller there. A great-uncle was president of the university—and her pre-school was at the Institute for Advanced Studies! Her father was an architect of great promise, but died when she was eight years old. Her mother's family had been medical missionaries and teachers in India for three generations before independence, something that, always associating India exclusively with the British Raj, I still find surprising for an American family to have done: one of them was even knighted. Alicia, Maggie's mother, exudes the intellectual conviction and social conscience that must have motivated them.

Maggie is a generation younger than I am, knowing about World War II, for example, source of some of my most vivid memories, only through history books. She's also several inches taller. We are in all respects a distinctly odd couple, but oddest of all in being so compatible. Once, when Nicholas was very young, we visited a church in Tuscany with a fresco of the Holy Family showing a curly-haired and chubby Jesus, a serene Mary, and a very, very old Joseph. I saw a tourist close by jerk his thumb in our direction and say, "It's them."

We'd met when we were both in a boat club on the Chesapeake Bay, and compatibility had ripened into something much more. I'd imagined her interest in me was sparked by the masterly way I used to handle the tiller. Only later did she say she thought I looked so helpless that she felt I needed someone to look after me. She reads dauntingly fast, and studied architecture at Catholic University in Washington, D.C., where she was known for reliably coming up with some of the most innovative ideas and the untidiest drawings. Although given to diffidence about her scholastic achievements, literary allusions are rarely lost on her and her curiosity extends to both high- and low-brow. She seems to me to have an understanding that goes beyond cleverness, and she has taken from her reading and contacts with other people not just the quotations and the popular jargon but the essential messages on how to live. She is—how shall I put it?—a spasmodic housekeeper and her reaction to a smoke detector giving an alarm is to turn it off. At the slightest murmur on the baby monitor, however, she would get up uncomplainingly in the middle of the night to provide whatever comfort was needed.

A Presbyterian, she is to my mind the best kind of believer. She has faith without self-righteousness, allowing that others can find answers by different paths. She doesn't go to church, except occasionally to please her family, and has never tried to convert me to religion. But she knows the scriptures well enough for them to be not just words in a good book, but a means of illuminating daily life. So, when Nicholas died, she didn't discard her beliefs or wonder if God was punishing her, but calmly reminded herself that in her faith death is a transformation, not an end, and it is the soul, not the body, that endures. "Nicholas is where everything makes sense," she said to a reporter even in those first numbing hours.

The inscription on an award given to her in Sicily sums up this combination of softness and determination. "She was able to bear up against the most bitter and poignant sorrow ever conceivable, maintaining her dignified composure and turning her own and her family's tragedy into an example of courage and humanity to Italy and the whole world." She is in private as she is in public. I have never once heard her express bitterness at Nicholas' death or rail at her misfortune.

At home, she has remained the essential unifying force, loving without cloying, tolerant but not lax, and not allowing the loss to warp our daily lives, although she is aware every moment that we have lost an essential ingredient. As John Buchan said of someone he admired, she has both light and warmth in her.

I've always thought of Eleanor as being like an English spring day, with sunshine and rain mixed together, and occasional outbursts of thunder and lightning. Laughter and tears follow each other in rapid succession and sometimes overlap. It's that mixture, the ability to feel sorrow keenly, but to see the rainbow too, that has helped her through the overturning of her life with so few obvious scars. She was also helped by a strong mind and an iron will.

Some may see in the circumstances of her birth the origins of those features. Nicholas, unwilling to come into the world, had at first been induced with the drugs Maggie had been so reluctant to take and, when those didn't work, was a cesarean birth. He grew up strong and straight, but Maggie wanted her next child to be born as naturally as possible. California is rich in doctors and midwives who feel the same way, and she found in our area an experienced couple, Donald and his wife, Nan, dedicated proponents of natural birth. I was the only doubtful member of the party, but not sufficiently so to have much influence.

Once labor starts, I was told, there may not be a lot of time to get to the hospital in Santa Rosa, so keep alert. I did all I could: I bought new tires for the car and waited. But not for long. One morning Maggie announced that labor had started, and a few minutes later that the contractions had strengthened considerably. We called the midwife, but by the time she arrived she saw we might not get to the hospital in time. I'd already alerted the doctor, but now we called again and asked him to come to the house.

I had no idea what to do—on the three previous occasions when I'd become a father, the nurses seemed to prefer it that way—and Maggie, calm as always, simply said everything would be okay and just make sure Nicholas had his breakfast. I had, however, seen Jimmy Stewart, I think, deliver a baby in the back of a prairie schooner and I remembered he called for lots of hot water. When Don and Nan arrived, there were gallons of it. I was told to turn them off and instead heat towels in the oven. This was something neither Jimmy Stewart nor I had ever been told, and I managed to burn them. In those few minutes, however, a baby girl arrived and, though very fearful of hurting her, I was given the honor of cutting the umbilical cord. "We need more girls like this," Nan said. "This will be a strong woman."

Less than five years later, she needed all that strength. She awakened at the moment we discovered Nicholas had been shot. She came out of a sound sleep to a policeman shouting in alarm and an ambulance pulling up to the car. The limp body of her brother, who had seemed to be sleeping too, was carried out, put on a stretcher, and taken away. The three of us were ushered into the car of a stranger who spoke scarcely any English, driven along pitch-black roads, and interrogated by the police. She sat through the long drive to Sicily, the bleak days of waiting, and the sad journey home. For a girl of four years, the shock of this and all that followed is hard to comprehend. Much of it presumably was simply mystifying, much else numbing.

Maggie remembered this period in something she wrote a few months later: "I kept Eleanor close—in part to comfort her, but also to comfort myself. I knew Nicholas' dying was one of the possible outcomes, but I just focused on the moment. I remember telling Eleanor that, as Nicholas got better, we could look forward to his sitting up and then moving into a wheelchair." It was horrible to think of him being paralyzed, she added, but fearing something worse, it was something to hope for. "Eleanor has been my greatest consolation. She's helped keep us on track as a family. We couldn't skip Halloween or Thanksgiving or Christmas. And there's still someone to wait for after school, to make lunch for, to nag about TV."

In those early days, the most routine decisions, such as where Eleanor should sleep, were a step into the unknown. Since she was born she had shared a room with Nicholas. Their beds were side by side. On the whole, it seemed right for her to remain there. But in those first few nights, we slept fitfully, miserable anyway, and listening to see if she would wake up frightened. Each night she slept through until breakfast, however, and has slept there ever since. In time, we took out Nicholas' bed, another wrenching experience, and reorganized the space. But some of the toys they both played with are still there, as are most of the books and, presumably, a host of memories. In the record of everything that has happened to us, Eleanor's fortitude has been an inspiring example.

Many people helped to ease the transition for her. Children and mothers from all over Italy and as far away as Australia have written and sent dolls and chocolates—and a koala bear. Schmoozer Small, a cat from San Francisco, sent a Valentine card the first year and has been a faithful suitor ever since. Andrea, who got Nicholas' heart, said he wanted Eleanor to think of him as her brother. Judy Ninman, a designer from Dallas, gave her a dress that made her feel like a princess. Bodega Bay children, with saintly expressions, treated her with gentle sadness until she and they reverted to the norm.

Maggie stated the principle, "We don't want her to think of herself as the sister of the little boy who was killed. She should have a life of her own and grow in her own way." That's what we've tried to do. In the early months I, in particular, had to guard against trying to force her into the pattern that made Nicholas such a joy to me. She isn't interested in trains. She doesn't resound to the chivalry in the Robin Hood stories. And so far she doesn't give a hoot about the ironies of history he and I had so much fun with.

On the other hand, she is a whiz with numbers and quick recognition, and has a fine memory. She reads as fast as many adults, spells like a champion, and when the California Transplant Donor Network arranged for her to throw out the first ball at a San Francisco Giants game, she did it with aplomb. She also has the usual quota of tantrums and is fast developing the irritating family habit of correcting the details of stories told to her. She is taking a gratifying interest in musicals and knows what's playing at the Roxy, who got pinched in the Astor Bar, and which way the Battery is. "Who's Frank Sinatra?" a friend of hers said the other day. Eleanor was incredulous. "Who's Frank Sinatra? He's my hero." "She's going to be okay," I thought.

She also knows about death in a way most other children of her age don't. Whenever she and Nicholas had shown some anxiety about being in a strange place or in a darkened room, I'd always felt quite at ease saying, "You can't come to any harm. We're here." Now that has a false ring, and I can't bring myself to say it to her. Even fairy tales have pitfalls. For a long time after Nicholas died, I sensed a tremor in her when I read to her about Cinderella or Snow White, young girls whose mothers have died. "How old will you get?" she asked me one day. "I'm already old," I told her. "No, but when will you get as old as you're going to get?" "When you're an old lady, I hope," I said. She smiled at the absurdity of it, but I'd have felt more comfortable fobbing her off if she hadn't seen mortality so clearly for herself. One day she asked happily, "If you could have anything you wanted in the whole world, what would it be?" As long as I can remember I've been able to come up with a dozen answers to that kind of question. But now I could think of only one thing, and that I felt I couldn't say and puncture her mood. She looked keenly at me for a moment while I hesitated, and then quickly moved on to something else.

I can't remember her ever trying to turn her loss to personal advantage by demanding special favors. I think you can say this was a two-way street. Maggie made no secret of the sadness Nicholas' going was causing and always enveloped Eleanor in love, but she made it clear that she would not be blackmailed into relaxing the standards of behavior we thought important. An extra ice cream, perhaps, or extra sessions in front of the television set, but being rude and impolite were no more acceptable than they had been before. On my side, I've rarely found it necessary to vocalize my love for the children. I've always thought they could tell. One night in Rome, however, Eleanor and I were dining by ourselves when she said something that seemed to me so perceptive beyond her years that I told her, "You know, Eleanor, I really love you." She blushed like a beetroot and made a show of looking modest, but I could tell she was delighted.

She appears to have taken the loss of a playmate with whom she often squabbled, but whom she loved dearly and was loved by in return, just about how I would have wished.

I was therefore less than enthusiastic about a suggestion that she should see a psychiatrist. But when Maggie was joined by Eleanor's doctor, David Fichman, and mine too, it became clear that it was the right thing to do. Besides looking for signs of disturbance that had eluded us as parents, a key reason for going was to establish a benchmark so there will be something to compare to if she does start to have troubles later. We were lucky with our doctors throughout. The highly respected child psychiatrist they recommended quickly succeeded in establishing a good rapport and came across vague feelings of guilt and anxiety that Eleanor had—consciously or not—kept from us. But in the end, the evidence seemed to confirm our overall impression: that her young mind, however it has been changed, has been strong enough to handle a potentially devastating trauma.

It soon had to handle another shock. Once the funeral was over, it was time to turn to the new kitten. Eleanor went with Maggie to the Humane Society, chose the worst-behaved of a litter and came home laden with as many accessories as if it were a new baby. I'm not sure who suggested the name, but as soon as Eleanor heard it, that's what it had to be: Angel. Eleanor loved him enough to make his life a misery and he retaliated by attacking reporters who came to interview us. Maggie called him a fallen angel.

But one night I heard a knock at the door and found Maggie talking to one of the neighbors who was telling her Angel had been killed by a passing car. We told Eleanor the next morning and, as she sobbed, she said, "I thought he'd have lived longer than this," a somber reflection of the way she had come to understand the impermanence of life. Maggie drew Angel's face on a rock for a headstone, and they buried him by the house. For the next few days, Eleanor showed her friends the new grave, sadly but with a hint of pride too. She asked about getting another cat, but we were traveling so much that we put it off, and she has mentioned it since then only from time to time, and then without much conviction. So far we have no new pet. I find myself wondering if she just got bored or if, more deeply, she didn't want to run the risk of yet another loss.

Eleanor is now older than Nicholas ever was. She is beginning to learn things he never heard of and explore ideas he couldn't have grasped. At some time he will change in her mind from being the elder brother, who led her through brightly colored fantasies, to the small second-grader in the photographs. Her memory of the details is already fading as she carves out a life for herself. But she hasn't forgotten yet. A few years ago, out on what had been a simple stroll with her and Nicholas near Banff in the Canadian Rockies, a snowstorm blew up. We had a clear way home and only a half mile or so to go, but Eleanor, until then carefree but now suddenly vulnerable, and wearing flimsy shoes as always, was plunged into misery, dragging her ill-shod feet through the snow. I egged her on, but she was so unhappy that I eventually picked her up and put her on my shoulders. She cheered up immediately. At the same time Nicholas, affected by her tears, started to run alongside us shouting encouragement: "Hi, Ellie, hi, Ellibobelli." She began to laugh, a little at first, then more and more. The more she did, the more Nicholas hammed it up, running around and yelling "Ellibobelli" every few steps. Once or twice after he died, I thought of calling her Ellibobelli, but it didn't seem right. Then one night she said to Maggie, "Do you remember, Mama, that day when I was cold and Nicholas called me Ellibobelli to make me laugh? Wasn't that nice of him? I wish he could say that to me again, I wish I could have a new brother and he'd say that to me. Remember Mama, when he kept running ahead and making me laugh? Remember?" I loved her for thinking of it. I thought too of what we would all have done with that memory if Nicholas had still been with us—furiously disputing the details, dragging in similar incidents, embellishing it. What a lot we'd lost, all of us. As it was, we simply smiled to ourselves and followed our own thoughts.

In "To a Louse," Robert Burns hopes we can see ourselves as others see us. I can tell him it can be quite deflating. I've always thought our house in Bodega Bay, with its wall of glass looking out to the ocean, quite breathtaking. Alas, people in glass houses shouldn't get cocky. *USA Today* called it "the small house by the ocean." Another writer described it as "modest." *The New York Times* pointed out that my office had a futon in it. (No longer. Every inch of bedding has been pressed into service in a house that needs all the sleep it can get.)

Bad though this was, the descriptions of our lives were more depressing still. A spate of articles contrasted the news coverage we had received with our previous obscurity. "Nothing had prepared them for this," said one. "They had done nothing to suggest the worldwide recognition that came to them," said another. "They had lived quietly," wrote a third. What had I been doing all my life? I wondered. Graduation from university at nineteen, word-perfect recall of (almost) every hit song from "On the Good Ship Lollipop" through the big band era, writer for some of the world's best newspapers, junior partner in a potentially blockbusting scoop from Moscow, number-one card-holding member one year of the Austrian Alpine Club (because of a clerical snafu). Secretly, I'd been proud of all this. Now what a louse I felt.

About the house, however, I am unrepentant. It's on the golf course by the eighteenth tee, reputedly one of the most difficult holes in northern California. I say reputedly because I have never played a round here. However, watching that tee and, without ever having to leave home, I feel I have participated in virtually the entire range of human emotions. Looking south, across the expanse of water on the far side of Point Reyes, the first land you'd come to would be

Antarctica. Out beyond Bodega Head, again with no land of any size in between, is Japan. Northwest across more water are Alaska and Siberia. That vast ocean dominates our weather. A mile inland it may be hot and sunny while we're in thick fog. Some days you can look through one window and see blue sky, turn around, and from another window see...nothing. The wind blows strongly, whenever it feels like it, and that is frequently. "The weather changes endlessly," someone on this coast advised us when we first came here. "Dress like an onion." The Goldilocks porridge of a climate helps make it for me the most beguiling place I've ever lived.

In winter, storms build out at sea, the sky blackens, the wind picks up enough to blow chairs over on the deck, and squalls whip the water by the rocks. Clouds that were miles away are suddenly blotting out everything. Then—whoosh—rain hits the windows like water from a hose pipe and thunders on the skylights. A few minutes later, I'll look up and see the sun dancing on the waves and the ocean as blue as the Pacific of legend. In the summer, the fog belt plays tricks all day long—closing in on the house like Jack the Ripper's London, then moving to play on the dunes, five minutes later way out at sea and the whole area basking in the sun.

A sign in the middle of our little town going north warns, "Tractor-semis over 30 feet kingpin to rear axle not advised next 154 miles." This may be as incomprehensible to you as it is to me. Still, the note of menace is clear. Another sign a few miles on the other side of the village gives similar advice for the next fifty-one miles south. They show how undeveloped the coast is although, using inland routes, it is an easy drive to San Francisco. Only a thousand people live here, and our doctor is a dozen miles away. Though tiny, it is familiar around the world as the setting for Alfred Hitchcock's *The Birds*, and few of the backdrops have changed much since then. To the south, sandy beaches interspersed with coves stretch for miles. You can walk to the next county—at low tide. Going north are high dunes and miles and miles of golden beaches. Inland, a line of green hills parallels the coast. The area has plenty of wildlife, is famous for its fish, and has a wider variety of birds than almost any other place in the United States. It is just a dot on the map, but a historically significant dot, marking the northern border of Spanish America and the southern border of Tsarist Russia's American colony. Both disappeared from California with the pioneer settlers and the gold rush, but the nearest river to the south is still the Estero Americano and to the north the Russian River. Those who named them would have no difficulty recognizing them today.

We came across it by chance. When I left the Investment Company Institute, in 1984, to start my own business—a public relations news service about investing—I thought about the optimal place to live. We were in Washington, D.C., then, and the obvious spot to go was at the focal point of the main financial centers. True to business school principles, I drew a map, with a heavy line from New York, another from Boston, smaller but still big from Chicago and Los Angeles, and lesser ones from various cities across the United States. I joined all these lines together, properly weighted, and found they met in the middle of Lake Erie. I threw the map away and we moved to San Francisco, where we wanted to live. After a year or so in a small office there, it gradually dawned on me—I'm a slow learner—that I could work from home and, when Nicholas was born and we needed more space, that we didn't even have to live in the city. I took to scouring the countryside, and eventually made it safely to Bodega Bay and a lasting infatuation.

For years Maggie acted—though it was not a very convincing performance—as my secretary and is still the office manager. The commute from breakfast table to office takes twenty seconds, and I have stuck rigidly to the only useful rule those business school books taught me about being self-employed: "Never work before breakfast. If you have to work before breakfast, get up early and have breakfast first." The people here, working or retired, are a mix of fisherman and lawyers, accountants and journalists, gardeners and builders, shopkeepers and farmers. A few have lived here nearly all their lives, but mostly they have come from all parts of the United States, with a sprinkling of Europeans, Mexicans, and Asians.

The local school is very small, so small that the six grades are combined into three classes. It has sixty students this year, three teachers who care about learning, a secretary, a principal who divides her time between Bodega Bay and Tomales, several miles away, where there is a sister school, and a squad of helpful parents. It seems chronically short of money, but has a heart and a head many a better-endowed school would be proud of. It also has a diverse group of kids who are close enough to the workaday world to have their feet on the ground, but who are also steadily absorbing those intellectual revelations that growing up in a thoughtful environment brings. Everyone has different ideas: too little this, too much that, and they are important issues.

Without them there wouldn't be a thoughtful environment. But the overall standard is summed up by the eulogy to Nicholas given by his teacher, Loretta Smith, which took the comments of the other children in his class and shaped them into a little work of art that helped give meaning and comfort in the face of violent death. In the confusing first years at school, could anything be more understanding?

In our misfortune, the entire community came together as one.

Early one morning, a few weeks after the shooting, there was an unusual flurry of calls. We let the first two or three go to the answering machine. But clearly something was happening. Maggie picked up the next one and was told, "They've arrested two men for your son's murder. How do you feel about it?" How did we feel? A little sick, really. There was relief, certainly, that they had been caught and the process could move forward. The men who attacked us were terrorists, and I was in no doubt that I wanted to see them held accountable. There was satisfaction that the confidence the police had expressed, that whoever did this would not get away with it, had been justified. But there was dejection too, knowing that the cardboard figures were now real people with families who on that day were presumably saying to themselves despairingly, "Why did this have to happen?"

CHAPTER EIGHT

WE GO BACK TO ITALY

One Saturday morning, a month or two after we arrived home from Italy, the phone rang. On the other end was an Italian, speaking English fluently and at express speed, who had learned the language first as a scullery maid in a working-class vacation camp in the north of England and second at one of the meccas of British education, St. Antony's College, Oxford. He was now The Cultural Adviser—I always thought of it with capital letters—to the Bonino-Pulejo Foundation, a prestigious charitable organization set up by the owners of *Gazzetta Del Sud,* the Messina-based newspaper. It embraces many causes, including scholarships for students in Sicily to study abroad. The money takes them to Cambridge and Harvard and Heidelberg, absorbing the best the world can teach, and then coming back to one of the poorest regions in Europe to improve the practice of medicine or chemistry or literary appreciation.

Each year, said the voice, identifying itself as Dr. Piero Orteca, we give a prize to a world-class scholar, the Bonino-Pulejo award. Last year it went to the co-discoverer of the AIDS virus. "This year..." I held my breath. "...it is going to..." I continued to hold. "...Ralf Dahrendorf, the political philosopher." I let out my breath. "That's nice," I said. "Ah, but that's not all," Piero continued. "This year for the first time we want to give a special prize for humanitarian actions of an equally high order, and we want to give it to your family. Do you accept?" Of course we accepted. This was a gratifying level of recognition.

"Now, for this, Mr. Green, we would like you and Margaret and Eleanor to be our guests. We will cover your expenses, everything. We will transport you around Sicily, wherever you want to go. You will meet Nicholas' recipients. You will attend a performance of the Paris ballet. You will stay in a beautiful hotel in Taormina. We will take you to the archaeological sites you never got to see on your first visit."

Several weeks later we went, and the visit fulfilled every promise Piero had made for it. They did send us all over Sicily, we did meet the recipients, we did have a box at the ballet. And we did stay at Taormina's version of heaven, the San Domenico Hotel, looking out over a turquoise sea and the snow-covered smoking mass of Mount Etna. We also visited most of the classical ruins we'd planned to see on our vacation.

This was our first visit back to Italy and journalists from all over Europe were at the hotel. So was ABC's *20/20* team, who subsequently traveled with us through long days and nights. Calls came in constantly—the BBC, French television, *Gente* magazine from Argentina, and a French journalist with a title I'd never seen before, "grand reporter." Harry Benson, a native of Glasgow, who in his young days was tough and smart enough to take most of the famous black-and-white photographs of the early Beatles, arrived from New York for *Life* magazine. Every few minutes we were asked, "How do you feel being back in Italy?" "How do you feel about meeting the recipients?" "How do you feel about the arrests?" In Taormina, walking down the narrow streets, packed with people, was like a royal progress. Mimi Murphy, *Life*'s reporter from Rome, said she saw Maggie, head and shoulders above the crowd, smiling and nodding and being mobbed like Princess Diana.

I'd previously told Piero that, on the rest day he'd planned before the main ceremony, I wanted to climb Mount Etna. He agreed and on that day we drove up into the snowfield for what was to be the start of the hike. As we got out of the car, reporters tumbled out of a procession of cars that had followed us, most dressed fittingly for a press conference in the hotel lounge—loafers, slacks, and open-necked shirts—but not for even the briefest encounter with nature. A few lit cigarettes to ward off the freshness of the air. I had a vision of climbing the trail accompanied by photographers lugging cameras and reporters holding notebooks in frostbitten fingers. Perhaps they did too. At any rate, without debate, we all moved into the restaurant at the foot of the climb, ate a hearty meal, and then drove down again to the warm sunshine.

Before we left, however, one man distinguished himself even in these unpromising conditions. With half a dozen other photographers looking on, Harry fastened on a fight with snowballs we were having and stage-managed it to catch one in the act of exploding on my head, Eleanor turning away in smarmy triumph, and Maggie laughing uproariously in the background. It became our Christmas card that year and, to judge by the volume of mail, touched a chord everywhere. "Your card told us however bad things are, there must be laughter," one school in Italy wrote.

In previous years, the annual Bonino-Pulejo awards were given at the university in Messina. This time, because of the interest, we were in the largest building in town, the Vittorio Emanuele Theater, and on that Saturday morning it was filled to capacity.

We were asked to wait in the hotel across the street, and it was with real pleasure that I saw there the desk clerk who on our last visit had fielded so stylishly the hurricane of phone calls from the highest offices in Italy and some of the world's most impatient people, senior journalists. He'd left the Europa for this other hotel and, standing behind the desk, was another reminder that when the occasion demands it, people everywhere rise to the challenge.

The biggest event of the morning was to be a meeting with the recipients—six of them, Andrea being still in the hospital with side effects from his heart transplant. We'd spoken on the telephone with one or two of them and been in a television linkup for a two-hour (!) prime-time Christmas program. But this was our first meeting and none of us knew what to expect.

Then, suddenly, they were there. One by one, they and their families came in and brought with them not one mood, but a whole palette. Some were shy, some ebullient, some restrained, some exuberant, some tearful, some beaming. Nothing perhaps could have demonstrated so clearly the explosive effects of transplantation. Domenica and Francesco could see properly again, Silvia was less dependent on her walking stick, Anna Maria and Tino were jumping about excitedly, and Maria Pia, dying four months earlier, was on the threshold of womanhood. We didn't speak the same language as the recipients, but we pumped hands, put our arms around them, kissed and were kissed, laughed and cried, were asked a flood of incomprehensible questions, and answered in kind. Nods and smiles and gestures did for words, and, across the language barrier, everything was clear.

Yes, they said, they all felt much better. Yes, they were enjoying life as they had not enjoyed it for years. Yes, their families could start living a normal life too. And, yes, yes, they loved Nicholas and would never forget him. We had expected mixed emotions from ourselves. But the relief in those faces overwhelmed the sadness.

As I looked at them I asked myself, "Did one little body do all this?" and, yes, it did. It had saved all those people from the devastation we have faced. Most families, I think, don't realize, as we didn't at the time, what a mighty gift they have in their hand when called on to make a decision about donation. Yet few people will ever have the chance to change the world as much as they can at that moment.

The theater was bursting with excitement. We were taken first into an enormous room full of children. I have never seen so many photographers in one small space. As they lined up in front of us, jostling for position, the flashes were like a summer's night exploding with fireflies. Through it all I heard Harry Benson's voice, "Reg, this way. Maggie, look down here." (He'd used the same technique at the O. J. Simpson trial, he told me later, on a man who had refused to be photographed.) We looked as bidden and, as usual, his pictures were the best of all.

The younger recipients had never seen anything remotely like it. "This is going to overwhelm them," I thought, "after all, these are people recovering from serious illness." I needn't have worried. They all took it in stride. Eleanor, too. A few weeks later I heard her saying to her dolls, "Look at me, click, look at me, click, click." These photographs made top-of-the-page stories around the world, deservedly, for in one image they captured a stunning victory of life over death. Often in those days people asked if I felt like a father to the recipients. It occurred to me to say "more like the Godfather." This was Sicily, however, and I resisted the impulse.

Lord Dahrendorf, the winner of the Bonino-Pulejo award, gave a characteristically thoughtful and questioning speech, and the forty students who received the awards were enthusiastically cheered by friends and families. But it was clear that the massive turnout was for the organ donation story. Well-known people were there from all over southern Italy: Nino Collarco, the hardworking head of the Bonino-Pulejo foundation, naturally, but also government officials, leading transplant surgeons, professors, artists, lawyers, and many people who had befriended us the last time we were in Messina. Alessandra, the doctor who had translated the medical terms for us and won all our hearts, was there and the head of the police who had been detailed to look after us at that time. Though an imposing figure with many men at his command, he had spent an hour on his cellular phone changing our flight home. I didn't dare tell him that as soon as we got to Rome the tickets he had arranged with such pain were canceled by the president's staff.

Then it was time for us to speak, and we did so to thunderous applause. Maggie mentioned that Nicholas had a set of U.S. cavalry soldiers and Indians that were so important to him he had taken them with him on vacation. They were in the car the night of the attack. They rarely fought each other, and when we had unpacked his things we found the two sides had been having a party and had exchanged clothes and weapons. I've often thought that, if Nicholas had been at the Battle of Little Bighorn, instead of General Custer, the history of the West might have been quite different. Maggie had lovingly put them all back in order, taking the bugles and gloves off the chiefs and the moccasins and headdresses off the soldiers. When she gave one to each of the recipients, they looked as though they had been handed a present from heaven.

A few days later we visited Maria Pia at her home, alongside the main railroad line to Palermo. In her room was a large photograph of Nicholas, next to which she puts a fresh flower every day. Guarding both was the little soldier. Trains thundered by night and day. To anyone unused to it, the sound was deafening. "Wouldn't Nicholas have loved this house?" Maggie whispered.

From the start, Maria Pia seemed to feel close to us. In the faces of her family, who clearly adored her, we could see the strain her illness had put on them. Now a load had been lifted and, though still unable to let go of worry, they reflected the relief of people coming back from the very edge of a calamity. Before we left, she gave me a pen. "It's so you can go on writing beautiful things about Nicholas," she said.

From there, we visited Tino at his school in Syracuse, where he was jumping around, singing, dancing, having to be warned not to overdo it. He was the class comic, we were told, though a comic who had been wasting away before his kidney transplant. We met his mother and aunt and his concerned teacher too, gracious ladies, but with the care-worn faces we were beginning to expect. I sat down at the next desk to Tino, feeling a little like a father on prize-giving day. I thought of all the games he'd play and all the gags he'd pull and, remembering a desk in another schoolroom, I felt my eyes fill with tears. I looked at him and saw tears in his eyes too. At this tender age, he'd understood. I put my arms round his shoulders and hugged him.

We also visited Palermo, the capital, to see the mayor, Leoluca Orlando, a legend in Italian politics for his campaign against the Mafia. We met in the city hall, and as usual a representative of each of the political parties—five of them in this case—made a formal speech. In this serious mood, Orlando presented us with the huge visitors' book which breathed old age and great events. I asked if Eleanor could sign too. His face broke into a grin and, tongue sticking out of her mouth and gripping the big ceremonial pen like a javelin, she wrote her name, alongside some of the most venerable signatures in Italy, in huge misshapen block capitals that ran to the end of the page like lemmings tumbling over a cliff. After that in other cities, when invited to sign a visitors' book, I often asked if they would like Eleanor to sign too. Such is the Italians' love of children that most seemed delighted and her laborious marker disfigures such books across the country. But it was Orlando's unfeigned pleasure that emboldened me to ask.

That day he was planning to address a meeting in a theater of several hundred children from every school in the city, each of which had adopted a historical monument and from now on would study it, read about the history of its time, and keep it clean. He asked us to go with him and we were submerged in an inspiring meeting of kids cheering their heritage, cheering the mayor, and cheering themselves hoarse at every mention of Nicholas. At the end, they spilled onto the stage, bright intelligent kids, crippled kids, mentally impaired kids, all wanting to meet us and say something nice. One strikingly beautiful girl of about thirteen was brought to us. She was blind and simply wanted to run her hands over our faces. I can still feel her gentle memorizing touch.

On the face of it, every day seemed to be a flirtation with death for the mayor. He travels in a convoy at breakneck speed around the seething streets, bumper to bumper with his escorts, sirens wailing, tires screeching. Even Gino Mauro, our impeccably calm driver, who glided us around Sicily as if on a magic carpet, smiled with relief when we reached the television station in one piece through the evening rush hour. Orlando and his wife, who, like him, has to cope with the possibility of sudden death every day, took us to lunch in a small exquisite restaurant. We were the only guests. For safety's sake they had picked a place that would normally have been closed that day, a Monday. The four of us talked a long time in that quiet, empty room, wonderful dishes coming out of nowhere, removed from all contact with the world, while outside the tiny square was crammed with police cars.

We all liked each other, and they invited us to dinner, ostensibly at their house. Whether that plan changed or if it was part of the incessant game of deception we never knew but, although we did go to dinner, it was not an intimate evening, but a grand affair in honor of fifty maitre d's from some of the most famous restaurants in Italy, and featuring one soaring course after another. Then we moved outside and reality came back. Bodyguards surrounded the mayor, we said "au revoir"—"good-bye" seemed ominous—and Gino drove us away first. A few hundred yards down the road a convoy of black cars roared by, going twice our speed, and disappeared into the night. At one time I would have thought it extravagant. But the memory of another quiet night made it seem quite natural.

We were up and away early next morning, heading for Agrigento, one of the places that was to have been a high spot of the vacation we had planned for the previous year. In all our travels through Sicily, we were escorted by a police car, which mostly just kept station ahead of us, but at times cleared traffic to keep up the momentum. Driving on the wrong side of the streets in the morning rush in Palermo is something you should try when your zest for life fades. It reached its peak when our small but determined convoy met another just like it intent on crossing our path at an already jammed intersection. Courtesy should have ruled—who cared whether the journey took one hour and forty minutes or one hour and forty-two minutes?—but a wave of triumph went through me when our police car bested their police car and we raced on to the next jammed intersection.

We had to stay in touch with our escort for another reason. Its trunk was filled with the stuffed animals Eleanor was given at each stop. We now had an entire Noah's ark, including a (nearly) life-sized elephant and a sleeping bag in the shape of a mouse. At every stop, the numbers grew, and every night we had to unload them from the police car, put them on a hotel trolley, sometimes two, and bring them down again the next morning. We tried to get Eleanor to give some of them up to children on the way, but she was adamant and in the end I liked the idea of returning to her own room with this horn of plenty, so she would always have a memory of Italy's unstinting generosity.

Sicily is divided into many different police jurisdictions and at each one, three or four times that day, the escort changed. We'd be bowling along when there would be a crackle on Gino's borrowed police walkie-talkie and we'd learn that at the bridge, just after the rocks, but before the big farmhouse, the new car would be waiting for us. When we got there, both police cars would be drawn up alongside each other, the new one's crew peering incredulously into the old one's trunk. Still, the changeover would take place—four beefy men gently handling pelicans and lions, monkeys and leopards—we'd shake hands all round and be rolling again.

Agrigento was all I'd expected and a bit more. The civic leaders met us, invited us to lunch, and then put us in care of an expert on the classical sites. There was quite a crowd, local journalists, the *20/20* crew, two detectives who would be our bodyguards while we were in their town, bemused tourists who had expected to have the place to themselves in February, and representatives of every segment of the local population. Despite the friendliness and the many television "takes"—none of which were used in the final program—it was an unsettling experience. This was a place we had looked forward to the previous summer. I'd been thinking then of all the things we would show the children in a way that would make it captivating. Now we were here with all that same knowledge and that same desire to share, but without a crucial member of the pageant.

Hereabouts Persephone was captured by the king of the underworld, breaking her mother's heart, a tale that made such an impression on Nicholas that he never got tired of hearing it. He'd listen gravely as she was allowed to return to earth for a few months each year, her arrival marking spring, the rebirth of life, and her departure the onset of winter. "Look," said Maggie, "there's Persephone's flower, almond blossom. Remember? It's the sign that new life is starting again." It was a lovely flower in the perfect setting and, looking at its message of death and renewal, I don't think any story from the classical world has ever affected me so deeply

The most satisfying way of seeing great sights to me has always been when I've been completely alone. When I found the temples were floodlit at night and that I could get in to see them, I could scarcely wait for darkness. I offered to go there by myself, but Gino wouldn't hear of it. In return I extracted a promise from him that he'd leave me at the entrance and I'd walk along the cobbled road, the sacred way, and meet him at the other end exactly forty minutes later. He was a little doubtful, but, as a man who also liked being alone, he understood. The temples are laid in a line on top of a spectacular hill, huge but delicately proportioned so that they seem to float. On that balmy flower-scented night, I saw them all in perfect solitude.

When I came to Juno's temple, I remembered something that had happened in Paestum. In the reading we'd done the previous summer, we'd often come across Juno—though more generally under her Greek name, Hera, Zeus' jealous wife—who punished every real or imagined slight with death and destruction. As we'd left Paestum, we stopped to look for a postcard. Among them I saw one of Hera's temple and said to Nicholas, "Let's not get this. I never thought much of her." I regretted it immediately. "I probably shouldn't have said that," I said, and laughed. It's a ridiculous fancy, of course, although some of the wisest scholars of the classical world would have made the connection when a few hours later Nicholas was struck down.

Now I leaned against one of the columns, almost prepared to believe in her supernatural powers. And, allowing for a moment that the ancient stories might be true after all, I thought about Nicholas and what Hera had done to him and to us. "Be careful," one part of my mind said. But it wouldn't do, and instead I said out loud, "You ought to be ashamed of yourself." It did me good. You have to stand up to bullies. I moved to the last building, drinking it all in, when my eye caught a movement flitting between the shadows of the cactus at the edge of a pool of light. It was one of the bodyguards and, it turned out, he'd been tailing me, unseen, every inch of the way. I've sometimes wondered what he made of my confrontation with the queen of heaven.

The Nicholas Effect Grows

Like the splitting of the atom, a botched robbery in a place most people have never heard of produced a worldwide fallout that continues to this day. Italians called it l'effetto Nicholas—the Nicholas effect—because, in the first few days after his death, the number of people signing organ donor cards there quadrupled. But the effect grew to proportions and took on shapes we could never have foreseen and, as it did, Maggie and I—and Eleanor too—made it our job to make it grow still more.

I remember saying to someone at the time that I wanted to squeeze the last drop of good out of this miserable affair. "Don't think of it like that," she said. "Think of it as a trickle turning into a stream, turning into a torrent, into a river and then into a flood." And that is how I do think of it now, thanks to the myriad demonstrations of human solidarity it has brought.

Hundreds and hundreds of people wrote letters that combined dejection at the cause and jubilation at the results. Strangers offered whatever help came naturally to them. The world's media dissected the story and found lessons for all mankind. Awards that in previous years went to some of the world's greatest thinkers and humanitarians were given in the name of a small boy who couldn't even do cursive writing. Men and women, boys and girls performed inspirational acts that had nothing to do with organ donation, but simply reflected a desire to pay back to the world something they vaguely felt they owed. And many people, who had scarcely thought about it before, realized with a shock that every year thousands of families, just like theirs, lost a member because other families, also like theirs, didn't donate the organs their loved ones no longer needed. Every response added a little to the flow.

CHAPTER NINE

HONORS FOR A SMALL BOY

From Sicily we flew home. Two weeks later, we were back in Italy. We hadn't planned it that way. No one in his right mind would. But the invitations were building and there were some we couldn't turn down. Once again we left home in the dark to catch the early flight to Newark, then overnight to Rome with, as before, dawn breaking over southern France and the peaks on Corsica going from gray to pink to orange.

This time we were on the way to receive a prize at the cathedral in Vibo Valentia, in Calabria, close to where Nicholas was killed, for what in Italian is called a *Testimonianza*, God's will working through human actions, a heady idea for an agnostic like me. The bishop's letter said it would offer "a moment of purification and reconciliation for the whole of Italy." In former years it had gone to, among others, Mother Teresa and Cardinal Glemp, the primate of Poland famed for standing up to Communist pressure.

Our plane to Calabria was due to take off shortly after we arrived in Rome, but technical difficulties with the aircraft delayed it, technical difficulties with a bus that was to take us out on the runway delayed us further, and technical difficulties with the baggage put us close to noon. Eventually we were seated and prepared to take off. Before we could move, however, there was one more announcement: a technical difficulty had occurred with air traffic control. Noon, it appeared, was the time set for their token strike, so we would have to wait. "We're just about to take off," the captain told the tower. "Sorry, you're out of time," they said. He tried again. "We've got the Green family aboard. They've come all the way from the United States. Can't you let us go?" "Wait a moment..."—a brief pause—then, "okay, you're cleared for takeoff." A burst of applause filled the aircraft. We took off, alone in the air, like a good deed in a naughty world, and looked down. In one of the busiest airports in the world, nothing else moved.

By the time we reached the airport near Vibo, the brass band that had been waiting since breakfast time had been sent home to have its lunch, but Don Onofrio Brindisi, dean of the cathedral, and local civic leaders were still braving the chill wind, and soon we were on our way. After a while, it came to me that we were passing through the section of road where the attack on our car had taken place. The driver, solicitous as virtually everybody we met in Italy was, gave no indication. When I asked him if this was the place, he deflected the question. Then I knew, of course, and recalled every detail in a flash.

We were taken to the 501 Hotel, high on a hill overlooking the sea, with the volcanic island of Stromboli a spectacular landmark in the distance. I had the eagerness to get on with things that I always associate with the new day after a night of traveling and, while Maggie and Eleanor went to bed—their association with night travel being a good sleep—I joined the sort of table I was beginning to get used to: a bishop, the chief of police, and an impressive scholar from the Vatican. Maggie and Eleanor were smarter than I was. Don Onofrio had prepared a schedule an American politician in an election year might have jibbed at—a fusillade of radio, press, and television interviews; school, hospital, and church meetings.

It was quite clear that many people in Calabria felt they had some share of blame for Nicholas' death, and it seemed important on our first visit back there to deal with this head-on. The first opportunity came almost immediately when we were asked to open an emigration museum. It was a haunting mirror image of the immigration ports of the New World, battered cardboard suitcases tied with string, well-used pots and pans, a carefully packed bridal gown, a few simple tools, and quirky personal items of no possible value to anyone but their miserably homesick owners. Together they summed up the boundless hopes of a new life and the desolation of being cut off from everything familiar. "Wait till they find out that relative of yours was governor of Ellis Island," I whispered to Maggie.

Out loud, I recalled that although the days of mass migration were over, the people of southern Italy could still follow their dreams as their ancestors who crossed the seas had done. The people in the audience were the true face of Calabria, we said, not the violent men who had fired on us. "You didn't pull the trigger," we told them. "You would have done anything in your power to stop Nicholas' killers." It was almost embarrassingly trite, but we meant it—you couldn't not mean it looking at those sad faces and the brave little bundles their forebears had carried—and it seemed to make an impression. Afterward, a journalist told us, "Keep saying those things. These people feel the rest of Italy is always dumping on them. Now, on top of all that, there's what happened to your son. They feel rotten. If you can help them keep their self-respect, you'll be doing something that's badly needed."

A quick visit to a nunnery—intended to be so quick it wasn't even on the itinerary—was prolonged by the quiet insistence that we couldn't leave without taking coffee and homemade cakes. One of the nuns came over and said she understood we might be making a movie. She asked if we knew how she might contact her cousin who lived in southern California and was in show business himself. "I'd like to write to him," she said. "My name is Sister Patrizia Sinatra."

At times in those early weeks, we had passing doubts about these activities. "Are we doing any good with all this? Are we just keeping busy to ward off our own emptiness? Are we exploiting the situation to be in the limelight?" I think both of us dug deeply to try to find the answer. Some of the moments in the public eye were exhilarating, of course, and the public approval of what we were doing was obvious. On the other hand, it was hard going too, physically and emotionally. But the overwhelming feeling we took away from most encounters, both in Italy and at home, was that good really was coming out of it: we could feel it in the air.

One morning in Calabria, we visited a day-care center for handicapped youths, a place that to many of them was like home. They stood by the door as we drove up, in a neat orderly line, but with that sense of bursting impatience the young have when they have been waiting a long time. They bore the marks of their affliction, some trembling, others breathing deeply, some standing rigidly to attention. There was something so humbling about it that, without waiting for the formality even the smallest Italian ceremonies demand, we found ourselves in their midst, hugging and gripping hands and laughing. They showed us round and fed us—again—and slowly and with difficulty explained what they did at the center. As we left, the director told us that few of them had slept properly for the past three nights, anticipating our visit and worried that it might be canceled. The neighborhood must have been very like that where the men who shot Nicholas were youths too. Perhaps someone with the dedication of the staff at this center might have made the crucial difference to them. After that visit, I don't think I ever had any serious doubts about what we were doing.

This was the last day before Lent, and the local children were getting ready for a massive fancy dress affair. We had heard about it weeks before and, one after another, local mothers had offered to supply a costume for Eleanor. As late as the day itself, they were pressing us to let them make one. "We can easily do it in time," they said. We refused all offers, however. We had our own plan. Maggie and I had thought of it simultaneously when we had come home through Newark on the last visit. We both had window seats, one behind the other, and we saw it at the same time. "Do you know what I think Eleanor should go as to the fancy dress party?" I leaned forward and asked Maggie, proud of my idea. "Yes," she said, "the Statue of Liberty." She found a bilious green sheet, stitched and sewed it into folds, and made a creditable crown and torch out of material covered by the same seasick color. She fished a heavy book off the shelves—the Italian dictionary we'd just bought—and that was that. On the day of the party Eleanor went off with newfound Italian friends while we did the round of meetings. We arrived at the cathedral as darkness fell. There, torch held high and bursting with pride, like the Pied Piper of Hamelin, she was leading a pulsating procession of cheering, dancing children, round and round the great square, all following the liberty lamp and all looking like infant immigrants to the land of McDisney.

"Tomorrow will be a busy day," I said to Don Onofrio as we said our farewells that night. "Tomorrow will be a glorious day," he said. It was. The first part was filled with preparations and meetings and large excited crowds and then a trip back to the hotel, dressing slowly and carefully as though getting ready for a first night. It was dark when we drove to the cathedral for the ceremony, but the square was a blaze of light and jammed with hundreds of people. We moved inside and began to walk down the long aisle, Don Onofrio behind us. He had warned us to walk slowly. "These people want to see you. Some will want to touch you. They all want to wish you well." We started at a slow walk, the congregation spilling into the aisle, smiling sadly, but mostly quite silent.

"More slowly," said Don Onofrio's voice from behind. "*Piano. Piano.*" And as we slowed, the crowd came bunching around us, stroking our arms and touching our hands. Some old ladies with lined faces and hunched figures, all in black, cupped our faces in their hardened hands, gazing deeply. Old men, shy at first, put out leathery hands and gripped with fierce intensity. We picked up the pace from time to time, shy ourselves, but each time there came from behind the quiet, insistent, "*Piano, piano.*" Every time we stopped, hands would come out of clusters of people close by, the nearer ones caressing, the farther ones barely touching with the fingertips.

Eventually we were all in place and the High Mass was celebrated, gloriously as Don Onofrio had said. The details of the *Testimonianza* ceremony were beyond us, but it was clear that a mystical event of great solemnity was taking place. We received it, unworthy obviously, but grateful. At the end, as at a wonderful party, no one wanted to leave, and we shook hands and hugged, it seemed, all the people we had not shaken hands with and hugged on our way in, as well as all those we had shaken hands with and hugged already. As a spiritual experience, it was one of the most satisfying in my life, the everlasting bonding with an eruption of human goodwill.

The next morning brought us back to earth. We drove first to Polistena, the town we had been taken to immediately after the shooting—at last we knew its name. We drove along the same autostrada, then up and up into the hills, living again the previous interminable journey. With a shock, I saw the hospital where Nicholas was taken first, in all its remembered details, except that now in mid-morning it was a place of businesslike comings and goings, not a floodlit nightmare. We met Giuseppe Ioppolo, the Good Samaritan, and his English teacher, Dr. Belnava, who had acted as our interpreter that night, and even the meticulous police inspector, Antonio Tramontana, who had taken our first statement. By day and on public display, he was still the same courteous representative of law and order we had met in his dark office.

Later we visited the home of a married couple who, through superhuman efforts, had managed to adopt a Russian boy suffering from who knows what horrors and then, finding he had a missing brother, had traced him and adopted him too. Despite the differences, everyone saw a connection between their story and ours. Then we drove down the coast alongside the legendary passage between Scylla and Charybdis, the rock and the whirlpool, that at one time had put both Ulysses and Nicholas Green on the edge of their seats with excitement. There were crowds everywhere, both adults and eager young faces from the local schools. From them we learned they were sending money and gifts to a poverty-stricken village in Cameroon whose central feature is now called, in Italian, the Nicholas Green Well.

As I came out of a building in Reggio di Calabria that night, I saw the crescent moon hanging over the straits of Messina. It was a harmless ritual in my family, when I was a boy, to wish on the new moon. It is seen beautifully over the ocean from our house in Bodega Bay and, carrying on the tradition, I used to make a show of it for our children, bowing elaborately seven times and making a wish that was *never* to be told. I knew wishes have a way of turning out badly, so the things I asked for were for the most part impeccably self-righteous.

I did have a recurring wish for myself, however, and feel free to tell it now: that I should live until Nicholas was old enough to be at college. In London, my best friend, Bob Hugill, the wittiest and most generous man I've ever known, married Beryl, who already had a son, Jonathan. He loved them as only a man with a huge heart can and when his own son, Walter, was born he was, he said, "besotted." But Bob died, and everyone suffered cruelly. "By the time Nicholas goes away to college, he will be sturdy enough to deal with that kind of thing," I reasoned. So I determined to do whatever I could to live that long—eating properly, exercising (moderately), always fastening my seatbelt. But to be on the safe side I played the game of asking the moon for help too. Now, seeing it there hanging innocently over the town where he died, having granted the substance of the wish, was a mockery I was unprepared for. Since then, I have never made a wish for anything.

We left Calabria to attend an event arranged for us in the town of Terni, the birthplace of St. Valentine, in the region of Umbria. The organizers wanted to honor the power of love, and they chose to see it in our story. We learned that one reason why Valentine became the symbol for love was because he encouraged marriage between Christians and nonbelievers. That seemed very appropriate in view of our marriage, a Presbyterian and a north of England heathen.

Near Terni are the falls of Marmore, one of those mixtures of history and spectacle our family loves. They were created by the Romans, who made a channel in the mountains above the town to divert water to the Tiber, and we'd been promised an unforgettable sight. Alas, when we arrived for the viewing, it was a very long but very thin trickle, the water having been cut off at the hydroelectric dam upstream. "Don't worry," said Mr. Paparelli, our considerate guide from the tourist office, "we've opened the dam for you." And in a few minutes the trickle turned into a stream, into a torrent, into a river, and in the end into a flood of white water reaching up to the sky.

The ceremony was held in yet another packed hall and this time, whenever Nicholas was mentioned, in total silence. I had come across a valentine card he had made at pre-school, and it had seemed right to bring it to this meeting. It had all the awkwardness of a child beyond his limits. "I don't suppose it has much artistic merit," I said. Holding it up, I looked at the message: "I love you, Daddy." It was hard to go on. "But to me it is now more precious than any Michelangelo."

Terni gave us one more thing. We were in the aftermath of a stabbing that had taken place at a soccer game in the north of Italy. The papers were full of stories about young thugs. On the way back to Rome, we saw coachload after coachload of fans, pulled over, waiting to be frisked by the police. As we sat down to lunch, a visiting soccer team came in and sat nearby, boisterous as sports teams are on game day. I suppose we all looked over at them once or twice, wondering about them. As they stood up to go, two of them walked over to our table. Now what? But in their hands were a box of chocolates for Eleanor and a great bunch of spring flowers for Maggie. "We will never forget you," they said.

Back in Rome, we wandered among the ruins of the Forum, the first time we had been there since that hot day in September with Nicholas when, his face flushed and beads of sweat standing on his forehead, his greatest desire had been an ice cream. I remembered how, to cheer him up, Maggie made a small crown of laurel leaves. The ancient symbol had revived his spirits, and he walked proudly through the triumphal arch.

At last we were able to visit the only recipient we hadn't met, Andrea, who was still in the hospital. He was with his mother and father, not surprisingly, since they had kept a vigil for months, and his mother had slept at the hospital in those frightening weeks before and after the heart transplant. Andrea smiled and chatted, but despite the public attention he had been receiving—including visits from some of his soccer heroes—he seemed a little overwhelmed. Still, he warmed to Eleanor and dutifully kissed her for the cameras. He was still suffering from side effects of the treatment, so we didn't stay long. Before we left, however, we spoke to the chief surgeon of the team who had performed the transplant, Carlo Marcelletti. Andrea's heart had been like lead, he said. "But Nicholas had a first-class heart." Yes, we nodded, we already knew that.

Among other groups, we were now working with the Italian chapter of TRIO, the international organization representing organ recipients. Its president, Egidio de Luca, had contacted us months before, explained that he was a liver recipient, and asked us to be honorary presidents of TRIO Italia. We accepted readily. No pay or power, but no work either, we thought. There we were wrong or, more strictly, half wrong. There was certainly no pay and only symbolic power, but the incessant labor they put us, and themselves, through on Italian visits over a period of more than two years, was enough to satisfy a nineteenth-century factory owner.

On this visit, a new idea was tried out: a public service television spot in Italian with a simple theme, "*Un trapianto è un atto d'amore.*" A transplant is an act of love. It took a whole morning to film and cordoned off most of the ground floor of the famous Forum Hotel, the hotel management going from pride to tolerance to suppressed fury as the whole lobby was time and again shushed into silence. I read my

Italian script phonetically from a poster covered with large, childlike block capitals held up behind the camera.

The advertising agency was doing all this free, but, catching the sense of commitment, was treating it as though it were a campaign for Fiat. The first take seemed to go haltingly, but at the end everyone, camerapeople, producer, production assistant, and sound technician, crowded round. "That was great, Reg," they said. "You really got the accent." The second sounded better and the producer added enthusiastically, "It's coming along fine. Just don't look as though you're reading the words." The third brought more praise, "Marvelous, though don't look quite so grim." And the fourth, "Splendid. But keep your hands still." It was then I realized how far we were from even a modest success. I don't remember the number of takes, but it was in the twenties, I think, while the rich and famous mutely checked in and out of the hotel. Despite all the team's talents, I can't believe the result made much of an impression in Italy. But it did on me. I can still recite the entire script like a phonetic robot, including the sign-off, "*Un tra-pi-an-to è un at-to da-mor-e.*"

On what was to have been our last night in Rome, we had a meeting in a massive room filled to capacity with politicians, doctors, and television and print journalists. I ended my talk with a quotation that seemed apt in this place, Shakespeare's Cleopatra preparing to die:

> *"Let's do it after the high Roman fashion*
> *And make death proud to take us."*

I said I thought death would have been very proud to take Nicholas.

That ended the program, but the man sitting next to me introduced himself as Mino Damato, one of the best-known television interviewers in Italy, a thinking man who ran his own shows in every detail from camera angles to makeup. "I'm starting a new series on Sunday. It will be a wonderful occasion and millions of people will see it. I'd like you and Maggie to be in it. We'll change your airline reservation, get you a hotel, and take you to the airport on Monday morning. What do you say?" I looked at Maggie. She nodded. "Yes," we said. Suddenly we had time on our hands, the first in months. The next morning we got up slowly and had two cups of tea.

The lull didn't last, however, and in the next few days we had a series of meetings, the first of which was a television interview with a

London station arranged by Reuters, the news agency. Driving us to the studio outside central Rome was one of their journalists, Alex, who knew everyone in the media business in Rome and all the shortcuts, and referred to everyone by their first names. We were supposed to stop outside the great iron gates of the studio, but, hearing who we were, the guards waved us through. "Even Prince Charles had to walk from there," Alex told us.

Over our weak objections, she told us she would arrange a private tour of the Vatican museum. "It's usually only for kings and people like that, but they'll do it in this case," she said, and she was right. Accompanied only by scholarly guides, we walked along those kilometers of corridors the next day, looking wherever we wanted at the thousands of treasures normally only glimpsed or not seen at all. It was like wandering through your own palace, stopping here for a better look or surprised there by some previously unknown masterpiece. Then into the Sistine Chapel, restored since we'd been there before and overwhelming. Even Eleanor, jaded with so much to see, thought it scrumptious. We drained the cup dry, conscious that seeing this alone was a once-in-three-lifetimes experience. Then we went into the robing room to look at a collection of ceremonial clothing that included the most sumptuous colors I have ever seen, all seemingly lit by an inner glow and each, we understood, worn for a different occasion. In this splendor, one of the guides was tempted by the devil and, picking up a papal miter, popped it on Eleanor's head. We were all poised between laughter and awe at the impiety of it, and as I looked at her sweet little face crowned by this exquisite hat, I had a vision of a new dynasty of popes: American, female, and first grade.

I went back to the Vatican the next day for a regular visit, along with hundreds of other tourists. Although some of the magic had gone, it was still powerful enough to override the crowding. That was reassuring: I wouldn't have wanted every visit to an art museum from now on to be ruined by not being able to see it like a king.

Being stopped in the streets in the small towns of Italy and given a hug had seemed astonishing at first, but we had become used to it. After all, we do stand out—an Amazon, a portly redhead, and a small girl complaining about having to go to another museum (after visiting the Louvre we renamed her Moaner Lisa). But in Rome we had expected to be anonymous. Not so. Television and newspapers had seen to that. In front of the Forum Hotel, the narrow street narrows still more so that barely one car can get through. At just this point, as we came out of the hotel one day, a car stopped and the driver jumped out, saying she'd recognized us. At length she told us how much she had been inspired by Nicholas' story. The line of cars had backed up out of sight, frustrated drivers were leaning out of windows, and the street was full of honking horns. Our new friend paid no attention, but, after many good wishes, got back in her car and drove away. As we stood on the sidewalk waiting for the traffic to thin—it seemed risky to cross in front of this murderous line—the driver of each passing car at first glared at us, then changed to smiles and cheerful waves.

From the hotel, we walked up the steep slope to the top of the Capitoline Hill, planning to cross it. It turned out to be the day of a taxi strike and a strike meeting was being held on the long flight of steps leading to the church. We heard the loud voices, then saw the barricades and started to turn back, when some people in the crowd shouted our name. In an instant the whole hill of men, two or three thousand of them, were clapping their hands above their heads, and shouting "*Viva Nicholas, viva Nicholas,*" and what had been acrimony turned to tenderness as we were escorted through the crowd. As we left, the *carabinieri* saluted, and we walked on. For a moment both sides of the barricades had come together.

Ben Williams, a friend since schooldays, told me once that, when he was young, his father had described how he had seen a Welsh rugby player catch the ball under his own goalposts and, in the dying minutes of a crucial game, run the length of the field to win the match. Ben said he never had any reason to doubt his father's word until he read much later that every Welshman alive at the time claims to have seen that game. I remembered that story whenever we got into a taxi in Rome: every driver told us he had been at the strike meeting that day. We didn't mind, of course. It was like becoming a little part of Welsh history.

Our new friend, Mino, turned out to be a perfect host. He'd suggested we move into an apartment he owned, and we went over there in someone's van and waited as friends struggled up the stairs with a bed for Eleanor, towels, cookware, and the other things absentee landlords don't need. But then, looking around, none of us could find a telephone, an absolute necessity for the kind of changeable life we were leading. We had no choice but go to a hotel instead, and all the household effects went down the stairs again. It turned out to be the

Leonardo da Vinci Hotel, and as soon as we went in we saw we were back with Jolly Hotels, a chain we'd become familiar with in other cities. It is widely known as the Jolly da Vinci, and since then I've never been able to think of Leonardo in any other mood.

In a sense, we now had the Roman vacation we'd missed: we saw St. Peter's early and late, the Pantheon and the Villa Borghese, and one night we walked to the Trevi fountain. When I'd passed it on my long night walk after Nicholas died, I'd remembered the custom of tossing in a coin by those wanting to return to Rome and had wondered if I would ever see Italy again. As we approached and heard the roar of the massive pumps, I put my hand over Eleanor's eyes and took her to the edge of the floodlit pool. "Now open," I said. It proved to be a moment of such joyous surprise that she wanted to go there every night and almost every night we did go. On the last night, throwing in a coin seemed the natural thing to do, but instead Maggie made a little boat out of a thousand-lira bill. It sailed bravely over the tumbling waters, ratifying the bond that had grown between Italy and us in those few short months. For Eleanor who, by then five years old, knew the massive buying power of even a $20 bill, the sight of something with a thousand on it sailing away was an additional source of wonder. We didn't tell her there were 1,500 lira to the dollar.

The program we were preparing for so agreeably was an experiment, a new series called *Dreaming, Dreaming* in which people told their dreams and, as far as the powers of television allowed, enacted them live. It was a bold idea. Some dreams were ambitious, others disarmingly modest. One girl wanted to swim with dolphins and was taken into a pool with a group of them. Another wanted to go to a beauty salon used by movie stars. The scenes lacked the finesse of an edited adventure, with slow starts and the kind of dead time that gives a normal prime-time producer bad vibes. But it made up for it by the tenseness of real life, of not knowing if this or that dream would turn out well or badly.

Courageously, Mino put Maggie and me up there without notes or props, at the peak viewing hour of the week on one of the largest TV channels in Italy and at the beginning of a series that was being billed as a turning point in his career. He didn't rehearse us in what we were going to say. Just look into the cameras, he told us, and talk from your hearts. We did and the letters that came in later said his faith had been rewarded. At the airport next morning, the Alitalia agent who took our tickets said, "Ah, so you're the famous Greens. I'm going to put you in *magnifica* class."

There was more to Mino than we knew at the time. He had adopted a beautiful three-year-old girl from Romania, one of the thousands of children there who contracted AIDS through contaminated blood transfusions. He nurtured her as only one who feels the gossamer-like fragility of life can. Widening his cause, he went to Romania repeatedly to help other children with AIDS, building a small hospital, sending toys, entertaining them. He sacrificed time and money, and risked his status as a spokesman for mainline television. But his daughter died and a light went out of his life. I saw him on my last visit to Rome, getting ready for yet another mission to Bucharest, sadder than before, but with a stature more imposing than when he was at the height of his popularity.

CHAPTER TEN

LETTERS FROM AROUND THE WORLD

We're all so used to complaining about illiteracy that the quality of the letters we received was a revelation. Many start by saying they can't find the words for what they feel, then say it with the simple eloquence that comes only from the heart. They filled boxes and boxes. They came from old and young, scholars and high school dropouts, right- and left-thinkers. Christians and Jews, Buddhists and Hindus spoke of Nicholas' story as a spiritual experience. Agnostics rejoiced in its humanity. Surgeons applauded it as an example to others. Recipients wept and cheered in the same sentence. We heard from presidential palaces and jails, American Legion posts and nunneries, pediatric wards and hospices, business leaders and labor unions. All seemed to be reaching to find the core of their beliefs and pass it on to comfort us. It was hard to believe these letters came out of a decision that had seemed so obvious to us. But as they arrived, day by day, their unwavering intensity told us we were part of something profound.

"My heart is breaking for you," said Gene Agan, with whom I'd enjoyed years of rollicking friendship untinged by any hint of solemnity. "It made me want to let go of my usual sense of privacy and share our family's story with you," one letter from a stranger said. A letter from Italy opened like this, "Who is writing is a boy, a university student, who is 22 years old—I am still today not able to forget what happened to you. I don't want to forget it—I feel as if I were directly involved." An American monk wrote, "I want to thank you for the inspiration, encouragement, and hope you have afforded me." Many letters were from parents, some who had lost children, some whose children had been saved from severe illness, some who had no tragic experience at all and said they couldn't imagine the anguish of such a loss. People seemed to have made a conscious effort to bare their souls so their attempt to soothe us would be more effective. One couple we know who long before had decided not to have children told us that, having seen what parental love could achieve, they now wondered if that decision wasn't the biggest mistake of their lives.

Many spoke of a mysterious transformation of sorrow into strength, darkness into light. "I will always remember you as people who interrupted an old pattern and began a new one," someone wrote. A retired general said Nicholas "is still alive...among all those who have understood—through your love action—how to overcome such a terrible tragedy and thus be able to truly realize the Gospel's word." A year after the shooting, an Italian woman wrote, "So many times Nicholas was with us during this year. Thinking of him is always an immense joy to my heart."

When I heard Ronald Reagan's decision to make public the onset of his Alzheimer's disease, I wrote to him, admiring his honest courage. He replied in what seems like an unforced personal statement, "While I was deeply grateful for your expression of sympathy for my illness, I can't help but ache for you and your wife as you cope with the sudden loss of your little boy. Although there are no words to ease your sorrow, I want you to know that you are in my prayers... Hopefully you will gain comfort in knowing that he is safe now in the arms of God." He added that our sympathy was making it easier for him to face whatever lay ahead. President Clinton kindly wrote on behalf of himself and the First Lady, and my notes show that when we replied Eleanor insisted that we tell them she now had a kitten.

Eternity was in many of these letters. "I will never forget Nicholas," said a father from Sausalito, California. An American mother living in Italy said she had learned that "a single unselfish act can change the world." And from another stranger, "Something special happened when Nicholas passed that seems to have created a shift in the

Universe." "You are in Italians' hearts and mind forever," said an American nun in Italy. We knew they meant it, but it was hard to think it. Never is a long time. I have to say, however, that although we still have a long way to go to never, after more than four years we're still getting letters that say exactly the same things.

"How gifted and honored you were to be guardians of an angel for seven long years. Most of us plead for merely a momentary visitation," said a Buddhist, the unearthliness compounded because the picture on the postcard she sent showed the exact spot on the cliff overlooking the Golden Gate Bridge where Maggie and I were married. "I want you to know that in your darkest hour you have taught me the meaning of wisdom and grace," one lady wrote.

Some of the expressions I'd scarcely seen before except in books, "tormented by your loss," "given us all hope," "changed my life." A Roman spoke of the classical virtues, "Thank you for bringing back those ancient feelings." Nicholas would have purred.

Most of the people breaking down the barriers were strangers. But many too were friends, familiarity with whom has always made anything but routine praise out of the question. Words that would normally have been laughed off in embarrassment instead took old relationships to a deeper level. "Mythical," wrote Maggie's Aunt Carol. "Biblical," said John Adams who, reared in Fleet Street like me, would normally have cringed if I'd ever tried to pay him anything other than the most trivial compliment. "Life, after all, is a serious business," they seemed to say. "There is right and wrong. For a moment, let soul look into soul."

Some elderly people obviously wanted to say something before it was too late, like a lady from Genoa who wrote affectionately. A few months later, the receptionist at the old people's home where she lived wrote to say she had died, but that writing to Nicholas' parents had warmed her last weeks. Many letters sounded as though they came from old friends. "We love you as if we know you since a long time," a doctor wrote from Sicily. "I have never written friendly correspondence to people I do not know," one Californian wrote. "I have never made gifts for people I do not know. I have never done anything like this before. When I said you had inspired me, I meant it."

I'm struck by how well those early letters seemed to understand Nicholas, having only our words to go on and a few snapshots we almost didn't take. They seemed to understand us too, why we did it, what we were thinking. The strength of the response, however, was a daily surprise. People often contacted us long after the event, saying they had wanted to write before, but were afraid of saying something inadequate. "Even now the words don't come any easier," one letter read, "but know that you have given me faith in humankind and hope for a gentler world." It isn't possible to read these letters without the sense of a momentous event having taken place. "As if to reaffirm all that we have been taught about compassion and the resilience of the human spirit—without joy, I'm sure—you reached out to those who needed you," an eloquent stranger said. A Bostonian I've always admired wrote, "I am sure Nicholas is in the company of the innocents, and among them he must also walk with pride in the knowledge that his death was an extension of hope for others rather than a vengeful quest." A phone message came from Sydney: "All Australia pours its heart out to you."

"Are they talking about us?" we kept asking ourselves.

Deborah, twenty-three years old, wrote from Bologna, "I got a friend who was died: his name was Roland. Nicholas had remembered me my Roland. You have a lesson of love and I don't forget Nicholas." Someone I had worked with, but never really knew, opened her heart about her eight-year-old daughter: "I hold Kate a little tighter, look more directly at her, put down the paper when she asks a question and treasure her more deeply...recognizing that should she be taken from me, I do not want to feel wanting in my love for her." And a father said something that sent a tingle through me, "You know, Nicholas would have been very proud of his family."

A few were anonymous, but passionately close for all that. On the grave one day we found a card from an Italian family who had been on vacation in San Francisco and had driven up specially to say thank you to Nicholas. They didn't leave their address, they weren't there to parade their emotions, but for weeks afterward I carried around the note they left: "Dear little Nicholas, we love you. God bless you to eternity, sweet child."

A package of letters arrived from a school in California's San Gabriel Valley where immigrants learn English. They expressed a unanimity that makes nonsense of national prejudices. "Mercy and love are desperately necessary in a world now being filled with brutality and violence," said a Taiwanese. "Heroes are people who give us dreams and inspirations," said one from Hong Kong. A Nicaraguan assured us, "You are not alone." Letters from Italians in all walks of life abolished national boundaries with equal ease. One said simply, "*Grazie, America.*" Wanda Ferragamo wrote to the American consulate in Florence, "Once again the traditional American generosity has not failed. Please allow me to express my great admiration for your wonderful country." A seventy-year-old man from Ravenna, twenty years old when the Allies liberated Italy, said it was then that for the first time he had met free men and had loved this country ever since. His brother, fourteen years old, was killed by mines abandoned by the Germans near his home. "I wish to tell my suffering to you, dear and good Mr. and Mrs. Green. Receive my tears and prayers."

The Little Sisters of the Poor in Messina wrote, saying they had given the clothes we left with them to a young boy "with no mother" and sent a photograph, a half-hidden face smiling from the green and blue anorak I'd walked beside so often. It was so uncannily like Nicholas that for an instant my heart leapt at the notion that, after all, the nuns might have managed a miracle.

Voices came out of the past. Letters from two cousins from my hometown in England, girls when I last saw them, leapt over the intervening fifty years of Fleet Street and marriage and emigration with memories of my unruly red curly hair. A girl who was at the same school all those years ago reminded me that her father was the goalkeeper for Accrington Stanley, the town's soccer team, the peak of life's possibilities it seemed to me at the time.

Some letters managed to bring a smile. Ed Loughman from New Rochelle said, "That little guy, St. George, must be looking down, perhaps quite puzzled how so much good can come out of such a devastating event." Ed's printed stationery invited you to contact him if you needed your handwriting analyzed. I was careful to send a typed reply.

Other letters were tragic. A single American woman told of the death of her adopted four-year-old daughter and the daily bleakness of her life. Now, she said, she could find a ray of comfort, imagining her child and Nicholas playing together in a place where there is no violence. Letters came from parents of children who had died of AIDS, children killed by drunk drivers, babies who had lived only a few days. Generally they didn't complain, weren't bitter, weren't maudlin, just filled with a sadness they felt compelled to share.

"We feel the impulse to be close to you," a letter from Turin began. "We had a loved and nice girl of 22, a brilliant university student...she left us in the worse way it can happen to a mother and father: she suicided. Since that day we are dragging our lives, in a house full of remember, where there is a room we quite don't dare to go in, where everything is still like it was that day." A mother says she and her husband live in daily terror of losing their daughter because of a rare congenital heart defect—and dare to hope Nicholas' example might contribute to finding her a new heart one day. If she reads this book, I hope she'll let us know: I still think about that girl. A forty-two-year-old man telephoned one night and said he recently went blind. "How do you stand it?" I asked. "It's very hard. And sometimes I think of suicide," he said. "But the thought that Nicholas helped those people to see again is giving me the strength to resist despair."

A desolate letter came from a mother whose son had died, "I find it hard to understand God's plans... I just cannot believe [my son] is not here with us any longer. Sometimes I can swear I hear his footsteps on the stairs, running up, or I can hear his joyful voice around the house... I have always spent my married life just caring for my children...and now I am empty-handed...some days I just would love to sit down and die." What can one say? Some letters were smudged, others ended abruptly. The reason was clear. "I am a father too and while I am writing these few words I can't keep back my tears. I apologize but we have lost our happiness too."

A sense of the unity of life is in every one of them and phrases that fill the memory. A young woman in Rome wrote, "Since when you have lost your son my heart has been beating quicker...today I think that people, common persons, can change the world. When you go and see Nicholas in the little graveyard place, please say this to him, 'Nicholas, they closed your eyes but you opened mine.' "

You can imagine what it meant to receive these letters, every additional one giving Nicholas' death more meaning, and each picking up a little piece of the burden of grief to make it less crushing.

CHAPTER ELEVEN

A DIALOGUE STARTS

From the start, we read and tried to answer every letter. In the first few days, they poured in with such force that we had to resort to a form letter, with a version in Italian translated for us by the Italian embassy. But as we sat at the dining room table every night, reading the twenty or thirty letters that had come in that day and preparing the responses, it became clear this didn't come near what was required. The letters were so personal that a set response was almost a cold shoulder. I found myself writing a postscript almost every time, picking up some part of the experience they had described or responding to some illuminating phrase. But soon I gave up the form letter completely. Some phrases, naturally, recur over and over. But I wanted to make each one a reply to the individuals behind the words, thinking myself into their unspoken questions.

When someone wrote from a place Nicholas had visited, I'd try to remember an incident to fix him in their own streets. Like the hot summer's day in Siena when the camera crew from an Austrian magazine came over to where we were sitting and asked Nicholas to dress up in a yellow woolen coat for their autumn fashion issue. We still have the photo of him, pouting, as only a young male can, with two beautiful young women trying to coax a smile.

When a twenty-nine-year-old from Verona said, "I think of Nicholas every night before I fall asleep," I told her he loved old cities and that on a day we'd spent in Verona we'd visited all the most celebrated sights—the amphitheater, the churches, Juliet's house. On the way home that night, I'd asked him what was the very best thing we'd done that day. "Lunch at McDonald's," he said unhesitatingly. A few weeks later, she wrote again to say she had taken her young cousin to McDonald's and told him the famous Nicholas and Eleanor had been there.

When a senior citizens' community in Washington state sent a poem and a picture of the Columbia River, I told them we had driven along the river at twilight a year earlier and how that huge body of water moving out to sea had made such an impression on Nicholas. There was something profound about that movement and I wonder if he could possibly have felt the pull Tennyson felt. I sent them a copy of "Crossing the Bar" and hope they identified with its majestic but soothing imagery. To as many people as possible I mentioned that Bodega Bay was the scene of *The Birds* to give them a sense of the place where he lived.

I tried to relate our interests to theirs without forcing it: to people from the mountains, I mentioned hikes we'd taken, to those in historical cities, the buildings we'd seen there. If they dedicated a new playground, I'd tell them about the games we played. It wasn't difficult; the memories came crowding in. When Eleanor had a birthday we told them what she did that day, when newspapers published articles we mailed clippings. Soon after *20/20* ran its program about our visit to Sicily, I was able to write to the children at Maria Pia's school. "You are famous all over the United States. One of the largest television programs—40 million people watch it!—included the song you wrote for us. We always thought that song was beautiful. Now everyone else knows it too."

Our replies produced a second round of stirring letters. One said, "The photograph you gave me is always in my diary: it is one of the greatest presents I have received in my life." A Sicilian woman living in Rome wrote, "Your letter provoked a special happiness that I seldom felt. Before going to bed I read it through, discovering each time something important and new. You taught me to find the dawn in the darkness." Many talked familiarly. "You mustn't get too busy, you need time to grieve," one wrote. And I replied, as one might to someone close, "Yes, we're busy, but there are enough black holes every day to satisfy all our needs." "Thank you for making me feel like your friend," said another, after I'd replied to his moving letter. But no thanks were called for. That's just how I did feel. All over Italy, I signed visitors' books, concert programs, or casts on broken limbs in hospitals simply as "*papà di Nicholas*" and no one seemed to want anything more formal. People still write to us about their vacations or a new baby—some of them called Nicholas—and sometimes the death of a parent. It has a family ring about it.

Some were obviously suffering. "I shall treasure your letter in the dark patches to come and it will help me find the sunshine," said one American lady. "Your card arrived on a day that was particularly hard for me. I thank you and Nicholas for teaching me in a way I cannot describe," said another. Others were joyful. An Italian couple wrote because they wanted to share with us the way the little Polish boy they've adopted has lit up their lives, and many told of someone they loved recovering from a serious illness, sometimes a transplant but often not.

We sent dozens of copies of photographs of Nicholas and were rewarded by deeply felt thank you notes. "I keep it on my desk so I see it all the time." "I have put it between the photos of my own two children." "I keep it in my wallet so it will always be with me." Later, in schools we visited, we came across some of the photos we'd sent, often in the entrance so every visitor can see them, or reproduced in local newspapers. Beautiful tasteful cards came from some people, a pleasure to gaze at; others were scribbles on scraps of paper. But in the hundreds and hundreds there was scarcely a false note. Some people couldn't find the words, but preferred that to glibness. "I just saw the article in *People*. It helped me somehow. I just thought I'd call... I just wanted to say... Take care."

Most letters said something about Eleanor. I told her I was sure she'd be getting offers of marriage and, whenever one was addressed to her, I asked what he was like. Many asked detailed questions or wanted a photograph. Even for those who just mentioned her, I was reluctant just to say, "She's fine, thanks." Rightly or not, I concluded that they'd like to know more than they were asking about the sad but spirited little girl they'd seen on television. So I told them about the kitten and, then later, that it had been killed by a car, and about the school she went to and what she ate for breakfast.

The first Christmas after Nicholas died, we sent a photocard, showing the three of us walking along our beach. It produced another deluge of letters, many praising its succinct message: Peace on Earth. That, indeed, was our sentiment, but it was also the maximum number of words the card company allowed at the price. That year we sent out something like six hundred cards. It seemed excessive, but in the second year Harry Benson's picture of our snowball fight on Mount Etna was too good not to use and, with new people writing, we went up to a thousand. The third year—will we always number them like this? Maggie asked—we cut back drastically, to a few hundred. Still, for people like us, who in some previous years had sent virtually no Christmas cards at all, this was still an undertaking of some magnitude.

One Italian scholar, knowing of Nicholas' interest in Julius Caesar, wrote to say he had just written a biography and had dedicated it to him. I thanked him for a wonderful gift and added, "In a small boy's way he had picked up a lot of information about Julius Caesar—he'd marched along Roman roads, walked in the mountains where the legions fought, and visited Roman camps. He had even crossed the Rubicon." The author's son, a journalist living in New York, called me later. "You have warmed an old man's heart," he said.

Some sent pictures of themselves or their house or neighborhood. They were plainly saying: this is the real us, not what happened to you. Some sent a piece of literature or a poem which had nothing to do with death or sorrow, but was just something of beauty. Simple sentences conjured up a whole family. "Your letter brought tears to my eyes and my 'macho' husband's." Or this one from a forty-year-old single woman in the diplomatic service who adopted a Russian half-Korean child, six months old with a hole in her heart and some problems with her kidney: "I am framing your photograph and hanging it in my office to remind those I care for—the employees and families of the U.S. Embassy—what being American and what foreign policy and foreign relations really mean." In all these encounters, it was a fact understood by both sides that we had gone through some profound experience together that made sharing confidences quite natural.

We got a few unusual requests for help, like the unemployed man in Sicily who heard we were going to make a movie and wanted to produce it for us and the Italian lady who asked for Madonna's address. But I can remember only one harsh letter. "What on earth were you doing on that dangerous stretch of road at night?" wrote Peter from Davis, California. "There are areas one hesitates driving in this country even during the day. The death of your son saddens me enormously. However, one fact stands out supremely: You, sir, are a very stupid man!!" In other circumstances, that could have hurt. Even the sympathy rang false. Having satisfied myself, however, that at around 10:30 p.m. on the most important road in the whole of Italy's deep south I could not reasonably have foreseen that our car would be mistaken for one filled with jewelry, I felt this was one letter I could justifiably ignore. In any event, I didn't see much likelihood of us becoming pen pals. It was balanced by a note from a man who said his family regularly traveled that route with his children asleep on the back seat "just like Nicholas."

Keeping track of these letters and the heartfelt gifts that came with them taxed our ill-organized resources. Classification was eclectic. Looking at the top letter in one pile, I see Maggie has crisply noted it can be found in the computer under NITMODSP (Nicholas, Italy, Modena, speech), nice and clear. The next one is identified only by her notation, "lovely brownies."

Some conversations were cut short. "I am quite ill with a liver cancer," one letter started. "Until this year I taught elementary school here in New Hampshire. It seems as if I might be more depressed, but then I hear of someone in even a more difficult situation. Your decision must have been very difficult. I thank you for it." Later that year, there was no reply to our Christmas card.

Another letter came from a "very grateful mother and grandmother who was able to celebrate a 61st birthday because of a loving family like you." She had received a transplant a year earlier. The following Christmas we sent her a card. Soon afterward her husband called to say she had died of cancer. "She knew she couldn't be cured when she wrote to you, but she didn't want to say so. When I saw your card it made me cry," he told us. "And now you're making me cry," I replied. I felt as though we'd lost somebody close. And, of course, we had.

Some letters came back undelivered. I worried about them more than I should, I suppose. They were only a tiny percentage, but I wanted to reply to everyone who had felt strongly enough to write to us. I hoped for a dialogue with each of them, brief necessarily, but enough for a genuine encounter that said, "Our paths will probably never cross again. But I want you to know you have touched something deep in us. That little piece of giving and taking will always be there." In the hundreds of letters I wrote, I never lost the feeling that these were special moments.

As it happens, many of those paths did cross again. Many people wrote a second or third time. Often at the end of organ donation meetings in this country or Italy, somebody will come up to say they were the people who had written to us about the park that had been opened for Nicholas or had sent a card for Eleanor. Meeting them in a crowd of people, they were sometimes difficult to identify, but I'd worked on those letters and after a few clues more often than not I'd remember the key points of their story. We'd shake hands, embrace, laugh more often than cry, and part, having kept alive a little flame.

All this time, telephone calls were coming in steadily. Many seemed surprised when Maggie or I answered, and it was hard not to feel like a celebrity after all. They could be difficult to handle, somebody crying softly at the other end, perhaps, or asking something urgent in an unknown language. Europeans frequently called in the middle of the night, saying, "Good afternoon." But I can't remember a single crank call, and even the most committed believers held back from preaching, offering instead help and counsel only if we should need it.

The early letters from Italy had indicated such a depth and breadth of feeling that I decided to write an "open letter to the Italian people," a grandiose expression I'd picked up from nineteenth-century history. By then I felt we were among a whole country of friends who would want to hear all the details. So I told them about the cemetery where Nicholas was buried and what the church was like and the rows of graves with the Italian names. I told them about the many acts of kindness we'd received since his death. And I told them I hoped everyone who was saddened by his story would find some inspirational act that would bring people closer together. I signed it: Proud Father of Nicholas.

I asked the Italian embassy to translate it, which they did graciously. Together we released it to the press. The result was overwhelming. The national newspapers in Italy ran it, mostly in full; it sparked a spate of letters to the press and became a subject for columnists and editorials. It did have one unfortunate result. Elegantly translated, it suggested not our near-illiteracy, but a command of the language fitting to someone who has gone to diplomatic school. The letters came back in droves—in colloquial Italian. Even here, however, as we plowed nightly through idiomatic phrases and complex tenses, there were compensations, and I learned to love envelopes addressed to *Orgoglioso Papà di Nicholas*.

Two years after the shooting a letter arrived, postmarked Quebec, from Mike McGarry, a friend from London whose whereabouts had been a mystery for twenty years. "I heard about the tragedy," it said, "but didn't know it was you. Six months later when I was visiting my daughter and son-in-law, he fished out a copy of *People* magazine from his briefcase and put it on the table. 'I've been carrying it around for months. I don't know why,' he said. I started to leaf through it and there was the article on you." A day or two after receiving his letter, I telephoned him. "What a coincidence," I said. "Our daughter thinks it was fate," he replied.

I've thought about issues like this many times since that night on the autostrada. What took us there at that exact time? Why, when that bullet was fired, did it go in that precise flight? Why did the car, rocking along at high speed, momentarily dip or rise in that fatal microsecond? Such questions touch the deepest mysteries, and we all have different opinions. Many people have written to us to say they see a purpose in this incident. For some it is a matter of faith, God's inscrutable will. Many, even those not particularly religious, seeing the electrifying effect the massacre of an innocent had around the world, conclude it couldn't be accidental. Some call it destiny.

By contrast, I have always been impressed by what seems to me to be the random nature of events. The most trivial decision made today—to park in one space at the grocery store rather than another, for example—affects every subsequent action in your life. You go through the store in a slightly different way depending on the space you took, by the time you get to the checkout counter you are in a slightly different order, as you get back on the road you are in a different traffic pattern. The consequences are magnified at every step so that by the time you arrive home the conversation you have with your family is different from what it would have been. By the end of the day, you have had thoughts and minor experiences different from those you would have had if you'd gone into that other parking spot. By the end of the week, some of that reshaping has become significant enough to make lasting differences.

From then on the paths diverge further and further, changing your life more and more. Think of how you met your wife or husband. What an unfathomable chain of events it was, starting from birth, that put you in just that place and in just that mood that lit the spark. And what about your children? What ever-changing combination of microscopic particles conceived them at that particular moment and gave them the personalities they have?

I look back to our vacation in Switzerland. We had planned to leave for Italy on September 27. The weather was poor, however, and with some trouble we managed to change our train reservations to the 26th. I remember getting off the phone and saying happily, "We did it. We can go a day earlier." I had started a sequence of events that would otherwise have been impossible. Even in the final few hours and minutes so many events could easily have gone a different way. On the night before the shooting, heading for Amalfi, where we had tentatively planned to find a hotel, we suddenly came across a huge traffic jam at an intersection. On an impulse I turned the car left on the quieter road to Positano where we stayed instead. Everything from then on was altered by that unreflecting decision.

As we left Paestum the next evening, thinking all the shops were shut, I caught a glimpse of a lighted window. The owner was just closing, but stayed open long enough to sell us fruit for the journey. A few moments later, we would have missed him. We stopped again soon after to fix the back seat of the car so the children could sleep more comfortably. Just before we got to the autostrada, I made a wrong turn, which cost us five minutes. A few hours later in Calabria, we pulled into a rest area at Pizzo, but almost immediately started off again.

If we had not done any one of those things, or countless others, all would have been different: a different part of the road, different traffic, a different lurch of the car. I now find myself thinking of those what-ifs. If I hadn't written to the family in Palermo and offered to exchange houses. If we'd chosen a different month. If I'd parked at the right of Safeway instead of the left.

Chapter Twelve

Other People's Stories

We had some striking early evidence of the impact Nicholas' death was having. Maria Shriver, who interviewed us a few days later, told us that all her life people have wanted to let her know where they were when they heard President Kennedy, her uncle, was shot. For those of us who were alive at the time, that moment remains perfectly clear, a measure of its unique impact. Now she was saying to us, "I was exercising with my husband when I heard Nicholas had been shot." Since then many others have said something like that: I heard it on the car radio when I was stuck in traffic, when I was in a hospital waiting room, just as I was leaving the World Bank meeting in Madrid. Someone I talked to three years later said, "I was driving back from a weekend in the country when the news came on. I looked over at my seven-year-old son and a shiver ran through me."

Many phone calls began hesitantly, "You don't know me... I just wanted to say... If there's anything I can do..." Once it was a man with a voice that took me back many years. "My name is Mitka and I felt I just had to speak to you... When I was a young boy, I was sent to a Nazi concentration camp. I read about your little boy and saw he was the age I was then. I feel so close to him and to you." He told me he was the campground host for the season at the nearby county park, and later I walked out to see him and his wife, Adrienne.

111

Mitka survived the horrors and made his way to the United States. He has success in obvious ways: a loving wife and family and enough zest for life to spend months a year away from home, responding to the needs of dozens of strangers. But his tale of being imprisoned, the splitting up of families, the recurring lottery of death or survival for another day, had a numbing familiarity. The large house where Jane and I lived in London had a dozen apartments, several of them rented to Polish Jews almost exactly my own age. Arriving in England after World War II, emaciated and without formal education for the whole of their high school years, they took university in their stride. Jerry became a mathematics professor, Roman an architect, Michael a first-rate accountant, and Ben an entrepreneur—and Britain's lightweight champion weightlifter.

They had lost fathers and mothers, brothers and sisters. They didn't talk about it much, but once Ben told me how he and his father had managed to stay together after they were captured and clung to the one hope of lasting out the war together. They almost made it. But in December 1944 in Buchenwald, they were finally separated, and, a few days before the end of the war, the father was shot trying to escape on one of the infamous death marches. As I walked back from Mitka's campsite that evening thinking of what they had all gone through, a cold wind blowing off the ocean made me shudder. Yet, in the end, theirs was the triumph. Instead of consuming themselves in bitterness, they understood pain in others and reached out to help. Their example has inspired me over the years, but never more than now.

Many other people we had never met came to us with stories that plumbed the depths. A mother in Texas spoke of her five-year-old son, who had died not long before. "I felt so helpless at not being able to relieve his pain. I could only talk to him and hold his hand and tell him he was going to a more beautiful place. He apologized to us the week before he died for having been ill and causing hardship to our family."

One day this letter arrived from another stranger. "When I was 12 weeks pregnant I started to hemorrhage. Waiting in the emergency room, a news flash came on the television. Little Nicholas Green had been taken away... My husband hugged me and said, 'Possibly his spirit will save our baby.' At that point we decided to name our baby Nikolas." But Nikolas died too, and his body was given to research. "It doesn't lessen the pain, but maybe he will help save other children," the letter closed. Some months later, we met the handsome young couple the letter came from. They were still childless and subsequently lost two more babies, but looking at them casually you would never have suspected the anguish they had gone through. Another two years passed, then one day a letter arrived with an exultant photograph showing a baby boy who had been carried for them by another woman. However you look at it, it deserves to be called a miracle, doesn't it?

In the last four years, we have had dozens of encounters like these that have reshaped our lives. The names alone read like a harmonious Tower of Babel: Nakaoka from Japan and Bautista from the Philippines, India's Malekar and Pakistan's Bashir, Kalinski and Jones, Helfgott and Iqbal, Ho, Melendez, and O'Reilly. We have shared experiences with the Los Angeles Lakers and the Compassionate Friends, the Australian Red Cross and the New Hampshire Department of Motor Vehicles, Saints Peter and Paul Church in San Francisco and Woodlands Community Temple in White Plains, athletic clubs and the National Italian-American Foundation, *carabinieri*, *gendarmes*, and traffic cops, politicians of all parties, and so on and on. Think of all those diverse cultural roots without any significant difference in how these people felt.

I've met my first coroner since I covered law courts as a cub reporter—only this time it was not a single coroner, but a whole professional association, what Inspector Morse would call a body of coroners. One small boy whose father is not at home sent me a Father's Day card. "He thought you'd be sad if you didn't get a card from a little boy today," his mother explained. A busy airline reservationist, as our business was coming to an end, suddenly said, "Are you the family that...?" and paused, uncertain how to go on. "Yes," I said quickly. "God bless you," she said, her voice breaking as she hung up.

One perfect summer's evening, I went to the cemetery to water Nicholas' grave, deep purple filling the quiet valley. No one is ever there at that time of day. Surprisingly, at the entrance a car was parked and in it were Amedeo Pignatelli, then the director of the San Francisco Italian Cultural Institute, his seventy-three-year-old mother on a visit from Rome, his lovely Thai wife, and his barefoot four-year-old son. This little cross-section of humanity, each with a different vision of Nicholas' story, had driven the sixty-five miles simply to visit him and were now going to drive straight back.

Even in the hectic naturalization process, there was an example of Old World courtesy. I'd taken the preparation for it seriously, not wanting to disgrace myself after studying history at three universities. I made sure to memorize the main constitutional amendments, and fierce contests with Eleanor had ensured I had all the state capitals at my fingertips. But I failed one question: "How many children do you have?" "One," I said, "Eleanor." "That's not what this application form says," the immigration officer countered. I wondered for a moment if I'd left Nicholas' name on the form. Then I remembered my grown children, Annie and Michael. "Sorry, three," glad not to have to involve a stranger, who had very little time and dozens of other people to see, in Nicholas' story. She didn't comment, but when it was all over she came with me to the door, held out her hand, and said softly, "We were all so very sorry to hear about your little boy. Good luck." She'd known all the time. And there was the clerk in the passport office, who called to say the check we'd sent was too small, but she would make up the difference and we could mail her the balance when we got around to it. Imagine.

We're still stopped by strangers in airports and stores and in the street. Booth operators on the Golden Gate Bridge often recognize us, though none has ever suggested remitting the toll. In restaurants, when I see people looking over at me curiously, I no longer check to see if I've spilled soup on my tie. A few weeks ago, a van drew alongside at some traffic lights. It was a warm day, and our windows were open. The driver looked across, waited a moment, then shouted, "Say, aren't you the guy...?" and his voice trailed off. "Yes," I said. "What a terrible thing that was," he said more quietly. "Terrible...but what a nice thing to do." We exchanged shy smiles, the lights changed, and he moved away.

We often meet them at filling stations. They usually finish pumping gas, pay, and then just before leaving come over. "Are you the parents of that little boy? I thought I recognized you. I just wanted you to know..." Then they get into their car and drive away quickly. They wanted to say it, but they didn't want to be brassy. No longer are they someone keeping you waiting in line: they're the real thing, people like you and me. All this can affect your behavior. To one of the two contenders for the hotly fought seat in a local election I was just a face in the crowd. The other called me "a great man." I voted unhesitatingly for him and advised my friends to do the same.

One day a man followed me out of the grocery store. "I was on the legal team that defended Polly Klaas' kidnapper," he said. "I felt I had to say hello. I think I can imagine what it's like at the trial in Italy." I sensed he was a little uneasy about his role in defending a vicious killer. I told him what I thought: "I wouldn't want anyone to go to jail because they weren't properly defended." It wasn't anything new to him, of course. He'd thought a lot about it. But I felt I owed it to him to say so and was rewarded by the feeling that a small bridge that didn't exist before was now in place.

At 7:15 one Sunday morning a few weeks later, the telephone rang and a man at the other end said he'd been reading an article in the *Los Angeles Times*. He was troubled by a sentence in it in which I'd said we didn't want vengeance. He wondered why not. I groaned inwardly. Being saintly before breakfast isn't me. But now this gentle, hesitant voice explained that his wife had been murdered recently and that he too didn't feel the rage he'd expected. He was disturbed, it appeared, by a nagging doubt that perhaps he was not reacting the way he should. He had cause to be angry. Returning from church one night, she was stabbed to death in her own driveway as he watched television. "If only I hadn't had the sound turned up, I might have heard her," he added. What an irony that this devoted man should find fault with himself. We talked for perhaps half an hour, sharing our responses, and I think it helped us both. As I put the phone down I reflected that, despite the commonly held view, the path of understanding is every bit as natural as the path of bitterness

Most of the people we met were strangers, but not all. Jack Bogle, chairman of the Vanguard Group, perhaps the most widely respected man in the mutual fund industry, wore a pacemaker when I first met him in the 1970s and played tennis with the punishing energy he brought to everything. "That's going to kill him," I thought. But no, he went on increasing in influence, fathering index mutual funds and conducting his crusade against anything he thought smacked of laxity. To him, the fiduciary responsibility in handling other people's money is an almost sacred trust. More than twenty years passed and at last even his battling heart was ready to give up. He was saved by one of those five thousand families in this country who, with no idea what the results will be, make their gift to the world. I wrote to him to say I couldn't think of a better result of transplantation than that it could save a man of his ethical and intellectual stature. His reply was typical: generous praise for donors, a sense of hope for the world, and a copy of his latest speech castigating mutual fund fees that he felt were too high.

Our new life has also uncovered the pains and victories of lives that the surface never hinted at. When the Italian consul general in San Francisco and his wife met us at the airport on our first homecoming, with that enveloping concern we'd already learned to expect from their countrymen, we had no idea they had lost a child of their own. A young television network producer, who spent most of a day at our home attending to the painstaking details of a long interview, it later turned out, had come straight from the funeral of her best friend. One young boy, sitting silently on his own at a meeting, was pointed out to me: his identical twin had been killed the year before riding a bicycle.

Without our story becoming known, we would have seen none of this. What do you see in the street, someone asks in a book I read a long time ago. It appears to be a man cleaning his car. But it isn't. It's a man thinking about his wife's infidelity. Now I too can see much more clearly that this isn't simply another driver pumping gas, but someone who underneath has all the fluctuating cares and hopes I have. It's been useful to be reminded that the annoying habits I see in others are the ones I readily excuse in myself. I've learned almost nothing about death in these years. It's still the same absolute mystery—the why, what, whereto—but I do think I've learned some things about life and one of them is the depth of suffering the ordinary person can go through while still doing all those mundane things that keep body and soul—and families—together.

There's also room for mix-ups. One day when I was sitting in a local restaurant with Jim Welsh, a friend on a visit from Australia, I noticed a woman at a nearby table pointing us out to a friend. As they left the friend came over, looked Jim deeply in the eyes and said, "You're my hero." "They're like that in America," I told him afterward. "You should come and live here."

In 1983, Katie Coolican, six years old and apparently perfectly healthy, was in her school playground when she suffered a catastrophic brain hemorrhage. When the little girl died, her mother,

Maggie, a nurse, and her father, Don, had no hesitation about donating her organs. Neither thought it was enough, however, and between them they have put in untold hours since then trying to ease the way for both donors and recipients. Even when we first became involved more than ten years later, many people in the transplant organizations were leery of donor families—they never knew what we were going to say—but in the early 1980s, it was much more difficult and Maggie Coolican had to struggle for years to make her voice heard. By sheer force of personality, she helped found the National Donor Family Council of the National Kidney Foundation, a support group for donor families which has grown from people sitting around the Coolicans' kitchen table to four thousand members.

It proved to be a unique voice. Traveling in the family car one day, and doing what she generally did on long journeys, sewing, a thought came to mind: "Why not ask donor families to send in squares to make into a quilt?" It succeeded beyond all expectations and is now one of the most moving props used in transplant meetings—hundreds of squares, each of them a separate love story and each sewn into place by Maggie herself.

There are pieces of T-shirts, football jerseys, a little boy's pajamas, a wedding dress, a christening gown. Some of the clothing is worn from long use, showing previous repairs from a minor accident, perhaps, that would have been forgotten long ago, but is now an enshrined part of family history. A few manage a touch of humor. Some squares are elaborately stitched, others rough hewn. A radiant little face peeps out of one square with a smile that says, "What a wonderful oyster the world is," but is accompanied by a chilling footnote: 1982–93. The quilt travels around the country breathing life into the medical statistics, and several statewide organ procurement groups now have their own. A children's version has been started so they too can remember parents or siblings in a way that hopefully helps them come to terms with death.

Maggie Coolican is one of a cavalcade of people in the transplant field who, often quite alone, have saved the lives of people they will never know. They don't fit any pattern I can see except, perhaps, their faint air of surprise that anyone should think they could behave any other way. Some are pioneering surgeons, like Thomas Starzl, whose dedication and imagination helped lead a revolution in transplantation, but who never forgot the person inside the patient. Starzl was named the most frequently cited scientist in clinical medicine in the last twenty years by the Institute for Scientific Information. But, when I asked a nurse who had worked with him what she remembered best, it wasn't his technical innovations or that he had performed the world's first liver transplant, but that he was likely to ask a resident doctor who had presented him with a chart of figures, "What color are her eyes?"

Many others came into the field by accident: Lisa Carroccio, for example, whose first question after she realized that a liver transplant had saved the life of her nine-month-old daughter, Marielle, was, "How will I ever pay this back?" Quick-witted and determined, she found the answer almost immediately and with Ronald, her husband, started a group to try to save other parents from the anguish they had gone through. The Children's Liver Alliance now has a newsletter going to 20,000 families and a web site, which tell where to get advice about liver ailments, how other families have coped with similar problems, and what new treatments are available. "Before Marielle had her transplant she had no hope of a normal life. At the end she was a frightening color of green. Now there's nothing she doesn't want to try," Lisa says. "If I can help parents find their way to a miracle like that, how could I not do it?"

Shania, a seven-month-old girl in Fiji, put that resolve to the test recently. She was dying of liver disease, but by one of those astonishing advances in transplantation, could be saved if her own liver was replaced by a small part of someone else's. It couldn't be done where she was, however, and the family had run out of all other options. It's the kind of impasse Lisa and her friends eat up. They persuaded an airline to offer free travel, brought the whole family to the United States, unearthed a contact to meet them at the Los Angeles airport who was not only the mother of a child with liver disease but who was from Fiji too, uncovered another mother who was a living donor to meet them on the east coast, and found a surgeon, Dr. James Piper, at Westchester County Medical Center, New York, who agreed to do the operation at no cost. Working against the clock, a huge black liver was taken from Shania's wasted body and a pink piece of her mother's put in its place. Both parts of what was one organ are now living normal lives. "She gave her child life a second time," Lisa says.

In Italy, Giorgio Brumat, who started AIDO, the main organ donation group there, had to work for years, almost single-handedly and with only the most primitive guidelines, to interest people who were either shocked or indifferent to transplantation. He became concerned, he told me, because, working for a pharmaceutical company and calling on hospitals, he couldn't bear to see such a waste of life, especially young life, that the new techniques could cure. I've often wondered, however, how much his natural compassion was focused by all that happened to his father who, as a young man in Austrian-controlled Italy, was a prisoner of war in Russia in the First World War and died when Giorgio was three years old. I imagine the vision of life being cut off in its prime has been with him since then. Now AIDO, with a million members and an army of devoted volunteers—from Aosta and Alessandria in the extreme northwest to Agrigento on the southern coast of Sicily—has helped save thousands of people from unnecessary death. It's a legacy his father could never have dreamed of.

When I first met Kenneth Moritsugu, the Deputy Surgeon General of the United States, he had already donated his late wife's organs, and his natural good humor came with an air of sadness. He was busy everywhere, organizing, speaking at conferences, running workshops. He described donation as "ordinary people doing extraordinary things." But that was not the end of it. Incredibly, two years later, one of his two daughters was killed by a car while crossing the street. He donated her organs too and still went on with his work of encouragement and education. I can't think of him as anything else than an extraordinary man doing extraordinary things.

Commitment comes in all forms. At a transplant meeting, I met a woman who has had five kidney transplants, one of which lasted for years. Instead of hiding away and worrying about the future, she is an active volunteer who hits head-on the fears of people on the waiting list. "Yes, your body can reject the new organ," she says. "But even if it does, that doesn't have to be the end of everything. Look at me."

"Do you know who your donor is?" I asked Mikie, a kidney recipient, at a tree-planting ceremony in San Francisco's Golden Gate Park. "Here she is," she answered, pointing to another young woman, about her own age, standing close by. "Were you best friends?" I asked, having come across this kind of selflessness among people who have grown up together. "No," she said. "She was my bank teller." It turned out to be literally true. One day at the bank, the teller, Mary, who knew her only casually had said, "You don't look so good. What's the matter?" and had found out that her kidneys were failing and no one in her family, all of whom had volunteered to help, was a match. Mary had then gone to the hospital, the University of California, San Francisco, Medical Center, volunteered to be a donor, and went through with it. "Why?" I asked. "I just felt it was the right thing to do," she said, with a conviction so absolute I wondered why I'd even asked.

Am I naïve, I wonder, in thinking people like these are much more common than we generally assume? Experience tells me they exist in every niche of society, quietly but steadily giving the rest of us a clearer view of the stars.

FAMILY PHOTOGRAPH

Maggie and Nicholas

Nicholas on
a family trip
to Wyoming

FAMILY PHOTOGRAPH

FAMILY PHOTOGRAPH

Reg and Nicholas in the French Alps

FAMILY PHOTOGRAPH

Nicholas as a
Canadian Mountie

FAMILY PHOTOGRAPH

Nicholas as
Robin Hood

FAMILY PHOTOGRAPH

Reg with Eleanor
and Nicholas

FAMILY PHOTOGRAPH

Nicholas in
Switzerland

© SANTA ROSA PRESS DEMOCRAT, PHOTOGRAPH BY JOHN BURGESS

Eleanor and
Maggie at
the funeral

© SANTA ROSA PRESS DEMOCRAT, PHOTOGRAPH BY JOHN BURGESS

Eleanor wipes
Maggie's tears

NICHOLAS GREEN

SEPTEMBER 9, 1987
OCTOBER 1, 1994

THOU ART A DEW-DROP,
WHICH THE MORN BRINGS FORTH,
ILL FITTED TO SUSTAIN UNKINDLY SHOCKS,
OR TO BE TRAILED ALONG THE SOILING EARTH
A GEM THAT GLITTERS WHILE IT LIVES,
AND NO FOREWARNING GIVES;
BUT AT THE TOUCH OF WRONG,
WITHOUT A STRIFE
SLIPS IN A MOMENT OUT OF LIFE.

WILLIAM WORDSWORTH

© HARRY BENSON 1995

Nicholas'
gravestone

COURTESY OF PRESIDENT SCALFARO'S PRESS OFFICE

The Greens being comforted by President Scalfaro of Italy

© HARRY BENSON 1995

Family snowball fight at Mount Etna

©RCS/OGGI

The Greens and organ recipients meet. Standing, left to right: Reg; Maggie; Andrea Mongiardo, recipient of Nicholas' heart; Francesco Mondello, cornea recipient; Tino Motta, kidney recipient; Anna Maria Di Ceglie, kidney recipient; Eleanor. Seated, left to right: Laura; Maria Pia Pedalà, liver recipient; Domenica Galletta, cornea recipient; Silvia Ciampi, pancreas recipient; Martin.

© RCS/TONY GENTILE

Domenica Galletta, cornea recipient

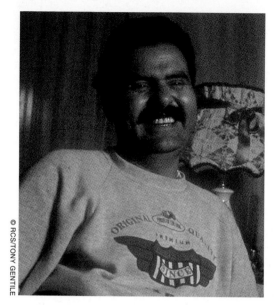

© RCS/TONY GENTILE

Francesco Mondello,
cornea recipient

© RCS/TONY GENTILE

Anna Maria Di Ceglie, kidney recipient

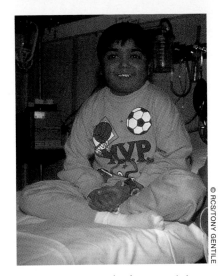

Andrea Mongiardo, heart recipient

Silvia Ciampi, recipient of islet cells

Maria Pia Pedalà, liver
recipient, as a student

© RCS/KATIA SACCONI

Maria Pia Pedalà with her
husband and new baby

FAMILY PHOTOGRAPH

Tino Motta, kidney
recipient, with
flowers for Eleanor

Italian children with a collection of bells for the
Children's Bell Tower

Pope John Paul II blessing the central bell

PROJECT SCULPTOR BRUCE HASSON
PHOTOGRAPH BY JOEL HACK, BODEGA BAY NAVIGATOR

Children's Bell Tower in Bodega Bay, California

© HARRY BENSON 1995

Sicilian schoolchildren singing in the street

© RCS/OGGI

The Greens on location. From left to right: Jamie Lee Curtis,
Gene Wexler who played Nicholas, Alan Bates, Hallie Eisenberg
who played Eleanor, Reg, Maggie, and Eleanor

SCULPTOR BRUCE HASSON, PHOTOGRAPH BY SCOTT MCCUE

"The Birds"
sculpture for
Calabria, Italy

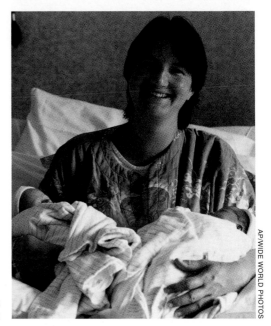

Maggie holding
Martin and Laura

AP/WIDE WORLD PHOTOS

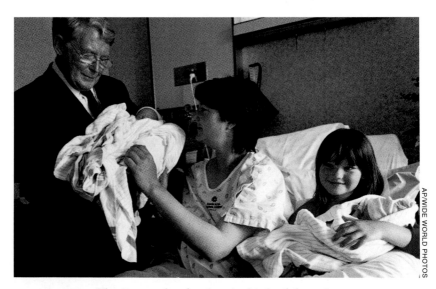

AP/WIDE WORLD PHOTOS

The Greens shortly after the birth of the twins

PHOTOGRAPH BY GIGI CAMANILE ©

The twins' first
birthday celebration

PHOTOGRAPH BY GIGI CAMANILE ©

Maggie and the
twins at the
Children's Bell Tower

PENNI GLADSTONE, SAN FRANCISCO EXAMINER © 1998

PHOTOGRAPH BY GIGI CAMANILE ©

The Greens at home

Chapter Thirteen

Talk Shows, Reporters, and Photographers

From the moment we entered the police station at Polistena, and the police showed their astonishment that we had been fired on, it was clear this was going to be a major news story. Before we went to bed that night, Maggie put into words what I'd been thinking: "We should tell whoever asks everything we know. It'll make it easier to catch the people who did this and it might help save someone else on that road."

The media did come in force, not just from southern Italy but the whole country, and phone calls from the United States and the rest of Europe soon followed. But all stories peak, and today's front-page news often can't find space on page 32 tomorrow. We were determined to keep interest alive as long as we possibly could. "If attention falls away soon," I thought, "this will be something people will remember for a while and think sadly of when reminded of it, but it will have no lasting effect." I wanted to etch it in people's minds. So, from the start, we were ready to talk to the press. In my view, all of us were after the same thing: to get to the bottom of this whole affair, whether it was the crime itself or the organ donor shortage or the psychological effects on a family of such a loss. Without ever discussing it, we also wanted the information to be as detailed and unadorned as possible. We had our own views, but we wanted everyone to read into it whatever they chose. It's what helped make it a universal story.

Having worked on daily papers for so long, I understood the need for speed. For news stories it is essential to answer as best you can there and then, not wait three days until you have confirmed it in detail. When Nicholas' story came to the world's attention, it came with a bang. As it turned out, the story had a tail like the Hale-Bopp comet, but the initial impact was what put it on front pages around the world. That first decision—to answer reporters' questions fully and immediately—was instinctive. The follow-up was deliberate and, I hope, thoughtfully worked out. So, once we were back home and while the calls were still coming to us, I started to initiate other media contacts. I wrote and telephoned and faxed. I sent clippings of our story in case they'd missed it and photos of some of the events such as the meeting with President Scalfaro. I tailored suggestions to suit their readers, mentioning that Nicholas was a Boy Scout to some publications, that he collected stamps to others.

Whenever we traveled to talk to organ and tissue donation groups, I let the local papers know. When we went back to Italy, I gave the flight number to the San Francisco television stations. We asked *Parents* magazine if they'd be interested in a mother's view. I tried *Parade* and CNN and women's magazines. I asked Grahame, my half-brother in England, to contact the newspaper in Accrington, the small town where I was born. I combed the reference books for publications that might be interested and began to call them, one after the other, mass circulation magazines, healthcare and religious publications, organ procurement newsletters, UNICEF. I telephoned rather than wrote so I could explain how I thought our story would interest their readers. I was encouraged to find that when they picked up the phone almost everyone knew what had happened to us.

I looked for new ways to tell the story. I used developments like the progress of the recipients to move it on, contacted Italian-speaking radio programs, wrote more and more articles for newsletters. All this in turn set up a chain reaction to new publications, some of which I'd never heard of. Journalists contacted us from Argentina and western Australia, Poland and Japan. An American friend in Nepal sent a clipping from a paper he'd seen there. Another read it in Kuwait, a third in Hong Kong. Children from Chernobyl, recuperating in Italy, knew the story of Nicholas. I like to think it gave them hope.

Many of the calls produced nothing but condolences. A few were quite cool, indicating they thought enough had already been written about what after all was only one donor family among thousands a year. By contrast, *Vanity Fair* rejected the idea with such delicacy that at first I thought they'd accepted it. But among the failures were triumphs. *Parents* magazine agreed and Maggie wrote a much-praised article for them called "Just Say Yes." In it she says how glad she is now to have neglected the laundry to play with Nicholas. "At bedtime he didn't ask for water but for a hug," she added. "I told him I'd never run out of hugs." A television crew did turn up at the airport to do an interview and, as a by-product, the flight attendants put us in first class. The *Accrington Observer* telephoned—at 2:00 one morning—and did a comprehensive piece. Ann Landers printed a letter I sent to her, and I got more calls from that than almost anything else I've ever written. The prestigious *Economist* magazine printed one too: none of my friends who claim to read it noticed. I've never dared show my British friends the article I wrote for the *Journal of the American Medical Association*, however: the subtitle was "A Piece of My Mind," to which the English schoolboy response is simple but effective, "Are you sure you can spare it?"

In *Scouting* magazine I painted this picture of Nicholas: "I never thought he would make a good Scout. Like his father, he seemed destined to be baffled by knots, tent pegs, and getting damp twigs to light. I daresay his entry for the pinewood derby was the ugliest in the United States, possibly in the history of the event. And he was always losing the slide for his neckerchief. I have a memory of him on a lake last summer. He'd so looked forward to taking a canoe trip that we gave him his life jacket and paddle and launched him. You're on your own, we told him. He didn't know it, but we watched him every second, ready with the other canoe to pick him up if anything went wrong. He just sat there, making ineffectual strokes with the paddle, carried along with the wind farther and farther away. In the end he just drifted, his mind consumed with some daring adventure, a hero alone in a canoe against the wilderness. He'll never learn the J-stroke, I thought, as we went out to tow him back. And, of course, he never did. But he had inside him the pure spirit of scouting. He hated to see others unhappy and wanted to help anybody in trouble. Even when doing jobs he didn't like, he tried his best. He was loyal to his friends, his family, and his toys." Letters poured in from Scouts asking how they could earn an organ donation patch for their uniform.

Just as those biblical figures begat a child which begat another which in turn begat a third, so these stories spawned others. I wrote articles for local papers, British papers, schools in Italy, magazines, more newsletters. Talented people who had never met Nicholas were writing about him too as if they knew him. The Sonoma County paper, the *Santa Rosa Press Democrat*, part of the *New York Times* group, covered the story at every stage with evocative writing and photographs that were used around the world: there's no chance now of shopping in Santa Rosa or any of the nearby towns without someone saying, "Don't I know you?" In the *San Francisco Examiner*, one of Stephanie Salter's articles captured the feeling so well that the editors allowed it to take up most of the front page and an entire inside one too. I left a copy with the Asian-American desk clerk at the airport hotel where we were staying on the Saturday night it came out. He called the room a few minutes later, scarcely able to talk for emotion.

I'd always felt *Reader's Digest* was a natural for the story. Reaching twenty-seven million readers in a score of languages justified a lot of effort, and I pursued the editors for months. At last they agreed to cover it and assigned it to a senior writer, Robert Kiener. Years before, when we came to the United States, the very first house I looked at was in *Reader's Digest*'s hometown in New York state. It was an attractive place, but here was something else I couldn't face telling my friends in Britain, that I would be living on Pleasant Avenue, Pleasantville. With his kindly manner, I could easily have mistaken Robert for Mr. Pleasant of Pleasant Avenue, Pleasantville, but in fact he was a probing journalist and a beautiful writer. Eventually he came with us to Italy and wrote an article of such close observation that it became the lead story in almost all the overseas editions from Russia to China, Australia to Hungary. If this isn't universality, you might say, it surely comes close. Nor did it end there. The professor of pediatric surgery at Bombay University Hospital, I heard later, was impressed enough to translate the whole article into Marathi, the local language, for even greater impact. "There are still another fifteen official languages in India and dozens of dialects," I reminded Rob. "This is no time to relax."

It was satisfying to see how writers of such different types had searched for the words that made the experience live for them. Organ and tissue donation was invariably treated seriously and sympathetically. In our first contacts with healthcare groups, we'd been told the press as a whole had almost ignored the subject, covering only stories of organs being sold or influential people jumping the line. Whatever the truth of that, what we saw now was the clear demonstration that donation could be not just news, but good news too. More than that, these stories spoke of what I'd felt from the earliest days: that Nicholas' death had sent an electric charge through the human spirit. Transplants, they showed, were doing more even than saving lives: they were helping bring people a little closer together.

So now when strangers tell us they signed their donor cards because of what happened to Nicholas, I reflect that a lot of it is due to nothing more than staying up late and writing letters to editors.

Television coverage was equally extensive. The morning talk shows were the most disruptive. At 7:09 a.m. you're unlikely to be scintillating. But with the time difference, it turned out to be 4:09 a.m. Pacific time. And for that we had to be sitting in our hardback Windsor chairs about thirty minutes earlier to make sure everything was working.

Even before that, the cameras and booms and mysterious black blinking boxes had to be set up. On those nights, we left the front door unlocked and tried to go to bed early. Typically, at around 2:00 a.m. the crew would arrive—shushing each other, setting up equipment with elaborate care but substantial noise, and occasionally tripping over Maggie's randomly placed furniture. Sleep was impossible and, after a while, we didn't try. We got up, made tea, and sat around getting in the way. Several times two or three of these competitive morning shows arrived one after the other, and the normally empty street in front of the house was lined with huge floodlit trucks, their generators filling the night air and bouncing signals off satellites.

In the order of earthly pleasures, looking closely into the face of Katie Couric or Jane Pauley as you wake up in the morning must surely rank high. But staring into a glass lens in the wee hours and trying to act natural is an experience of a different order. Certainly the medium is the message, imposing its own rules: instantaneous answers without the opportunity to back and fill as you do in a normal conversation, short takes that say only part of what you have in mind, answering something entirely different from what you were asked. I still find it disconcerting to be asked a two-part question, answer one part, pause for breath, and find the interviewer has moved on to something else. It goes against the grain too. One of the pleasures of going through life is to develop ever more subtle ways of expressing ideas. Now before a national audience—including your children's teachers— you lapse into hasty oversimplifications you'd be ashamed of over the breakfast table.

"Just think of Julie Andrews singing 'My Favorite Things,'" I advised Maggie before our first program. "Oh yeah, what's that?" she asked. "When the bee stings. When the sound bites," I said. It became our motto. Brevity and depth are friends, not enemies—think of the Gettysburg Address or any sonnet you learned at school. But most of us need time to refine a thought to its elements, and that's a luxury television guests don't usually get.

The impact, however, is greater than any other medium. Once, after a long interview with a wire service writer, which produced a delicately balanced and carefully researched story, I reflected that, while it would go to a thousand newspapers, the letters we'd get from two minutes on a television network would dwarf those from all those readers. Even on a dominant show like Oprah Winfrey's, which I knew commanded the loyalty of millions of viewers, I'm still surprised by the range of people who tell us they saw our interview, from schoolboys Eleanor's age to corporate executives I'd never dreamed would be watching television in the middle of the afternoon. But the impact is true too of local shows, and when people stop to shake hands at stores or airports or gas pumps, I'm sure it owes more to a fleeting image on a screen than anything they've read.

The coverage had a number of variations around a few basic themes: these people donated their son's organs and they don't regret it; transplantation crosses national borders; one death can save several lives—all of which we agreed with. A few talked about Nicholas living on through the recipients, which we didn't agree with in any literal sense, but our view remained that people should take from this story whatever they wanted. There was another side too—these are newspeople, after all. So, along with the perfectly sincere condolences and the sad looks, there's always someone who blurts out with genuine enthusiasm, "What a great story that was." They're right, of course. That's why they're interviewing you.

Instant communication has unexpected deficiencies. In the hectic wake of the shooting, one Italian paper added an "h" to Maggie's name. To this day, as reporters go back into the files to update the story, she often turns up as Margareth Green and sometimes, in Italy, Lady Margareth, an identity she has been quite unable to shake. I too have been transformed. I've been Reg almost all my life, shunning Reggie as too cuddly and Reginald as too stiff. But Reg was too difficult for the Italian press and Reginald is what I became for the first time outside my driver's license. Years ago, in a radio interview, I remember hearing Tex Beneke, Glenn Miller's lead singer, say he adopted his nickname in something like the second grade. Now, he said, any time someone sees him in an airport and says, "Hello, Gordon," he knows it must be a very old friend. By contrast, anyone who says, "It's Reginald Green, isn't it?" I've probably never met before. Like "Chattanooga Choo Choo," sung by Gordon Beneke, it lacks conviction.

The name may be catching on in Italy, however. One lady who was interested in what went on at the White House asked me if I knew Reginald Reagan. I should add it's only the latest trouble I've had with my very British name. My initials, R.F.D. (Reginald Frederick Douglas—ugh), frequently turned up as RED Green when I first came to this country and a mailhouse, misreading my scrawled signature, always addressed me as Dear Regifoo. The continual switching between national customs has given problems throughout, like the photographer who, pressing the claims of a British magazine, made what he thought was an unanswerable point in its favor: "It's the only one the Royals trust." We also had a phone call from a writer on what she said was the largest Dutch women's magazine and had 750,000 readers. I tried to imagine the 750,000 largest Dutch women.

All this activity was, for me, like being back in the rough-and-tumble of daily journalism. There was the same camaraderie among journalists and the differences in method that have always surprised me: some knew everything about our case, including our ages; others asked what happened. Some approached the whole episode of the attack with delicacy. Others hit it head-on: one wanted to know what were the exact words we said when we discovered Nicholas had been shot and seemed surprised that we didn't know. Some television studio sets were of opera house dimensions. Others were modest: in one noisy office I did a radio interview for a Spanish language radio station sitting in a broom closet with an interviewer and an interpreter.

The news coverage was the first surprise—its extent, its prominence, and its global reach. But the fulsome editorials and features were the second. *Life* magazine's first article said that while we had not hidden our grief from Eleanor we had taught her "—and they have taught the world—to create a miracle from a tragedy." Its second, by Brad Darrach, remains among the most touching of all the articles that have appeared in its eloquent wonder at life's mysteries. It obviously came from the heart. When, two years later, Brad died and I telephoned his wife, she said simply, "It was the kind of article he liked to write."

Eloquence and empathy came equally to Stephanie Salter in another *San Francisco Examiner* article. "The desire to wound back when wounded is one of humankind's most primitive violent instincts," she said. "The Greens did not surrender to it and, for that, they have inspired respect and awe in millions." In yet another feature, she added, "The Greens have continued to surprise and impress us as they've struggled, openly, to wring every ounce of good they can out of their boy's awful death. In a subtle, almost magical way, that is difficult to comprehend in the modern age, the Nicholas effect has begun to act like some potent medicinal vapor."

The *Minneapolis Star Tribune* editorialized, "Italians were stunned. They didn't expect such grace, least of all from Americans." The *Los Angeles Times* commented, "The Greens embraced people unknown to them. Amid heartbreaking loss they bore no bitterness." A Reuters story from Rome written by Philip Pulella said, "In a country where violent deaths are often followed by wailing, finger-pointing and threats of vendetta, the composure and serenity of the Green family forced even the most smug Italians to take a hard look in the mirror."

"They have taught us what it means to be civilized," said one talk show host. "We are truly in the debt of this couple." Columnists reached for extravagant analogies. "The Greens responded with remarkable warmth and love, reflecting in their actions and words the famous prayer of an Italian of many centuries ago—St. Francis of Assisi, who sought the grace to sow love where hatred flourished," said one. "It's important that St. Francis wasn't just against hatred; he was for love. So were the Greens." Although kindly meant, the absurdity of the comparison speaks for itself, but these hosannas show how deeply moved even the battle-hardened were.

The fact is that even those who had learned to cover saints and sinners with equal detachment were moved to tears by Nicholas' sacrifice. "In our jaded way, we thought we had seen just about everything. But we really hadn't," one television producer wrote. Ann Pleshette Murphy, then editor-in-chief of *Parents* magazine, wrote to Maggie after her article appeared, "I haven't denied my Nicholas or his sister Maddie an extra story or small treat since I read your simple, beautiful words," and Robin Montgomery, of *Guideposts*, added, "I have written many stories that have faded from my mind once written. But the story of Nicholas will forever remain in my heart."

And then there was one editorial from Italy that also holds a special place. "One day, the American boy's little sister will understand the reason for such a great clamor, and she will be proud not to have heroes in her family, but to have grown up breathing the values of solidarity and brotherhood." What a deluge it was and these are just a few of the drops. Clearly, some alchemy was at work, and we were determined not to lose touch with its source.

Over these years we have met an array of media people. Some of them are now friends. With others the meetings were brief but intense: in papers that still turn up, half-forgotten names, email addresses, phone and fax numbers float in and out. Some of them are the key to every activity in a place—such as the one person who had the itinerary for three tightly packed meetings in New Jersey—or the contact's beeper number at a TV station, with which you are whisked into a dressing room with a star on it and sandwiches in it, but without which you are just one of dozens waiting in line. I find these relics scattered over notebooks and calendars and yellow legal pads. Some are on several consecutive pages, then are gone without a trace. Is it still Bianca you have to see about picking up the limousine at Kennedy? Or was that Sylvia? Staring at the names, I can still recreate the sense of despondency I had when I realized I'd lost the painstakingly written-out schedule of a weeklong visit to Italy and with it the phone number of every contact there.

On one quick visit to Rome, I'd arranged to meet several journalists, one after the other. I was staying at the Ritz. Empty your mind of associations with the Ritz hotels in London and Paris. The first room I was given had no door. "There's no door?" the man at the front desk said when I told him. "No door?" He came with me to look, mumbling all the way to the third floor. But there was still no door. It turned out that it was being varnished, and they gave me another room. This one had a door, but now I almost choked on the smell of the newly applied varnish on it. I went to the front desk again. By now I was an obvious troublemaker: do you want a door or do you not want a door? But my status changed dramatically when he handed me a sheaf of messages later in the day and smiled like a co-conspirator: I'll be there at 8, Mimi. See you tonight, Paola. Be ready at 9, Antonella. See you after the theater, Olga.

All this coming and going to Italy produced expectations from new contacts back home too, like the planning committee for a major organ donation conference I was invited to join. "Will there be a lot of work?" I asked. "Oh, no, just a few conference calls." "Well, then, sure, I'd like to do it." "Oh, there's one thing. Do you think there's any chance you can ask the Pope to come?"

Except for the dailies, which are acutely aware of the unforgiving minute, photo sessions were always longer than press interviews, as the whole orchestra of expressions, positions, clothes, light, shade, background, and foreground were checked, double-checked, and changed. For a magazine spread, it could last most of the day. Just as everything was right, a telephone would ring or a cloud cover the sun. Two or three times for Italian magazines, it meant special effects, such as a birthday cake or Santa Claus outfits for the entire family.

No two photographers were alike. One was a Pulitzer Prize winner, another forgot to put film in. Some spent half an hour setting up the lighting, others came in, pulled faces at Eleanor, and got off twenty quick shots. Some came with an assistant who held the cameras, ran to get special equipment, and advised on clothing. Others were like a one-man band. Some we met only once, others like Gigi Campanile we saw often enough for him to have given up smoking twice. An Englishman who had answered an ad that said, "Come to sunny California and photograph movie stars," went straight from us to take pictures of a man who debriefed people abducted by extraterrestrial aliens. In all of these dealings, I can't remember a single example of obtrusiveness. Besides asking for general permission, some of them wanted to know if we'd mind a particular shot—Nicholas' bedroom, for example, or us holding a photograph of him.

For us, the standard had been set by Harry Benson, and the snowball fight on Mount Etna turned out to be typical of our other meetings with him. While his competitors watched approvingly, waiting their turn, he'd put us in the exact positions he wanted. The moment he'd taken his shots, and before anyone else could step in, he'd say commandingly, "Okay, Reg, stand up," or "Pick up Eleanor, Maggie," and destroy the careful arrangement he'd made. When he came to see us in Bodega Bay, he achieved a striking photo of all of us misty-eyed, by making us laugh till we cried at his falsetto version of "The Mountains of Mourne," and then suddenly snapping off a hail of pictures. One man in Italy, who was part of a group being photographed, was so overcome by Harry's style that he put his lighted cigarette in the pocket of his bright blue suit, from which a small circular hole and a wisp of smoke soon appeared.

But there were many other photographers, and we often sat on cold rainy beaches waiting for the sun to come out or in front of blazing fireplaces on hot days for Christmas editions. "Just be natural," we'd be told when a session was being organized. "Just don't wear navy blue or brown or plaid. No black or white, of course. Or grey. Don't be too bright. Don't all wear similar colors. And at some stage you'll need to have a change of clothes so it won't all look like it's one day." "Is that all?" we'd ask. "Yes, as I said, just be natural."

Late one night, we returned home from spending Thanksgiving with Maggie's family to find a message on the answering machine from a Czech photographer saying he wanted to come up the next morning from Los Angeles to photograph us by our Christmas tree for a family magazine. I called him when I woke to say we didn't have a tree yet. All we had was a tiny plant shaped like one. "Let's use that," he said. "I'll be there in the afternoon." When I'd put the phone down Maggie said, "You know, we could get our tree early this year." It seemed right: if this issue of the magazine was stressing the holy spirit, we needed the right props. After breakfast we went out, cut a tree only slightly smaller than the one in Rockefeller Plaza and, in a burst of energy, put it up. The photographer arrived soon after lunch. "Okay, let's see the dwarf tree," he said. We led him into the living room, now dominated by this Sherwood Forest of a Christmas tree. "Jesus Christ," he said.

As we traveled around, there were many reminders of the impact these photographs were having, and in Italy we were often stopped by someone wanting to take a picture of us. One day when I was walking in the Piazza Navona, a Japanese couple approached, smiled, and gestured with their camera. "So, it's got there too," I thought, "a place that doesn't even recognize brain death." I moved into position with one of the famous fountains behind me until I realized they wanted me to take a photo of them.

Photography gave me one other thing to think about. By this time, the snapshot I'd taken of Nicholas at the foot of the Matterhorn, a few days before his death, had appeared in magazines so often I thought I knew every detail. Someone sent an enlarged version, however, and looking at it one day I noticed for the first time two people in the distance, too small to see in the usual size. Like the figures on Keats' urn, they are immortal, never aging, strolling forever together on a sunlit path on that lovely afternoon and to this day blissfully unaware of an impending tragedy.

Everywhere we went in Italy the media went too, at least someone from ANSA, the Italian news agency, and a camera crew from the local television station. On bigger occasions, we became accustomed to a thick crowd pointing microphones and tape recorders at us. Many of the questions were quite direct. On our first visit back to Italy, one TV interviewer asked, "Are you planning to have more children?" Most, however, were of a more open nature. How do you feel? Or, how do you feel today? Or, for a change, what are your feelings now? In a small town near Venice, I had the nicest question I've ever heard from a newspaper: "If you were me, what would you ask?"

They displayed none of the pushing and shoving we've all heard about. In the early days, many of them would send the hotel desk clerk to ask our permission to take pictures. I was never sure whether a refusal would have been effective, but it was a pleasing gesture. One kind family, appropriately, bought a doll for Eleanor that talked with the aid of a microphone, and in Terni, surrounded by a crush of reporters, a small pink plastic microphone was thrust at me. I looked down to see a small smiling girl asking, "How do you feel?"

Clearly, in Italy there was much greater room for misunderstanding: the language, the culture, the laws were all a mystery. Unable to read Italian above the pace of a snail, and with about as much understanding, the nuances escaped us, and we had to rely on the feedback from the next batch of questions to know if we'd made ourselves clear. There were some obvious communication disasters. On the same day, one newspaper came out with a prominent story, "Green Family Forgives Killers," and another, "We Will Never Forgive His Killers." Then there was the reporter who sent a list of questions, noting that the following Tuesday was his "deathline."

Television came with its own problems, like the crowded news day when we were standing outside a school in Sicily, waiting to give a live television interview, forbidden to move and surrounded by a couple of hundred children and their parents, none of whom wanted to move either so as not to lose their place on camera. We waited a half hour, an hour, an hour and a half, in summery clothes, getting colder and colder as darkness came on, trying to keep Eleanor warm and still, and not scowling enough to ruin our image. The boys began to chase the girls, mothers tried to quiet fast-cooling babies.

Every few minutes, the interviewer was told from Rome, "Let's get ready." The crowd stiffened, the publicity seekers crowded more closely around us, the weak and infirm were pushed into the background. It was a Darwinian world ruled by the survival of the stage-struck. A few tense moments would pass until the announcer said, "We're now going to the United States. Hold it there, Sicily." One enterprising but very small man stood next to me, gripping my arm every time it looked as if I was about to be interviewed, then pushed his way through the thick crowd to Maggie when it was her turn. There her height was decisively against him, but all the time she was on camera she said it felt as though someone was climbing up her back.

CHAPTER FOURTEEN

DONORS AND RECIPIENTS: THE KNIFE EDGE

On the platform at a conference in San Diego, two women sat next to each other. One was American, the mother of two-year-old boy recently rescued from almost certain death by a heart transplant. The other was Mexican, the mother of a two-year-old boy who had died. It was his heart that had saved the other boy's life. Both women were on the verge of tears.

The American family had lived through a long nightmare, their only child moving, inexorably it seemed, toward death. "I was afraid to hold him even when it was time to say good-bye. He looked so gray and limp," the mother told a weeping audience of two hundred nurses.

As the end approached, the other little boy was found barely alive, face down in a pool of water in Mexicali. His name was Martin, and he had been born in the United States of Mexican parents. The medical community in San Diego moved heaven and earth to bring him to a hospital there and, when permission was given, sent an ambulance for him. It was in vain. The round-cheeked cherubic-looking boy died. Brokenhearted, exhausted by their efforts, emotionally drained, his parents nevertheless agreed to donate his organs. Why? I asked his mother. "She was brought up to try to help others," a relative who was interpreting for her said simply and unselfconsciously. It was palpably true. Now they sat on the platform, one mother still stunned by her loss, the other saved but awed that she should have gained so much from another's tragedy. "I'll spend my life trying to thank her," she said.

Everywhere we go these days, we come across that kind of knife edge of death and salvation. As I came out of a hotel in Modena one day, a young man stopped me to say his eight-month-old cousin had received a transplant after her parents were interviewed on the Maurizio Costanzo television show, a program that had been sparked by our interview. He wanted us to know his family was grateful. That same night at a donor meeting a doctor mentioned an eight-month-old baby. "That was a beautiful story," I commented. "No, not that one," he replied. "This one died. The parents donated the organs."

In a tiny village in the north of Italy on a rain-soaked Sunday afternoon, I was asked to lead a discussion of donor families. I agreed with a sinking heart: group therapy is foreign to my nature. I'm as unfitted to give advice as I am to take it. In similar sessions I've found myself in over the years I haven't felt better at the end, and I doubt I've told anyone else anything they haven't already worked out for themselves. In this case, there were about thirty of us, from a dozen families. It was as bad as I'd feared, two or three who wanted to talk, most of the rest sitting in gloomy silence. One young woman, who had lost her husband, struggled through sobs to weigh the good results of donating against the crushing loss. Who better than the rest of us there to commend her, but who better than we to know the futility of saying so? Almost none of them knew who their recipients were: I couldn't tell if they were resigned or resentful or simply didn't care. But there was an air of deep dejection over the discussion.

A few days later, during an Italian television program I was on, one of the other guests, a recipient, said blithely he had no interest in knowing who his donor was. To him that was history. He felt like a new man, his business was doing well, and the illness that had nearly finished him off just a nightmare. To my mind came an image of the impassive faces of those heartsick people, the bare room, the hard chairs, and the rain beating on the windows. It seemed like a different world, but it was just the knife's other edge.

Some recipients, however, do go to extraordinary lengths to find their donor's family—researching newspapers, perhaps, to pinpoint a particular car accident on a certain night. Some then charge ahead; they can't wait to say, "Thank you—you saved my life." Many others are shy, unwilling to do anything that might reawaken memories. So they hold off, making do with the scraps of information they've pieced together, and sometimes never do write or make that call, despite knowing with near certainty that they owe their lives to this someone who is a stranger only in name.

Similarly, many donor families choose not to meet the recipients. Some are in a sort of shock for months or years. Some don't want to do anything until they feel ready to smile again. Others are fearful, worried they won't like them, afraid they'll like them too much, frightened they may have to go through their grief all over again if the transplant fails. Still others don't ever feel involved: they see as pure coincidence whatever it was that brought the two families together in what, strictly speaking, can't even be called an encounter. Their attitude is simple: "Let's try to put our own lives back together and let them get on with theirs."

The most dramatic meetings of donor families and recipients are on television programs when the two are brought together for the first time. It can be hokey and more like the last act of a soap opera than real life. But I can speak to the power of it also. Before the show, the two sides are carefully segregated. Both are nervous as kittens, far more so than usual for people going on television for the first time. They sigh a lot, hold hands with relatives, gaze into space. The meetings themselves, however, are generally a love fest. The hostess gives the buildup, the donor family member on stage twists a Kleenex in her hands, the curtain parts, the recipient enters, and both parties forget the world. They hug, cry, stroke, gaze at each other adoringly. After the show, they take innumerable pictures, show each other family photos, swap anecdotes. They are self-selected of course—they chose to go on the program—and the first enthusiasm may not last. But I've seen enough of them now to know they can be the sort of moment when the earth shakes.

Certainly, knowing Nicholas' recipients has enriched our experience far beyond anything we would have known. They are now part of our lives and we of theirs. They are still careful with us, not wanting to stir up the pain, but we always try to see them if we are anywhere near where they live and they always seem pleased to see us. It's not like being with close relatives—we don't know them that well—but they do feel like part of an extended family. Even from the beginning, however, we never thought of Nicholas living on through them. These were now their organs and as Maggie once said, "I wished Nicholas would have lived a long time. Now I wish the same for his heart."

Dozens of people have been involved in their recovery, all the way from the removal of the organs in Messina to the after-care they still receive. We have become friendly with some of them, including two transplant team leaders, Raffaello Cortesini and Carlo Marcelletti, who are world-class physicians. But many more we are never likely to meet, and through this book I want to thank them too for the skills and dedication they mostly practice anonymously, but which, in this case, showed the world the astonishing power of modern medicine.

We often hear from the recipients at Christmas or Easter or perhaps they'll send a card if they travel on vacation. The messages between us are rarely long: not knowing the language is more frustrating in talking to them than it is with anyone else. It would be nice to chat freely, surprising each other with little revelations about ourselves. We'd like to tell them more about Nicholas, and I'm sure they'd eat it up, and Eleanor too, whom they've known as long as they've known us. From time to time they give us a scare, when we hear of a setback in their health or a suggestion of a problem we hadn't heard of before. But so far, at any rate, these have been temporary upsets and, overridingly, these are people participating in life in ways impossible to them for years.

When I last saw her in Rome, Silvia, though still blighted by the after-effects of diabetes, was feeling independent enough to have moved into an apartment of her own. Domenica not only can see her daughter Laura's face clearly—no longer a baby's face—but also that of little Antonio, born to her twenty months after she got her new cornea. Mindful of how memories fade, a television interviewer asked her four years after the transplant, "Do you think of Nicholas often?" "All the time," she said in her unaffected way. Francesco, in his mid-forties, is not only back watching rugby but playing it—as I told him, the doctors may be able to cure you, but they obviously can't make you smart. The youngest ones, Anna Maria and Tino, tiny when we saw them first, have grown and matured. Andrea, having had six operations on his own heart, all of which had failed, looks like any normal boy now that he has another boy's heart inside him. And Maria Pia, who at nineteen years old had been given up for dead, married Salvatore in the full bloom of womanhood and in the spring of 1998 had a baby—a boy, whom they have called Nicholas.

It may seem grandiose, but the scene in the Jimmy Stewart movie *It's a Wonderful Life* comes to mind—where, after trying to commit suicide, George Bailey is shown what life would have been like if he had never been born: his hometown corrupted and in the grip of the local miser, people dead who would have lived, his wife an old maid. I sometimes think of transplants that way—not just lives saved, but lives that would never have been, marriages that would not have taken place, consequences flowing for generations to come. All from one simple decision.

The basic rule in this country is to allow the two sides to meet, but only if both families choose to. Yet some donor family members, who had to wrestle with a decision that racked them and distressed other members of their family, have never had so much as an unsigned letter from someone who is living today, thanks to them. We're complex creatures and simple ingratitude probably doesn't begin to explain such lapses in civility. Vague feelings of guilt at living when another died, apprehension that the other side will make emotional demands, and, perhaps, a feeling of not measuring up to their scrutiny seem to me to be more likely. But, if nothing else, my hope would be that every recipient would somehow get a message through to make it clear that as life came out of death, it did so not just bravely, but gratefully too.

I have to add that unresponsive recipients are rare. The ones we see are usually among the most dedicated campaigners to be found anywhere, who make raising awareness of the shortage of donors their crusade and do everything from the humblest to the most influential jobs with the special energy of the reborn, speaking, organizing, checking schedules, talking to legislators, licking stamps. Others follow their own expertise, helping disadvantaged children, perhaps, or giving away works of art they've made. They tell us, some serious, some ebullient, they are trying to "give something back." They act as though they borrowed something and can't rest until they've paid it off at an above-market rate of interest. Perhaps the donor families who have deflected attempts to meet are missing something valuable also. At most meet-ings of recipients, someone will say to us, "I don't know who my donor was, but every day I say, 'Thank you.' Can I say thanks to you instead?" From other recipients nearby, there is generally a murmur of approval. But it is surely a poor substitute for the real thing.

Watching the reactions of living donors who have donated an organ to someone very sick is to be convinced once and for all that to give is more blessed than to receive. On one visit to Italy, I met a gra-cious count and his wife and their muscular twenty-something-year-old son, who showed a group of us around their home, a castle that has been in the family since the fifteenth century. Four years earlier, the young man had been on dialysis four hours a day, three days a week, and was weakening perceptibly until his mother gave him one of her kidneys. Now he looked strong enough to defend the family seat against any invader, and she smiled radiantly as though someone had conferred a great privilege on her.

One spring day I sat in a surgically scrubbed room in Sicily with a thirty-eight-year-old mother of four who had received a new heart six days before. "You can't touch the patient," I'd been told, but someone relented and brought in two pairs of rubber gloves. The impulse to hold hands was strong: this woman now had the heart of a twenty-year-old student from Rome, Marta Russo, whose parents donated her organs after she had been shot.

I could see in her all the mixture of emotions a transplant opera-tion brings on: relieved beyond words that she was now not going to leave her young children, but heavily burdened by the thought of hav-ing been saved by another family's suffering, and still oppressed, as many Italians are, by Nicholas' death. She murmured her mixture of thanks and sorrow, and I held her hand tightly, feeling life through the gloves.

We were not alone, however. Looking through the window at us, television cameras and reporters were massed, and in our hands we held microphones, covered with cloth to keep up some semblance of sterility. In Sicily, where transplantation rates are among the lowest in Europe, the surgeons had wanted to lose no opportunity to publicize what donations can do and neither did I. Later that night, it seemed to be working. On a dark street in Catania a woman stopped me to say, "I saw you on television tonight. I'm glad those parents did that." As for Marta, the prime minister attended her funeral, she was given her degree posthumously and an organ and tissue donation group has been set up in her name. I don't know how her mother and father feel about all this. But in that hospital room was the tangible proof that their decision has transformed the world for six other people.

This was not an isolated case. By 1998, donation rates in Italy had more than doubled since the year before Nicholas died. Although there are always multiple causes for changes of that magnitude, it seems clear that his example has helped save the lives of thousands of people. Dr. Starzl sent us a copy of an official Italian report on the rise of donations. "It's amazing to me to realize that what you did changed the emotional climate of an entire nation," he commented.

Letters and meetings put faces on the statistics. A woman writing from Bethesda, Maryland, said she had recently heard from her cousin, who lives in Italy. He had been waiting for a transplant since 1987. "Thanks to Nicholas Green, I finally have a new kidney and a new life," he told her. "I feel in my heart I received my lung and new life because of the publicity of your wonderful gift." A California man wrote, "I was told I should have heard the angels sing. I was that close to death." And Dr. Frederick Grover, head of Cardiothoracic Surgery at Colorado Health Sciences, commented, "We could never as an organ transplant group in this country raise enough money to publicize, in the way that you have done, the importance of organ donation."

More and more often, a shy couple will be introduced to us at meetings in Italy who say, almost inaudibly, that one of their children had talked of donating. Soon afterward there was a tragedy, generally a road accident, and the parents, sorrowfully but without doubts, followed the child's wishes. The greatest hope is with the young. Some are mature students with all the determination of youth to right the world. Others are tiny schoolchildren. They understand only that a little boy did something very good, and they want to be very good too. Not only do the young make the decision for themselves, but they often change the opinion of their parents and even grandparents.

The decision to donate does not take the pain away, however. Arriving for a talk to the city government at a small town near Rome, I was shown first into a large committee room. A dozen or so people sat there, including a young man, eighteen years old, huddled in his overcoat, hands thrust into his pockets, coat collar turned up. His eyes were focused on something far away. I recognized that shivering feeling, and my heart sank. "This boy's parents and sister were killed in a car accident this week," someone said. "He wanted to meet you." We embraced, awkwardly, his body stiff inside the overcoat. A newspaper clipping was on the table with photographs of a laughing girl, thirteen years old, sitting proudly with her older brother and their youthful parents. The headline read: "*Famiglia decimata.*" On his own, as the family's sole survivor, the boy had decided to donate the organs. "They would have wanted it," he said. I stumbled through a few consoling phrases, but felt their uselessness. He will, I hope, always feel glad of his decision. But his life has been shattered and, as you read these words, he is still out there in a world emptier than he could ever have imagined.

In every country, the decision of who is to receive donated parts produces disagreements and suspicion. Should they go to the sickest? Those with the best chance of surviving? Those who have been on the waiting list longest? Most countries, including the United States, now have elaborate rules, but they are bedeviled by hairsplitting distinctions which give everybody involved a great deal of heartache. I once attended a meeting of one of the organ donor groups which was trying to refine the priorities. Its governing board of impressively qualified men and women spent hours wrestling with meticulous definitions that, compared to the larger issues, were of minute significance, except that for some individuals on the borderline it would determine if they lived or died. It is one of those problems that would simply disappear if enough organs were available.

Hospitals in the United States are now required to inform the organ procurement groups of patient deaths, and the hope is that, along with programs to heighten awareness, donations can rise accordingly. Even minor changes in procedures might have a substantial effect. The discrepancy in donation rates between different regions in this country shows some things work well and others don't. Obvious? Certainly. So surely some of the solutions should be too.

Meanwhile, the shortage of donors and the high success rates of transplant operations push families across the world to whatever solution they can find. Even those who at first refuse to believe a new organ is necessary can become among the most determined once they are convinced it is the only cure. The mother who says, "You've got to be kidding," when told her child can only survive with a new liver is transformed into someone who asks persistently, then desperately, "Why can't you do it now? Can't you see she's dying?" I met an Italian whose mother lived in Moscow for twelve months waiting for a liver, which she eventually received. The cost, obviously, was horrendous, but he still has a mother.

There are heartbreaks among those who want to donate too. In southern Italy, a man came into a restaurant where we were having lunch between meetings. "He wants to meet you," the owner said. "He's not an educated man. He works in the fields over there," pointing to some rough land with a few poor buildings on it. "His son died recently in a motorcycle accident. He said if anything happened to him he wanted to give his organs, like your son. But when the father tried, they could only take the eyes. Now he's sad." I said something to him about all the good he had done giving two people the chance to see again, but he shrugged it off. He seemed so dejected I felt I had to say something more. I turned to the interpreter. "Please say that even though giving the organs made us feel better, I still miss Nicholas so much that I cry a little every day." "He understands," came the quiet reply. "But not being able to do what his son asked was like losing him a second time."

It's a subject that seems to make everyone cry. You'd expect it of donor families, and we do cry in public from time to time, though I think we all try to set a good example and these are generally quick tears that can be mastered. But the voice of a meeting organizer, crisply reading a list of names, will suddenly crack and you realize that throughout the details of working out who sits where, she's been fighting some deep emotion. Many recipients weep bucketsful—humbly, as they think how many trained people it took to bring them back from the very edge, gratefully, for the family who made the decision, and painfully, knowing someone had to die so they could live. Just the memory of what their families did for them on the birthday they never expected to live to see can bring it on.

Surgeons call transplantation delicate work, work that has to be done quickly, technically exacting work, but everyday work for all that. They must be right: some 85 percent of transplant operations are successful. To me, however, it is still science fiction, and I'm lost in admiration for whatever combination of skill and spirit keeps them doing it day after day. I'd always imagined they would be proof against tears, however. Yet, at a meeting I attended, a surgeon built like a football player, reading aloud a letter from a patient, simply stopped, unable to finish it.

Of all those involved, the organ procurement nurses must have one of the most difficult tasks in the whole of medicine, having to approach families at the most tragic moment of their lives with a request that offends or shocks many of them. I often think of a spring evening in Charleston, South Carolina—a day to remind you why the settlers fell so in love with this beautiful area that they felt compelled to create a city worthy of it. Ruthie Stockwell, a transplant coordinator I'd just met, seemed ill at ease. It seemed incongruous, on that gentle Sunday, in a pretty young woman on her way to a charming restaurant—and in good company, obviously.

What's the matter? I asked. "I have four patients right now who need a transplant badly, one very badly," she said. "I try to distance myself from all this, but these are real people and we don't have donors for any of them. You feel so helpless." One of them was a fifty-one-year-old woman with a husband and a thirty-year-old son. "Just a couple of weeks ago she developed sinus trouble, nothing serious, but enough to make her go to the doctor. He noticed signs of jaundice and referred her to a specialist. 'You need a transplant,' he told her. 'It's the only way to save your life.' At first the family was in complete denial. 'Thanks for the advice,' they said, 'but she'll get better. We don't need anything drastic like a transplant.' " In just two weeks, however, she deteriorated alarmingly. "We could lose her tonight," Ruthie commented and tears sprang to her eyes. We joined the rest of the group, and the conversation turned to other things. But in the middle of dinner, Ruthie's beeper went off. She left to make a call and came back a few minutes later looking like a rainbow, tears and smiles in equal profusion. "We've got a donor," she said and tucked into her half-finished blackened shrimp and Cajun sauce.

While we ate, the chief liver transplant surgeon, Dr. Baliga, flew to Tennessee in one of the small jets under permanent contract to the Medical University of South Carolina. He removed the liver of a young boy, who had died in a car accident that day, and flew back again. By 4:30 a.m., the rest of the medical team had assembled, and the transplant operation began on the fast-sinking patient. At 7:30, I was with Mark Ruppel, another member of the transplant team, on our way to do a radio interview when his car phone rang. "Ruthie? What's up?" he asked. "Oh no. What kind of problem?" A tremor ran through me. "I know they were informed," Mark was saying. "Yes, tell them it's *forty* bagels." Besides coordinating the team, staying up half the night and crying about people unknown to her a few days before, Ruthie was apparently the backstop for catering too.

That afternoon, I looked at the darkened room where the transplant patient was still asleep. "We got the liver in prime condition, with very little time on ice," said Dr. Sindhi, the team's other transplant surgeon. "When it's that way it's like having fresh vegetables." Although he'd been at work all night, he was still worrying a little about her. "We want her to wake up soon. There's always the danger of fluid getting on the brain." The donor's other organs had also been recovered and transplanted to patients in Tennessee.

As I flew home that night, I thought of the chance events that had led to this reversal of fortunes for two families. One coming into the light after a nightmare, the other darkened beyond any possibility of relief. What a fearful lottery it all is. I can only hope those parents will find some solace in knowing that, at the end, that little boy helped someone in desperate need when no one else in the world could.

"Some people's stories haunt you," a transplant coordinator said to me one evening. We were sitting at dusk near the water's edge on the Gulf Coast. "I had one patient, a very young woman. She'd had a pitiful life, pitiful, but it seemed she was just getting things in order, taking care of her eighteen-month-old child, all she had. It brought out the best in her. Then one day the little girl was killed in a car accident. It was devastating for everyone. For me too: I had to keep saying to myself, 'We mustn't give way.' We talked, this young mother and I, about a lot of things, and in the end she said, 'I want to donate the organs. It's the only thing that will get me through.' Well, she did and now she's going back to school. She's even offered to do volunteer work for us." By now twilight had turned to darkness and, sitting there in silence, I shuddered that such agony should be. "Come on," my new friend said. "Let's not mope. She saved something from the rubble."

Every decision to donate produces on average three or four organs. So families faced with brain death have a clear choice: they have the chance to save three or four other families from the devastation they themselves are going through or, equally, condemn them to a lifetime of sorrow. Then there are the tissues, which sound less dramatic, but which, among other things, can cure blindness, relieve the agony of severe burns, and avoid amputations. I sometimes wonder how any other decision is possible.

At present, donations are still too hard for most people, however. In Denver, a nurse who had been involved in many transplants, told me that, after her mother died, she took a deep breath and asked her father, "Shouldn't we donate her organs?" He looked at her in disbelief. "Hasn't your mother suffered enough?" he asked. Few people say it as baldly as that, but that underlying thought is one reason why people can't bring themselves to make the choice. There are many others— the fear of upsetting other family members, a numbness that paralyzes decision-making, or just a sense that somehow the process is disrespectful.

Some families who don't donate feel they haven't been treated well. They complain they weren't given enough time to absorb the fact of death before they were asked to donate or they never saw the right person. Stories of people coming out of comas after months feed their fear of making a terrible and irrevocable mistake. No one, they say, told them that brain death is death, pure and simple, not a new word for a transitory state. It's easy to see how this can happen. In a hospital with hundreds of stories being played out at any time, real and imagined lapses are bound to occur.

Other families have a strong objection rooted in beliefs or deep feelings, and I would not want to try to talk such people over: this is an intensely personal matter. Everyone, however, is a potential recipient, and that thought often makes people thinking seriously about donation for the first time uncomfortably aware of a moral dilemma: if they object in principle to giving to the pool, by what principle are they justified in taking from it? "A few people I meet take a principled stand against donations," a chaplain told me. "But I've yet to meet any parents who would refuse a transplant for their own child."

But brain death is generally associated with sudden death, and I think that what determines the decision of most families is not a question of belief or of administrative procedures. Instead they arrive at a hospital to find that someone they love, who was in perfect health the last time they saw them, is now dead or dying. Their minds are in turmoil. Many are distraught. Some are angry with themselves for somehow not having prevented it. "If only I hadn't given him so much freedom, this might never have happened," some parents say. "If only I hadn't been so strict," say others. They are struggling at the same time to come to grips with the mystery of death and a loneliness they sense will never go away. On top of that, to be asked to make a decision they have never thought about is just too much. Worried about doing something they may regret forever, and often unable in time to consult other family members, they do the safe thing and say no.

Yet I can't believe the consequences are what they would have wanted. I often think of something a transplant coordinator said as we traveled together to catch an early morning flight. She had been on duty when a small boy was killed in a road accident. "The parents were in a terrible state. It took everything I had to even ask them if they would consider donating. They wouldn't discuss it. They were angry I'd even mentioned it." She couldn't persist, of course. "I could see what they were going through. Their world had collapsed. But I had to fight back the tears. All I could think of was that, on the third floor of that same hospital, a mother and father just like these were sitting at the bedside of their little boy, who was dying that night too, praying that somehow he might be saved. But he did die, because a new heart didn't arrive in time. So, instead of one tragedy, there were two—and one, we know, could have been prevented." I can still hear the wondering sadness in her voice coming through the darkness of the airport bus.

I don't know if it's just our involvement, but nowadays I seem to see references to transplants in places I would never have expected: top-of-the-page stories, for example, or specialist magazines outside the medical field, even comic strips, where recently in our local paper a donor gave Humpty Dumpty a new eggshell. Some associations of car dealers are beginning to make organ and tissue donation one of their projects, a breakthrough for a group that has traditionally shied away from any publicity about car accidents. After years of discussion and unnumbered committee meetings, the U.S. Postal Service now has an organ and tissue donation stamp.

Donor families haven't changed much—by and large, they go their own way—but the climate around them has. Among many other places, I think of a cinema, packed to the doors, in a Sicilian town, small and remote enough that even visitors from Messina call it "deepest Sicily." In the audience were a man and woman who, some years before, had donated the organs of their five-year-old daughter, a gentle little creature whose photograph they gave us. Not long ago they could have expected hostility and incomprehension. They now found themselves being honored. They sat anonymously in the audience, were introduced to thunderous cheers and quickly sat down again as if embarrassed by all the attention—and later went home, as they do every night, to a house that has lost its magic.

Signing the donor card is a big step. It is a clear statement of intent. It's also easy to do: many organizations have them, and in many states drivers can simply add a note to their license indicating their decision. Sometimes it's enough. But more often something else is needed. When death comes without warning, family members often don't remember if there was a card or where it is. For many, it is too painful to look for it. By far the most effective step is to talk about donation to other family members while death is just a distant concept. It's as if you'd said: when I die I'd like you to give money to this charity or I want you to put this message on my headstone. Not only do we do it, but we do it with alacrity as a last shared act. Similarly for donating organs and tissues. A simple declaration that this is what you want is likely to be sufficient. The analogy is often made with putting on seat belts: not long ago few of us did it, now only a few don't. We're not at the seat belt stage with transplants—that's why ten people on the waiting list die every day in the United States alone—but I believe it would take only a small shift in public behavior to put us there.

The most original idea we've heard of since we went into this field has come from the American Society of Transplant Surgeons, which appointed an innovative public relations agency, run by Milt Benjamin, a former foreign editor of the *Washington Post* and *Newsweek*, and worked out with him an imaginative but blindingly simple new program. Instead of signing a donor card, which is a solitary act, the surgeons suggested a "family pledge," by which members of a family would say, in effect, "If something were to happen to me, I'd want you to donate." In non-traumatic conditions, when the issues can be examined calmly, there would normally be some sort of family talk, perfunctory if the household already knew about organ and tissue donation, more detailed if anyone wanted to know more, and perhaps quite protracted if some members didn't agree. But in the end those who did agree would sign and would then probably forget about it. The pledge has no legal standing. But when death came for that family, perhaps much sooner than anyone expected, at that moment, when most people are caught off guard, a memory should stir for those who signed. "Do you remember?" one of them might say. "This is what he said he would want us to do." A discussion months or years before could relieve the next of kin of what, for those who are unprepared, can be an agonizing decision.

This, anyway, is how Maggie and I saw it, and we gratefully accepted the offer to become co-chairs of the program. Milt has proved to be a dream to work with for his expertise alone. But he has an additional qualification. Like so many who throw themselves into a task that demands more of them than they can reasonably be expected to give, he has a family motivation—Jennifer, his daughter, a diabetic, having been saved by a pancreas and kidney transplant when it seemed nothing else could have worked.

The program began ambitiously, initially concentrating on politicians, whose participation is seen as a first step in influencing many others. From the start we made no distinction between right and left. We quickly signed up state governors and their families from Nevada to New Jersey, U.S. senators and members of congress, mayors, and state legislators. We took it to every organization in the transplant field we could think of and, among many others, the American Red Cross has made it one of their key projects. Now we are trying to interest show business people, sports personalities, and role models of all kinds. To us the program contains the seeds of a major change, for it rests on a proposition anyone can understand: just as any family, anxiously waiting for a transplant for one of its members, hopes another family will come to its aid, shouldn't they be prepared to help others if the situation is reversed?

Encouragingly, people seem to be taking the whole issue more seriously and asking all the important questions: How can the doctors be sure he won't recover? Does it really make the recipients healthy or are they going to be basket cases all their lives? Most frightening of all, suppose he isn't really dead? It's not a situation to be taken lightly. Imagine being uncertain afterward. The key to all these questions is that people must be able to trust the medical team if they are to be cooperative. Just as discussing donations with their family is the most important thing potential donors can do, so earning trust is the most important thing the hospital can do.

One of the key questions people ask goes to the heart of this: if they know I'm willing to donate her organs, will they try less hard to save her? To this, I can only say that in the last four years of meeting doctors and nurses all over this country and overseas in large and modern and small and aged hospitals, I have never heard a remark or caught an inference that they did not do everything they could to save a patient, whether a potential donor or not. Skills vary, clearly, and levels of dedication, but I have not the slightest evidence that patients are at higher risk if they have indicated a willingness to donate.

As for the effectiveness of transplants, before the operation most recipients are usually desperately ill. You have to be ill to get to the top of those long waiting lists: many are hooked up to machines, knowing death may come at any time, others are out of work or going blind, unable to concentrate or do anything useful. Think only of diabetes, which sounds less threatening than heart or liver disease, but can be a miserable life without salt or fresh fruit or fat. Many diabetics can't stand up or eat properly because of severe stomach pains. Think of not being able to see well enough to dial a telephone or never being able to go anywhere without a beeper in case the organ you need goes to someone else. And, underneath it all, to have the daily fear that the disintegration will go on spreading and spreading.

But unlike normal therapy, where progress can be painfully slow, organ recipients surprisingly often bounce back to life rapidly. We have toured hospitals where patients who were dying of kidney failure a week earlier are now sitting up and moving around. Many leave the hospital within days and are quickly back into a working life. Nor is this just a temporary improvement. We recently met a woman who, when young, had to kneel down to rest three times between the parking lot and her apartment, but, with a transplanted kidney, has lived an active life for the last twenty-eight years.

When I first began to read about this subject, I was astonished to hear of a man who, dependent on a respirator, comatose, and weighing only ninety-eight pounds, progressed from moving around the house to five-kilometer races, then two years later to hiking in the Swiss Alps. Or another, now leading a vigorous life, who was so weak that he could make a sandwich only in stages: after reaching for the bread he'd rest, cut it and rest again, spread on the peanut butter and rest some more. By that time, he said, he was often too tired to eat. Or Kelly Perkins who, once so sick she had to be carried to bed, climbed the 14,494-foot Mount Whitney, the highest peak in the 48 states, two years after receiving a new heart and, a few months later at the age of thirty-six, Mount Fuji. There, at the summit of Japan's sacred mountain, she scattered the ashes of her forty-year-old donor.

But equally striking is the revival of their spirits. They look younger, feel younger, act younger—and by any test other than pure chronology, they are younger. Why not? They are back in the mainstream. They have lost the deflation that comes with having to rely continuously on others for help. Best of all, people who have felt the presence of death day and night can now renew their confidence in life. "It seems trite," Tony Benedi, the former president of TRIO International, said hesitantly, being a man who doesn't speak tritely, "but coming out of hospital I seemed to feel the breeze on my face and see the clouds moving across the sky for the first time."

It's all new enough that the results still surprise us. The first successful kidney transplant was done in 1954, the first liver transplant in 1963. In 1968, one of Christiaan Barnard's patients lived three weeks with a new heart. As recently as the early 1980s, anyone over fifty-five was widely considered too high a risk for a transplant. Since then technical skills have improved dramatically, rejection rates have declined sharply, and matching donor organs with recipients is far more sophisticated. These aren't experiments any more. Every year, 20,000 Americans receive organ transplants and 600,000 receive tissue transplants. These operations are not a cure-all, however, and many things can go wrong then and later. The longer people are on the list, the more likely there will be complications. Some people need two or more transplants, others are too far gone to benefit from the healthiest new organ. I am reminded of this every time I walk through a hospital and imagine the roller-coaster emotions of families who have had a last-minute reprieve and then discover the transplant isn't working. It came to mind when I saw a tiny baby crying desperately in the arms of a worried mother in a hospital in South Carolina. "Didn't the transplant work?" I asked the nurse. "Oh, yes," she said. "But now she has diaper rash." At that age, who can differentiate between a failing heart and a sore bottom?

But organ and tissue donation has a dimension outside medicine. White men are alive today because they have inside them the hearts of black women, Mexican children breathe with Anglo lungs, religious skeptics have Quaker kidneys, Democrats see the world through Republican corneas—and vice versa. Human parts are interchangeable and transplants leap all the conventional barriers. I think of it as a helping hand in the dark from a stranger. Could anything make it clearer that what divides us as people is trifling compared to what we have in common?

CHAPTER FIFTEEN

A SPATE OF AWARDS

In Miami Children's Hospital, the average age of the patients is two years. Some, just a few days old, are in tiny plastic bags of the size that you might pick up in a convenience store. Some gasp desperately for breath or lie there too weak to move. Others, astonishingly soon after major surgery, are looking, breathing, and acting like any normal child.

We were there to go into the hospital's hall of fame, an honor that in previous years went to people of the rank of Jonas Salk and Walt Disney. But the sick children were the reality behind the glitter. As you walk around the wards, you are constantly reminded what is in the balance as, even for children with simple fractures, parents, brothers, and sisters stand around the little beds with tearful, frightened faces. With luck, a few days later you see the same faces, but radiant now, as they carry their little bundles home, newly reminded that they are irreplaceable. Tragically, some of these bundles—including some who need a transplant—don't make it home. Donations by parents of the organs and tissues of tiny children are rare. They are understandably crushed by their loss—but then so too is another family praying for a deliverance they feel slipping from their grasp.

The hospital, recreated in 1986, is the vision of David Walters, an entrepreneur and the first Catholic to become American ambassador to the Vatican, who almost single-handedly converted a rundown hospital previously supported by show business people into one of the top children's hospitals in the country. He was motivated by the loss of his six-year-old granddaughter Shannon Joy to leukemia during her stay in the old hospital. A well-known fundraiser, he says friends who see him coming cross to the other side of the street. Having seen his tenaciousness, I'd guess such a feeble response would only increase the amount he hits them for.

Like all successful fundraisers, Walters has an eye for human weakness and sat me next to Gina Lollobrigida and Eleanor next to Lambchop, all of us that year's inductees. It was very grand and, as usual, very humbling, such as when Lambchop's owner, Shari Lewis, who spent a lifetime making children happy, said about her award, "When I think of what the Greens did, I don't feel worthy of it." Not long afterward, she died, but I see her occasionally on a children's television show, still earning her place in the hall of fame. Gina, as I now call her (to myself), was too much in demand for us to talk much but, as it happens, I saw more of her the next day, when we traveled to the airport together to catch the plane to Rome, and found she was quite familiar with Nicholas' story. The relationship ended there, however, as I headed into coach class and she, fittingly, into *magnifica*.

This was one of a spate of awards that is still continuing. They came in such numbers from Italy that Maggie wondered if there'd be any left for anyone else. When we heard from a reporter we were to receive a gold medal from the president, we thought there must be a mistake. "We already have that one," we told him. No, he said, this is another and it's the highest of all. It was hard to think of any Italian medal outranking the president's own gift, but it turned out to be the *Medaglia d'Oro al Merito Civile*, generally translated as the gold medal for civic virtue, the highest civilian decoration. The foreign ministry's records turned up no evidence that it had ever gone to a foreigner before.

The medal is so rarely given that, astonishingly, for a parallel to our case the diplomatic corps referred to Giorgio Perlasca, an Italian businessman in Hungary in World War II who, using a Spanish diplomatic passport he had somehow acquired, falsified the papers of hundreds, some say thousands, of Jews to save them from being sent to concentration camps. That we should find ourselves in the company of a man who had defied death and torture day after day doesn't seem right. But there they are, two gold medals, not like a lone wartime hero, but side by side like old family members and, of course, among our most valued possessions.

Other awards had practical value, such as the scholarship fund some kind friends in the mutual fund industry set up. By hard labor that only masochism can explain, and the warmheartedness of individuals and fund companies, they have now raised more than $150,000 to send students abroad for short study courses. With the help of the National Alliance for Excellence, a strong-minded organization started by two mothers of gifted children, the scholarship has attracted some awesomely qualified college students, equally at home in arts and sciences and community service, at the threshold of careers as concert violinists, nuclear physicists, or opera singers.

To channel our own efforts, we set up the Nicholas Green Foundation, which, like the Rockefeller Foundation, can contribute to a wide range of good causes and is mainly funded by family money. Only the scale is different. The main focus of ours is to expand the understanding of organ and tissue donation, but it has had two notable achievements in other areas. First, together with the scholarship fund, it is financing a program run by the National Association for Gifted Children to give an award each year to an outstanding student from the third to sixth grade in every state. The aim is to stimulate children in arts and athletics as well as academic subjects and to draw attention to the educational needs of talented students everywhere. Encouraging children like Nicholas makes this an especially satisfying effort.

The second of these big projects moved us into the rarefied atmosphere of the Fulbright Commission, the world's most prestigious cultural exchange group. With them, we evolved a program to bring transplant doctors from southern Italy—where organ donation rates are still a fraction of those in most of Europe—to the United States to study the most advanced techniques. Over the years, we hope emerging doctors will come to the best medical schools here, returning home afterward where their skills are desperately needed. The project, the initiative of Larry Gray, executive director of Fulbright in Italy, and funded initially by our foundation, is called the Fulbright-Nicholas Green grant, only the second time in the commission's fifty years in Italy that its name has been linked with an individual's. Some of Italy's leading citizens, including two of the last five prime ministers, were Fulbright exchange students. Once again Nicholas found himself in good company.

Other awards are practical in a different sense. Across Italy, parks, nature trails, and schools have been named for him. The scale always seems to be the biggest, the quality the highest, that the group organizing it can aspire to. At one end, the largest hospital group in Italy is now the Nicholas Green Hospital and, at the other, the owner of a small bakery in Sicily put his staff of three in coveralls with "*Grazie Nicholas*" sewn lovingly on them. When a lime tree was planted in Bari, it was in the Piazza Garibaldi. When Florence looked for a site for the cheerful Nicholas Green playground, it put it close to the Piazzale Kennedy. The Istituto Scudi di St. Martino gave us their silver *scudo*, a tiny replica of a breastplate in honor of St. Martin, who in legend cut his cloak in two to share with a beggar. As we walked back from a meeting in one small town, I said to Maggie, "You know, that was a cross-section of the whole town." "No," she said, "that was the whole town." Italy's prime minister at the time, Mr. Romano Prodi, thought enough of the little Nicholas Green Park in Lecco to pay it a personal visit and when, two years later at a White House dinner in his honor, I showed him a photograph taken of him at the site, he asked with unfeigned pleasure, "Can I keep it?" Later that night, I introduced myself to Sophia Loren, whose beauty dominated a room full of handsome women like an empress. "We Italians feel very close to you," she said. Phew.

Awards also provided another chance to have the sort of dialogue the letters had produced. When a musical academy in Concesio, Brescia, wrote offering their annual prize, named for Pope Paul VI, who was born there, I was able to tell them that when we had visited nearby Bolzano I showed Nicholas a house where Mozart had stayed. "He was touched by the idea of someone dead so long ago still bringing pleasure to the world," I wrote. "That seems very appropriate now."

One day a poem arrived that I remembered from my schooldays, Leigh Hunt's "Abou Ben Adhem." It came from yet another stranger, Ray Gottsacker, who had the happy idea of sending a framed print to people he thinks have done something worthy. The poem tells how Abou woke one night to find an angel writing in a book the names of "those who love the Lord." To his surprise, Abou's name was not there, so instead he asked the angel to write his name as one who loved his fellow men.

> "...*The next night*
> *It came again, with a great wakening light*
> *And show'd the names whom love of God had blessed,*
> *And, lo! Ben Adhem's name led all the rest.*"

For someone who calls himself a humanist, it's one of the most satisfying presents I've ever had.

Shortly afterward, however, the Italian Catholic Federation gave us their Pope John XXIII award, and I told some of my fellow men I would have to become a little less accessible to them.

One day we had a call from Lufthansa. "Sixteen crates from Italy have arrived. Please ask your import broker to contact us." For us, who buy so little on our foreign trips that we invariably fill in our customs forms "nothing to declare," this was another world. It turned out to be a special consignment put together by the Bonino-Pulejo Foundation from things sent to them from all over Sicily, and they were boxes rather than crates. But they filled the station wagon to the gunwales, and when we got them home the house looked like Citizen Kane's basement. Some genuine crates did arrive on other occasions, however, including one containing a painting addressed to Mr. Reginald Fragile and Brittle Green. I wondered if the Regifoo mailhouse was involved.

They were part of a flood of gifts of all kinds, whose only common feature was that they seemed to come from deep down, as though everyone wanted to give what they valued most in themselves. The foodstuffs were the nicest of their kind, and all fattening: creamy chocolates, marzipan shaped like bananas and apples, homemade marmalade, and liqueurs so fierce a headhunter in Borneo couldn't have stomached them. Sicilians sent puppets, Neapolitans nougat. Courmayeur, the village at the foot of Mont Blanc, sent its finest make of ice ax.

One man gave us a history of Japan he had written, another his history of the Eskimos. Both are in Italian and impenetrable. The only clearly understandable thing about either of them is that they were a part of themselves the authors wanted us to have. Towns send books about themselves, lavishly illustrated histories if they have them, pages and pages of economic statistics if they don't.

The story of Eleanor asking for a kitten, which I'd mentioned to a reporter at the hotel in Messina, reverberated around Italy. The reporter bought her a toy cat himself so she wouldn't have to wait until she went home. Cat photographs, drawings, poems, envelopes with cat motifs, cat stories, dozens in all, arrived. Antonio Ciccone, an Italian artist well known for his cat drawings, sent a whole book of them.

Many paintings of Nicholas arrived and, though based only on newspaper photographs, were dotted with the symbols he took most pleasure in, as though the painters had taken the trouble to find out about him—Venice, Halloween, dressing up to play a role, things normally only a child's own family would have known about. I blessed the decision to carry the camera on those hikes in Switzerland. One massive painting, forwarded by the Sporting Club in Verona, from an artist who said he preferred to remain anonymous, being only an amateur, captured the likeness so well, even to the smiling eyes, that when we took it out of its crate both of us exclaimed simultaneously, "It's him." Then there was a masterpiece from Anna Bonomo, from Catania, for whom good deeds are a way of life. When she gave us this painting, she said she had grown to know him so well she could hardly bear to part with it: it was as though he was finally going away. But she did part with it, and it hangs at home where I see it every day and marvel at human generosity.

Music of all kinds was written about Nicholas by people we didn't know: a haunting piano sonata by Luciano Lunardon, a series of piano pieces by Dianne Forsythe, folk songs by Maura Susanna in Italy and Peter Rawitsch in Albany, even a full-scale work for chorus and orchestra by Angela Montemurro Lentini, whose husband conducted the first performance for us in the cathedral in Vibo Valentia. Two busts came, by Marisa Panero and Anton da Cudan, which capture his spirit so well that I still find myself running my hand through the tangled hair or gently touching the cheeks, and for a moment he is there. Poems poured in, sometimes one from every student in a high-school class, and even the saddest seemed to end on a note of hope. Our favorite poet, however, is a friend who lives in Bodega Bay, Jeremy Raikes. This is how he starts a tribute to the little friend he describes as the "quintessential" boy:

"Now he can be laid to rest,
this boy who bore with life so brief,
and left the world to be impressed
by more than sorrow's stifling grief."

A shy craftsman in Sicily gave us a toy soldier, Julius Caesar, which he had made with meticulous attention to detail, not just the uniform, but the character in the face too. "I read that Nicholas had studied him. So have I. Working on this made me feel close to your son," he said. It's on our shelves and I look after it as carefully as if I was his personal bodyguard.

When I asked Jay Hamburger, a photographer who wrote to us from Houston, why he felt so moved, he said, "Transplantation goes off the spectrum at both ends. The death of a child is the biggest loss anyone can contemplate and saving a life the biggest gift anyone can give." It turned out that he knows about territory off the spectrum himself. Virtually every Sunday for more than six years, he and a group of friends have cooked two hundred dinners in his kitchen. Then they drive to parks and bridges and dumpsters to feed the homeless. When Jay saw *Nicholas' Gift*, the television movie, a phrase from it stuck in his mind, when I'm shown slipping the coin into Nicholas' pocket after he died and saying it was "to pay the ferryman" to cross the River Styx. Years before, Jay had taken a photograph of a boy and a man in a canoe in a golden sunset on the Amazon. "I never knew what to do with it," he told us. But now the answer came, and the silhouette of a small boy being carried across a vast expanse of dark water to a dimly perceived shore glows mysteriously on our living room wall. He called it "Nicholas and the Ferryman."

CHAPTER SIXTEEN

ITALY REMEMBERS

Although each of them was different, the dozen or more times we went to Italy in the four years after Nicholas' death had a basic theme: bursts of intense living surrounded by fatigue. Our usual flight from San Francisco meant getting up at around 4:00 a.m., traveling during most of the daylight hours to Newark, hurrying to make a connection there, flying all night, waiting for another flight from Rome, and then going straight into a lunch meeting with a lot of details to absorb.

Our hosts were solicitousness itself, presenting baskets of flowers to Maggie, dolls to Eleanor, and pieces of paper with crowded itineraries to me. The mayor, the prefect, the chief of police, the head of the local hospital board, representatives perhaps of the tourist board or the gas company, and their spouses, would often be waiting on the tarmac, smiling and gracious. Some of these people we never saw again. They had played their part in the welcome and had gone back to making a living. Others would be with us on long journeys, especially professional drivers. All of them were highly skilled and the cars highly powered. We overtook other speeding vehicles on the autostrada as if they were standing still, and were blind to traffic signs. We always raced, whether early or late for appointments. One Sunday morning at 5:00, the driver kept the needle at 120 miles an hour for most of the forty miles to the Bologna airport. I arrived with ninety minutes to spare. On long journeys, car phones rang frequently and drivers would carry on conversations at seventy miles an hour.

The driver we met most often, and perhaps the most intrepid of the whole fearless species, as well as the most loyal and attentive, was Luigi Taurisano, built like a good-natured fireplug, but as gentle as a nursemaid. A friend of Anna Lagana, then vice president of TRIO Italia, Luigi owned a large car sales business near Rome, but when we came to Italy he dropped everything and ferried us around, however early in the morning or late at night. At airports, hotels, and busy restaurants he was invaluable, his oblong shape miraculously finding its way to the front of any line. As a young man he had followed his father's footsteps, a firefighter famous enough to have a street in Rome named for him. The walls of his office are covered with commendations, firefighting apparatus, scrolls, a plaque for saving the life of a young girl who had fallen into a well, and a personalized photograph of the Pope. On his desk, more prominently displayed than any of these, is a photograph taken with us in Florence. With all that competition, it is a compliment in a class of its own.

Eleanor was always more interested in the girl in the well and wanted me to extract all the details. "That girl is now a woman living in Naples with three children," he added. Eleanor beamed. "What else did you do?" she asked. "I rescued a horse that had fallen in a well too," he said. Her happiness was complete. I complimented him once when he jumped out of the car to direct traffic around a hidden danger in the road. "I'm just a little fireman," he said. Maybe. But with the heart of a lion and the generosity of a prince.

The itineraries varied, but the texture was generally the same, very closely woven. A day might go as follows: 8:30 radio interview, 9:00 meet bishop, 9:30 visit school for speeches and performance by children, 11:00 meet city government, 12:00 television interview, 13:00 lunch and free until 16:00 (an illusion, this, the lunch consisting of several courses and several speeches and generally ending very late), 16:00 tour of hospital, 17:30 interview by local newspaper, 20:00 meeting organized by local transplant groups.

In the early days, we perpetually ran late, often went into meetings expecting to give a talk to healthcare workers and found ourselves in front of a couple of hundred schoolchildren, and repeatedly got lost in complicated city centers. Commemorating a newly planted tree in the tiny village of Sapanaro, in Sicily, we arrived at dusk on a cold

February day, scandalously late. As we walked the last quarter of a mile from the tree to the central square, the sidewalk was jammed with people from all over the area. "Did you see those people's faces? Many of them had tears in their eyes," our interpreter said later. "Yes," we pointed out, "they'd been waiting in the freezing cold for hours."

Communication depended on local conditions. In some places, professionals translated simultaneously. In others, the English teacher or the head of the tourist bureau would find herself in front of several hundred people and television lights, having to work her way through topics she knew little about—with words like immunosuppression—and in a language where most of her training was in irregular verbs or directing visitors to the nearest beach. The meeting locations were anywhere custom dictated: an army base, an opera house, a park. In Florence one meeting filled the Palazzo Vecchio, in Verona the largest theater, in Grotte, Sicily, a children's playground.

Maggie made a determined attempt to follow the presentations in Italian. I didn't. Having the work done by the interpreter was much more satisfactory. Press photographs in the following day's papers often showed us at a long table—eight faces, including Maggie's, all looking at the speaker, I facing the other way with a good-looking young woman whispering in my ear. Monolingualism has its benefits.

In the middle of one night, a fax arrived from Italy. That itself was not unusual. Later I found the senders were mortified to think that, having miscalculated the time difference, they had wakened us. In fact, we slept through it—as we have slept through dozens of others—and found it only at breakfast time. What was unusual was that it was an invitation from a Nicola Sama, one of the coaches of a soccer team of "chicks" from a village not far from Venice, called Villaverla, which had arranged a Nicholas Green soccer tournament. The idea of spending a weekend near Venice with a soccer mom and her friends obviously had a lot going for it. It happened to fall next to a trip I'd already planned to Modena, so I sent back a fax saying Maggie was earthbound with household duties, but indicated that taking tea with a group of young ladies like them would be a pleasure. Things moved swiftly. I was the first off the plane in Milan, the first to collect my luggage, the first through customs. What I didn't know, however, is that in Italy Nicola is a man's name, and instead of five athletic young women I was met by five burly men.

They were, however, a delight, all five, and on the three-hour drive to their home it was like being with old friends. They let me easily into their jokes, including references to Nicola's beautiful wife being much too good for him. When he turned to me to say they shouldn't be surprised at his good fortune because his name meant "winner" in Greek, I felt at ease enough to say that was already clear to me and that it was obviously his wife who was the loser.

I learned that Nicola had felt compelled to do something positive after Nicholas died. "Through sport we can spread the message to children in a way they can understand," he said. It turned out that he was from Calabria and was troubled by that now familiar sense of personal responsibility. But his colleagues were northern Italians, and Nicola's idea had ignited a flame in them all. This was the third year of the tournament, and this time sixteen teams were involved, ranging from eight to twelve years old. The team Nicola coached, Novoledo, was called the Nicholas Green team and his name was on the shirts they played in. "How old are they?" I asked. "The age Nicholas is now," he said, and in this strong, tough man I caught yet another glimpse of the mixture of thoughtfulness and tenderness that has gone into all these commemorative ideas.

I'd understood there would be a small ceremony on the Saturday morning before the games started, but in fact the sports ground was overflowing—children in soccer kit, parents, grandparents, nuns, nurses, organ donation groups, TV teams, and the commander of the American paratroopers stationed in the area. Many of the children had written messages to us and those who could not write had drawn blooming flowers or sunlit clouds. I was given a boxful of these messages as a present, but a larger number had been attached to balloons. In a huge bunch they floated high into the sky, separating as contrary winds caught them. They would come down randomly over a wide area, and whoever picked them up would read two or three words of anonymous love from the skies.

There were other events, but at last it was Sunday afternoon and the Novoledo team was getting ready to play. They were in a tie for first place, and a win would clinch the tournament. They were the home team, and the atmosphere was electric. The games, six a side, ten minutes a half, were played in a large gym, and every seat was taken, every inch of standing room filled. Specially favored guests lined the touchline and at moments of high drama spilled onto the playing area. Kids were hanging from every piece of apparatus. I was allowed to sit on the coaches' bench and, as the noise mounted, I was aware of a special interest building around me. From the corner of my eye, I was aware of fingers pointing in my direction and whispers, "There he is." "It's him." I'd deliberately kept out of the way, not wanting to take anything from the players, but this was too much to ignore. I turned around to smile appreciatively and saw Fabio Viviani, one of Vicenza's top players, at the center of attention. I returned to obscurity.

The game began exactly on time: this was serious business. It was obvious from the start it was going to be a hard match, and though played at a furious pace neither side could get the vital edge. My heart was in my mouth. The visitor's striker, a strong forceful boy, looked dangerous every time he got the ball and sure enough, as the first half wore on, the right winger crossed the ball in classic style high into the goal area and he headed it in. This was bad. A single goal could easily settle a game of this sort. But Novoledo kept cool, and four minutes later was rewarded when a crashing shot gave the goalkeeper no chance. I cheered myself hoarse.

I spent almost all the rest of the game on my feet as the ball went from end to end. But then in the second half, the home team—the Nicholas Green team—scored its second and third goals to win the game and the tournament. We hugged and cheered and shouted like World Cup winners. I was given the honor of presenting the cup, and pointing to the blue shirts, made my two-word speech, "*Viva Nicholas.*" The rafters rang loudly enough to put a twinkle in a faraway star.

A few months later, I met them all again—Beppe, Bob, Franco, Bruno, and Nicola, along with Gianpietro and Marilisa, the town's mayor. I think of them now as my pals from Villaverla. We laughed and joked as before. Then Franco said quietly, "Do you remember the coach we met? Two weeks later his son was in a road accident. He was killed." The table fell silent, as we all thought about that stirring, glittering day, a day in a boy's life that could have brought a smile even in old age.

"The family donated the organs," Franco added. For a moment, it seemed irrelevant in the face of such a loss. Then I remembered the children I'd seen in Italy being eaten away as just one vital organ steadily deteriorated. Now three or four of them would live. Nicola's tournament had won its biggest victory.

The nine-hour time difference between California and Italy is a killer. You go to bed while they are on their way to work. When you start work, they are preparing to go home. You stay up until midnight to telephone them as they arrive in the morning and find they've been held up in the rush hour. You get up in the middle of the night and they are at lunch. We were astonished to find some fax machines had the same work schedule—surely they weren't caught in traffic too?—only later discovering the ones we were calling were manually operated. My office being at home, we have no similar defense. At times of breaking news, or when someone overseas forgets the earth is round, the telephone will ring in the middle of the night. It's often less aggravating to answer it than leaving it to the answering machine, which booms out incomprehensible messages with inaudible names and phone numbers without the area code. Our industrious little fax machine is on duty through the night too, and sometimes I find it in the morning with yards of paper coming from it.

But this is only part of the problem. We have every reason to learn Italian. It would enrich every contact there, make us feel less helpless, and allow us to play a more effective role in discussions. Maggie tries more than I do, but against long odds. Our failure is due partly to the fact that we're looked after like babies whenever we go there and so act like babies too, waiting to be fed by interpreters and hosts who go out of their way to speak English.

The letters come with hazards of their own. I can still see Maggie during the first few weeks, sitting at the dining room table, on one side a pile of letters and on the other a pocket-sized Italian dictionary lent by Lois, our next-door neighbor. After more than four years, we can get the hang of most of them, but, oh, those nuances. We regularly get our heads together: Are they inviting us to a future opening or are they telling us they just had one? Are they sending photos to us or do they want us to send photos to them? The difficulties are compounded by what we understand is a point of Italian etiquette. Personal letters, it says, should be handwritten. If I were Signorina Manners, I would advise against this. Much of the handwriting is diminutive and baffling. At the end of one solemn television program, I was asked if I had one last word to say to the Italian people. "Yes," I said. "Please write legibly."

There were other problems. A doctor sent a letter addressed to the mayor of Bodega Bay: there isn't one, but the post office sent it to us. It read, "Dear Mayor, I'd suggest you change the name of Bodega Bay for Bodega Nick. Do it please." A lady with a heart of gold, who has written many times and still keeps in touch, said this: "*Ciao* Eleanor. To wish as much well. To like I cat's? To send much basin. Greeting of family." Others were clearer, but not word perfect. One man wrote, "I have received with great pleasure your moving mind," and another, "I embrace you Mrs. Reginald and Margaret." One woman in Italy wrote that her son had been educated at Ann Ardor, which sounded like a good place for a young man to study. Sometimes the expressions gained in intensity from their flaws. "We make you with all sure hearts the best wishes," two sisters from Verona wrote. And who could find fault with this? "I don't forget to you and to Nicholas. He's always in my heart with you. Very kiss to Eleanor. Lovely Debora."

With only a minimal understanding of the language, I'd compensate at meetings in Italy by playing the lovely phonetics in my head, especially the lilting "ch" sound—*cinque, cento, cinquanta*. Once I heard a new word—it sounded like "Cherry Bralley." It cropped up every few sentences, enlivening the turgid rhetoric with thoughts of orchards in bloom, and I let it run happily through my mind, until it came to me that it was *cerebrale*, the brain—and, therefore, brain death.

I saw how these mistakes could happen the other way around. Over lunch, an Italian senator asked someone in the group, "What is the Italian for 'waste'?" "*Rifiuti*," someone said, "trash." He explained he wanted to be clear what I'd meant at the meeting that morning by saying the death of people waiting for a transplant because an organ did not arrive in time was "a terrible waste." I've imagined him since then telling fellow legislators I talk terrible trash. Meanwhile, on my side, I continued to demolish the Italian language.

One of our interpreters told me of a cross to Nicholas that was put up in Calabria. It says simply, "Forgive us." As we'd said from the start, it had never occurred to us to blame Italy. It could have happened anywhere, as the hundred chapters of the Parents of Murdered Children in the United States attest. But time and again, I found myself having to reassure people who seemed to feel they were at fault. Even Professor Giuseppe Nistico, the cultivated president of the Calabrian assembly, wrote to us, "I feel deeply ashamed for the premature death of Nicholas. But he will continue to live with us and no one is going to forget him."

One morning in a hotel restaurant in Salerno, I looked up from the powdered croissants to see standing at my table not the spruced waiter, but an unshaven, unbrushed older man, looking earnestly at me. He was a hotel employee from one of the unphotogenic departments and well outside his own territory. He waited to be spoken to but when I smiled the words tumbled out: "*Papà di Nicholas*? I saw you through the door. I knew it was you. I wanted to speak to you. I wanted to say how sorry I am. Do you need anything? Can I help you with your baggage?" Unthinkably, he even strayed on to the waiter's turf. "Can I get you some more breakfast, some juice?" And before he left: "Good-bye, Mr. Green, we always remember Nicholas." It was typical of hundreds of encounters, a desire to help without hurting.

Regional presidents and farmworkers invited us to stay with them. Restaurant owners would open a bottle of wine they said they'd been saving for an occasion worthy of it. Teachers wrote songs for their students to sing to Eleanor. A man standing in front of a sidewalk bar stopped me as I walked by. "*Papà di Nicholas*? I thought so. Will you have a drink?" and chose a Mexican beer to remind me of home.

Everyone seemed to relate the story to their beliefs. One day in Venice, when I was looking at a mosaic of St. Nicholas in St. Mark's, I turned to find a monsignor standing close by, who smiled in recognition. "I was just thinking it doesn't look much like our Nicholas," I said. "Oh, I think it does," he answered, "as he is now." Often when I go to pay for a coffee, the café owner will say, "There's no charge." When that happens, I've taken to giving them a photo of Nicholas.

Then they make me feel as though I've overpaid. Maggie had a suggestion: "You ought to take some ten by sixes and see if they're good for a full meal." One lunchtime I arrived late at the hotel. "I'm sorry, sir, the restaurant is closed. But I can get you a sandwich," the hotel clerk said. From the inner office there was a shout, and the clerk spoke again, "Mr. Green, for you the restaurant is open." I ate gratefully, but quickly, so as not to make them regret their flexibility. On the way up to the room afterward I met a waiter carrying the smallest sandwich I have ever seen. "The restaurant is closed so this lady has to eat in her room," he explained. "She's Miss Italy."

We became accustomed to being approached, though even now it's a surprise when hearty men in Italy shake hands with tears in their eyes and leather-jacketed youths smoking cigarettes stop to say a kind word. Some men, like Pietro, a member of the *carabinieri* in Rome, go much further. His letter read, "I have a son of name Francesco of 4 years ago and when born me the new son his name to be, in honor a your son, Nicholas. Still thank you Green family." Months later he wrote exuberantly that he was now the proud father of Nicholas Torchia. I hope many people ask that little boy how he got his name.

"The whole world knows your story," David Wolper, the movie director, had said, and at times in Italy it seemed to be literally true. Often when I called Alitalia and gave my name, the first words were something like, "How is your little girl?" Even the professionals were affected. Sue Patterson, the U.S. consul general in Florence, who has handled dozens of difficult situations, spoke tenderly but calmly in a speech she was giving about Nicholas. But as she came to the quotation from *Romeo and Juliet* she'd chosen—"and, when he shall die, take him and cut him out in little stars and he will make the face of heaven so fine that all the world will be in love with night"—her voice quivered and for a moment she had to stop.

"I've read everything about you," a disconcerting number of people in Italy said. They knew our ages, the children's birthdays, anecdotes I'd told and forgotten. Many have seen *The Birds* and almost feel as if they have been to Bodega Bay. These are not just people with time on their hands. "We followed your story hour by hour," said the owner of a damaged Palladian mansion in Vicenza, who has devoted his life to restoring it. "I know where you've been and what you've been doing," a middle-aged lady confided. It could be quite unnerving. When I came back to one hotel late at night, a note from the maid lay on the bed: "Thank you for being like you are." For once, I thought, I must have left the bathroom tidy.

We knew about Italian warmth, but their correctness was a surprise. We saw it all over the country, however, little niceties of manner intended to protect against life's bruisings. When the small town of Gioia Tauro in Calabria planned a series of activities, it asked us to come in these words, "We realize that to fulfill our wish you should confront many discomforts. Nevertheless, a little hope spurs us to believe that you might contemplate our invitation." It's hard to refuse, isn't it? And in fact we did go.

The entire export department of the BASF company in Cinisello Balsamo near Milan wrote to us several times. We exchanged photographs and floated vague plans to meet. On a freezing day when we opened the Nicholas Green Park in Lecco, we found out later, a few of them had taken the long trip, sat through the proceedings, and gone home again without introducing themselves. "We didn't want to intrude," they said when we asked why.

That same night, we had dinner at a hotel in a village on the side of the lake. We lingered over the meal and sat around the cozy lounge afterward, reluctant to step out into the piercing wind. When eventually we hurried to the car, a young woman stepped out of the shadows. "I'm a nurse," she said. "I saw in the newspaper you'd be coming to dinner here. I just wanted to say thank you to you and your son." "How long have you been waiting?" we asked. "Oh, not long. Half an hour maybe." "Why didn't you come in?" "I didn't want to get in the way," she said. I don't know what the correct response is, but I put my arms around her and hugged her tightly. I don't know her name and I can't think we'll ever meet again. But equally, I don't think I'll ever forget that mixture of gentle courtesy and strength of purpose.

These were people I'd never seen before, but those we came to know quite well were equally restrained. In the middle school at Motta S. Anastasia, near Catania, there are two clocks, one conventional, the other labeled "Bodega Bay time," and each day, I imagine, some students feel the Pacific coast giving them a little tug. It's there because the principal, Dr. Giuseppe Aderno, has thrown himself into our story. On the day before we were to attend a meeting at his school, he said he would drive to our hotel, an hour or so away, to go over some details. We assured him it was unnecessary, but he insisted. Usually meticulous about timekeeping, he was late. "I'm sorry," he said when I met him in the lobby. "My mother died today." He stayed forty minutes, going over the arrangements, making sure we knew enough to feel comfortable. Only when he was satisfied we had no questions did he excuse himself and get into his car for the lonely ride home. At school the next day, I'd prepared a few sentences to let him know how moved we were by his dedication. But as I tried to say it, the tears welled up and for once I couldn't force myself to go on.

Another surprise is how stoic Italians often are. In long declamatory meetings, I find myself envying them. While I fidget, doodle, write tomorrow's speech, and check the program fifty times to see how much there still is to get through, they retreat silently into some inner life where rhetoric hasn't been invented. I met one soul mate, however, an interpreter who kept muttering "too long," "sit down," and when a speaker turned to yet another page of type, "oh no."

Undaunted by the rows of glazed donuts staring back at them, some speakers would make a point, repeat it, and then say it again. "Don't translate all this," I'd tell the interpreters, "just the gist." After minutes of impassioned talking but not a word from the interpreter, I'd whisper, "What's he saying?" "Nothing," came the reply with depressing frequency. Or, if pressed, "It's what he said before but in different words." Even an interpreter who works mainly with the European Commission, and whose job has entailed years of numbing meetings on the allowable fish catch in the Barents Sea, was struck by the emptiness of some of the speechifying. Somehow, it seemed, there were those who had found a platform in organ and tissue donation, but couldn't see one human being in the endless tables of statistics.

Other meetings, however, were feverish with excitement. I think, for example, of the school in the small agricultural town of Vittoria, Sicily, where we arrived at 8:30 in the evening. The school had dedicated a library to Nicholas and, late as it was, the place was jammed with children of mostly eight to twelve and their parents. The crowd spilled onto the street, lined the staircase and the hallways, and were jammed tight in the library itself. Every time I stood up to receive a new poem to Nicholas or a book on local history, I had to avoid hot little fingers spread out on the floor. The speeches, few and short, were loudly cheered, rising to a crescendo every time Nicholas' name was mentioned. But when I came to give my talk, it was heard in a silence befitting the Library of Congress. I'd cut it short, feeling I shouldn't overstrain young children late at night, but now I think could have gone on and on and their attention would not have waned. Somehow through their teachers and parents, their minds had gone to the core of the subject, seeing it not as a showcase for grand words, but a tale of suffering and idealism.

Happily, there were many more successes than disappointments. The one in Vittoria was a local initiative, but others were massive affairs, like the competition held all over Sicily for essays on transplantation on Nicholas Green Day. In the Catania region alone, seventy local schools competed. I don't suppose the essays broke much new ground, but, on this evidence, involving young minds in a project in which they have to do some serious study, putting them in a competition with other schools and then having a public presentation complete with rock groups and sickeningly sweet food, is one of the most effective ways of having some lasting results. As for emotion, it beat the Super Bowl.

I was not often alone on these tours, but one Sunday in spring I found the time to go back to Positano, drawn by a desire to recreate Nicholas' last happy hours. The hotelkeeper's wife remembered him playing with her four-year-old son, now seven. "He was an affectionate boy, I could see," she said. I had lunch looking over the same sparkling sea, and I now know exactly how many steps there are to the beach. I've decided not to put it down here, however. One day, who knows, on some vast ethereal staircase, I might get the chance to quiz Nicholas again.

Normally, however, these were tightly packed days, beginning early, moving around, making and listening to speeches, often getting back to the hotel after midnight. On one such night in Syracuse, a middle-aged man was in the lobby. He had the air of someone who has been waiting a long time on an unlikely errand. "I was hoping you'd come with me. Just for a few minutes," he said. "I want to take you to a disco." We'd become used to unusual proposals but this seemed outlandish. I couldn't possibly come, I told him. "We have to be up at 5:30 to move on."

"I know it's strange," he said. "But two young men have written a song for Nicholas and they want to play it for you." I didn't have the heart to refuse. We drove for a few minutes to "The Disco Speakeasy," which like its counterparts everywhere was filled with young people laughing, drinking, and listening to loud music. As we went in, the music died away and, after a word of welcome, the two performers played and sang their pulsating tribute to Nicholas, the words incomprehensible, but the sincerity crystal clear. When they had finished, there was a moment's pause, then a roar of approval and the entire audience was around the three of us on the tiny stage, hugging, smiling, crying, patting our backs, shaking our hands. No sacred music could have been more uplifting.

Time and again we found emotions like these swept over all the barriers, but they reached a peak in the little fishing town of Bagnara Calabra, where the last event in the annual festival was a variety show in a huge tent pitched in the main square. It was already packed to capacity when we arrived, but, with scores of people waiting outside, more and more plastic chairs were being brought in, lengthening the rows until they touched the canvas at each side and pushing the rows closer and closer together. In the front row, our knees were jammed up against the stage. I'd been told that at this event I would have to give the most important speech of our weeklong visit to southern Italy. Many awards were being made, but ours was the big one and our whole tour had been built around it.

Aim for a ten-minute talk, they told me; everyone will be there from the president of the Calabrian assembly down—and there he was, sitting next to us, legs painfully sandwiched like ours, hot like us, deafened by the music like us, and apparently pleased to be there. I wanted to do my best that night. This was low-income Calabria, close to where the shooting took place, at the heart of those conflicting emotions it had aroused of shame and guilt on one side, fierce local pride and a feeling of being pilloried by the world on the other. I'd decided days before that the speech would be about the bells people from all over Italy were sending for the children's tower we had built in Bodega Bay. I wanted to say this established a bond between us, and I'd asked someone to find me a school bell to give them an inkling of what we'd done.

The first glance told me this wasn't the audience for a ten-minute speech. They were here to enjoy a show and only at the end would the awards be given. They were excited to be seeing some well-known Italian entertainers—Calabrians mainly, who'd made it in Rome—excited by the transformation of their little town, excited by Saturday night. Scrunched between the president on one side and Eleanor on Maggie's lap on the other, the stage in front and someone's knees in my back, I began to pare my notes. After every song or comedy routine there was tumultuous applause, and it became clearer and clearer that anything that broke the mood would be a disaster. A picture came into my mind of an English vicar walking on stage to give thanks at the end of a Punch and Judy show.

At last the slapstick and the rock groups were finished, and those of us to be honored trooped up on stage. The audience was kind, applauding politely and listening as one after another said thank you. But the tension had dropped dramatically, and a long speech in English was going to put it away. I mentally cut another paragraph and tried desperately to think of a joke. Then it was time for our prize. It came with kind words about Nicholas, obviously from the heart, and listened to with more attention than we had the right to expect. But the fun was over, and the audience was ready to go home. I was asked to say "a few words" and mentally cut a few more phrases. By now I'd got it down to a minute or so.

As I stepped forward, however, the answer came. "I have only one thing to say," I said and stopped. The interpreter looked surprised, but said it in Italian and then waited too. "*Viva Nicholas*," I said loudly and rang the bell a few fast peals. There was a moment's silence, then a roar came back, "*Viva Nicholas, viva Nicholas,*" and I saw the crowd rising, row after row, like waves, hands clapping above their heads, cheering and shouting. I rang the bell again, then stopped, but the cheers went on. People were climbing on their chairs, children being picked up for a better view. I held the bell at arm's length and rang it again and again and again. The cheers were deafening. At last I moved off the stage and the hands came out, very old and very young hands, peasant and presidential hands, touching, stroking, patting. No one, it seemed, wanted to leave. Nicholas had done it again.

CHAPTER SEVENTEEN

FRENCH TV, A EUROPEAN BATTLE, AND THE WORLD GAMES

One evening, rather late, the phone rang. "My name is Jerome Pin, this is the television station, Tay Ef Uh, and we were hoping you could come for a program on transplants we are preparing." "We'll do it if we don't have anything else on then," I said. I always said that. I didn't think we should turn down any television program: you reached masses of people you couldn't get to any other way. But what was Tay Ef Uh? "I'm speaking from Paris," the voice said. Now it was clear. TF1, French Television 1.

The proposal was ambitious. An organ donation day for the whole of France had been declared, the first ever, and TF1 was putting on a two-hour program at prime time, including bringing as many as possible of Nicholas' recipients and their families to Paris. From the United States, Chet Szuber and his wife, Jeanne, would be there too. Dangerously ill, he had received the heart of his own daughter, Patti, when she was killed in a road accident.

This was the first of a series of trips overseas outside Italy, but by now we had our travel routine worked out. Some hotels near the San Francisco airport, we'd found, offered free parking for up to two weeks. Staying there the night before the flight was less expensive than using a regular parking lot. Travelodge became our preference: good rates for Dad and an adjacent International House of Pancakes for Eleanor. The waiters have the initials, IHOP, on their uniforms. I pointed them out to Eleanor. "It says I hop. Tell them we're going to France and ask if he has frogs' legs." It went right over her head. "No, Daddy, I want pancakes. With lots of syrup," she said. Nicholas would have got it, I thought sadly. And then he'd have kept saying it for the rest of the day. Maybe something was stirring, however. TF1 had booked us into the Appia Hotel, and, although this was not as long a flight as southern Italy, Eleanor was cranky on the ride into Paris. "We're 'ere at last," I said as we turned into the Rue des Deux Gares and stopped at the Appia. "Let's hope you'll be 'appier 'ere." She smiled, filed it away, and to my intense gratification said it half a dozen times over the next few days.

We were just in time for lunch—and our first interview, with *France Dimanche*, a weekly tabloid that, along with the Szubers' unique story, made it into a full-page article. We did a series of interviews in the next two or three days and a press conference with Dr. Christian Cabrol, the first surgeon in France to transplant a heart and the most eminent member of its transplant community. "I can't tell you how much you have done to make the idea of transplantation more acceptable," he told us. It was another of those surprises coming from someone who had moved mountains in the same cause, and I told him so. "Oh, my fame is largely symbolic," he said. "I can't believe that," I said. "But I'm sure ours is."

The program had been built round an idea, but an idea that didn't seem particularly clever to us. Viewers were asked to phone in during the show and request a special donor card. It cost money to do that, about seventy-five cents, I think, a penalty that seemed likely be a deterrent in a country that, like the United States, can't attract enough donors even by the most painless methods. The program, however, proved to be very powerful, the most affecting we'd been on until then. A strikingly beautiful woman told how she had received a transplant and since then had given birth to the two delectable blonde children who ran around the set all evening. Another woman had given up her defective lungs and sound heart to receive a new one of each: she sat next to the woman who now has her former heart. Five of our recipients and their families were on the set with us, a mass of people that said more about transplantation than a thousand words. The drive for donor cards had begun before the show started, but during those two hours, and in the next few days, a few hundred thousand people called in. Obviously we had been wrong about the effectiveness of the idea. It showed again that once people's emotions are engaged, donation rates can soar.

We had met the Szubers in New York and had been impressed by the straightforward way they told their story. "I was against it at first," said Jeanne, who was faced with the decision immediately after the death of her daughter. "I didn't want to lose him too." Now her husband was sufficiently recovered to be running a tree farm. I had wondered how he felt about all this, in good health for the first time in years, but at such a disastrous cost. In Paris we saw the answer. Chet was on stage at the press conference, quietly self-controlled as usual, talking in an abstract way about the shortage of donors. But as he was about to finish he started to say something about Patti. The mere mention of her name was enough to fill his eyes with tears and end his statement brokenly.

We got to know them quite well. They are kind, considerate people with a good sense of humor, which was tested in us all by the problems of moving a group of people in three languages to places that were expecting us hours earlier. An elaborate game evolved to deal with this, in which he was an enlisted man with scarcely any idea of what he was doing and I a junior officer who had no idea at all. "Corporal Szuber," I'd say in an impenetrable traffic jam around the Arc de Triomphe. "Take a few men and sort that lot out." He'd ask me questions about the program arrangements with the dumb insolence of one who knows you haven't the slightest notion of what they are. If he caught me sitting alone, he'd want to know if I planned to eat with the rank and file that night. "Can't stomach this barrack room food, corporal," I told him as we entered the famous restaurant *Paris Match* magazine had chosen for us. It was very childish, but it brought us quite close and took our minds off what we were there for. Near the end, after we were laughing at a good crack he'd made, he went on, "You thought I was just a dumb, ignorant, tree-hugging old dope, didn't you?" "I never, ever said tree-hugging," I assured him.

We had scheduled a few extra days to stay with Maggie's stepsister, Betsy, then living in Brussels. Laurent, her husband, knowing our minds, had already arranged two interviews. It was yet another illustration of the influence of this story that, in a country that had no connection with Nicholas and one of the highest rates of donations in Europe, it could still command full-page coverage.

While we were there we went to the reenactment of the Battle of Waterloo and missed Nicholas badly. He'd have wanted to know everything: why were the English soldiers hiding behind that hill, why were there so many different uniforms, who were those ladies following the soldiers around? He'd have recognized Napoleon's horse: he'd seen a replica in the army museum in Paris; he knew from his grandfather what the bagpipes were for; and he knew about the lightly armed cavalry from "The Charge of the Light Brigade." How I wished I could have shown him the difference between them and the heavy brigade. And, of course, in answer to his infectious curiosity we'd have told him everything we'd learned in two separate lifetimes. By the time he came away, he'd have known more about Waterloo than many a college history major.

In the square in front of the Gothic-style town hall in Manchester, England, a thousand athletes from thirty-five countries had gathered for the opening ceremony of an international games event. Like the Olympics, each team carried its country's flag. Some teams, such as the U.S., had many members. Iceland had one. Some competitors were born athletes, bouncing on their toes, impatient to start. Others were in it for the fun. The common element was that, at one time, none of them could have dreamed of being there. All had received a transplant and had needed to become fit enough to face the physical and mental stress of a well-publicized week of contests, the World Transplant Games.

Fernando Rodriguez from Argentina spent seven years in a wheelchair before being given a new heart. He was there to compete in the 1,500-meter race and 5-kilometer walk. Paula Burke, a new mother of twins, received a kidney from her father twenty years ago and had gone on to become a badminton champion. Mark Cocks, from Australia, was once a top-class tennis player, but at twenty-two his kidneys began to fail. At one time he was blind and needed two transplants, one from his sister Julie. Since then he has competed regularly in these games. Jerry Conrad from Arkansas had two heart transplants and was in his seventh games. Anders Billstrom of Sweden had come with his father and mother, each of whom had donated a kidney.

"At one time many contestants were often too ill to take serious exercise, never mind engage in competitive sport," Christiaan Barnard, who was there, commented. Now they were competing in a full range of the classic events, including the 5,000 meters, 4 × 400 relay, and the shot put with a sixteen-pound weight. The 50-meter dash included a two-to-five-year group, all of them recipients. There was an air of serious purpose about it. "Track and field rules will be enforced," the program of the similar U.S. national transplantation games warns. "Competitors will be disqualified for failure to observe the rules."

Not all of them went full out. Eleanor's most enduring memory of the Lord Mayor of Manchester's buffet dinner was that by the time she got to the chocolate cake the competitors had eaten it all, and enough cigarettes were being lit to bring on the need for a heart transplant for any athletic coach. But the overall impression was of men and women once at death's door chasing loose balls around the tennis court, fighting fatigue in grueling long distance races, and pushing themselves to the limit in the swimming pool, as their supporters, who were sometimes their donor families, yelled themselves hoarse with pride.

We were in Manchester—where I grew up—at the invitation of Tom Sackville, then the member of the British government directly responsible for the organ and tissue donation program. He had written earlier in the year, starting by saying what so many others have said, "I feel compelled to write to you," and adding, "I wondered if you would consider helping promote the new organ donation register."

This is not an invitation one can turn down lightly—it crossed my mind there might be a knighthood in it—and a few weeks later the offer was reinforced when Richard Branson, chairman of Virgin Atlantic, offered to provide tickets to London. Normally we travel everywhere in coach class and were not fazed when we discovered Virgin does not have a first class. It turned out, however, that it does have an upper class and there we lounged the long flight through, eating meals that, if I may put it so, are on a different plane from those we have become used to on other airlines.

On arrival in Manchester, reality returned quickly as we moved into student accommodation along with the crowds of competitors.

Everything was clean and neat, but it just wasn't upper class any more. That came home strongly in the refectory where I found the set dinner was chicken with potatoes, green beans, and carrots. I didn't feel like eating chicken, so asked instead if there was something else. "Yes, dear, you can have the vegetarian," said the motherly server who ladled it out: potatoes, beans, carrots, and no chicken.

We were there primarily to do interviews, and they went according to plan in Manchester and London, including one for South African television. For some interviews, we were with two British families who had also donated organs when their children died. I talked to both fathers, strong, clear-sighted men dealing, like me, with something for which they had had no preparation. Neither was given to demonstrativeness and communicated quietly the pain of ultimate separation. "It's the first thing I think of every morning," Joe, an ex-miner, told me. How familiar that was. He and his wife, Florence, had donated their daughter Joanne's organs because, seeing a television ad, she had filled in a donor's card.

Martin, the other father, told me his son, Nicky, was riding his bicycle and had been hit by a truck. "I don't know how it happened. You just don't know who to blame." "Well," I said, "you blame yourself when these things happen, don't you?" "You do," he said quietly and, through his composure, I glimpsed the doubts that torture all of us who have said to ourselves sentences that start: "If only..."

Even in unusual settings overseas, almost everyone we talked to seemed to know at least the rudiments of Nicholas' story. Nearly four years after he died, we were in the far north of Queensland, Australia. We'd done some media interviews in Sydney, but that was more than a thousand miles away and we were now on vacation. One day, walking along a tiny trail through the tropical rain forest, we passed a group of people. Nothing was said and they disappeared from view, but two or three minutes later we heard shouts through the dense vegetation, "Green, Green," and looking back made out a forest of waving arms without heads or bodies attached and then a chant, *"Auguri, auguri,"* "Good luck, good luck." They turned out to be an Italian choir touring Australia, so perhaps the coincidence wasn't that remarkable. Still, it will go down as our family's version of Stanley's meeting with Livingstone: "Lady Margareth and Mr. Reginald, we presume."

Chapter Eighteen

Speeches and More Speeches

Speaking to large audiences suddenly became a big part of our lives. I'd had some experience, but it was not always the most promising. Long ago I was a member of an international committee which met regularly in Europe. It was very formal—simultaneous translations in French, German, and English, microphones at every place, highly polished tables. At one session in Paris, after traveling overnight from Washington, I heard a voice say, "Well, we'll come back to the American delegation later," and realized that the entire room was looking at me as I woke from a contented sleep. In organ donation I now had a new topic, but often still traveled overnight, and I had to keep that kind of hazard in mind. Who knew what a conference of coroners might do to a prostrate body?

Within a few weeks of Nicholas' death, the World Children's Transplant Fund invited us to speak at their annual dinner. The effect of Nicholas' story was powerful, a room full of men in well-cut tuxedos and women in beautiful evening dresses crying quietly. Jerry Buss, owner of the Los Angeles Lakers, who was being honored for his contributions to the organ transplant cause, stood up to reply. He mentioned Nicholas and started to tell a story of his own son's life-threatening illness and subsequent recovery, but, overcome by the fearful idea of young death, couldn't finish it.

The children's fund was started by Mark Kroeker, a Los Angeles deputy police chief, after he had tried forcefully, then desperately, to save the life of a young girl from Argentina, Veronica Arguello. In the end, after three liver transplants, she died. But what might have crushed others only persuaded him to do more, and now the group he started in sorrow for one faraway family brings inexpressible relief to others.

Among the people who crowded round our table at the end of the evening was a member of the Lakers' squad. "You've changed my mind tonight. I'm going to sign that donor card tomorrow," he said. Emotional responses are fragile and, when the mood wore off, perhaps he wouldn't do anything. But the degree of conviction in that voice, repeated by others dozens and dozens of times over the following months, has convinced me that something is changing.

Other invitations followed swiftly, first from LifeGift, the organ procurement group in Fort Worth, who made it difficult to say no—"I want you to get them up on their feet and then down on their knees," one of the organizers told us—and then the Circle of Life in Dallas, who were planning a lunchtime meeting of a thousand influential people, transplant surgeons and hospital administrators, bankers and industrialists, civic leaders and healthcare workers. Tom Landry, the legendary Dallas Cowboys coach, and his wife, Alicia, were there too, keeping an imminent personal tragedy to themselves. Their daughter, Lisa, when pregnant, had been found to have cancer. She was told she could be treated, but would lose her baby. She steadfastly refused, gave birth to a beautiful baby girl, and then had a liver transplant. The cancer came back, however, and when we were in Dallas she was weakening fast. Neither of the Landrys said a word publicly, but a few weeks later she died, without regrets for her decision. "Lisa said those years with her daughter were the happiest of her life," Alicia told us.

I had doubts about the arrangements for this speech, the timing being so tight between the opening at 11:30 a.m. and the end, fixed absolutely for 1:00. "We'll be trying to talk over the clatter of a thousand plates and the munching of 32,000 teeth," I thought. I needn't have worried. The audience ate salad, main course, and dessert with military precision and heard the introductory remarks while sipping coffee quietly. Tom Landry talked briefly, though still without a word about his daughter, who must have been tugging his heartstrings. As Maggie spoke, I looked around at the mass of faces and reflected that in that huge ballroom the only thing I could hear was falling tears. At the end, a line of doctors came to the podium to say thank you. It still seems odd: the thanks surely should go the other way. It was yet another illustration that we had been handed an opportunity we just had to make the most of.

For a long time, the three of us traveled to all these meetings. But as time went by and they showed no sign of tailing off, we felt we couldn't keep pulling Eleanor out of school. So more and more I went on my own, though missing them badly.

If you're speaking at meeting after meeting, it's impossible not to repeat whole passages over and over. But no parrot carries conviction, and we kept on trying to evolve the talks. As we met new people and heard other inspiring or deflating experiences, they added to the texture. Talks had to be shaped to the wide variety of listeners, young, old, professional, amateur, recipients, donor families. Remarkably, however, the message itself seemed as appropriate when talking to surgeons with years of experience in transplantation as it was to people who had never given it a thought. Struck by the way the subject seemed to go beyond surgery, elevating people's aspirations and taking them to a vision of a better world, I often ended the talk with a paraphrase of a quotation I'd learned long ago, "We're all standing in the mud, but we can all look at the stars."

The mood varied, however. Often the talk was punctuated with laughs, and for a while it seemed as if I'd secured some detachment from the story. But then I'd find myself embarked on an innocuous sentence that from out of nowhere had my eyes brimming with tears. Simply looking at the people in the front rows dabbing their eyes could bring it on. I thought of how Senator Muskie's career had crashed after he cried at a public meeting, and I skirted all the danger areas when I was talking to schoolchildren. I still remember how, as teenagers, Peter Wiseman and I quickly looked away when we caught each other crying at a movie. I imagine there are groups all over the world who meet and share tears, but it was all new to me.

Time was scarce and it was obvious that we needed some way of packaging our message and sending it around the country. That was when I thought of making a video. For years I'd been friendly with Corporate Productions, a Hollywood company—well, Toluca Lake, actually, near Hollywood—and thought they were the best documentary filmmakers I'd ever come across. They'd made dozens of movies for companies such as IBM and Chevron and nonprofit organizations like Guide Dogs of America. I called Dick Ridgeway, one of the partners, and Jack Jones, their elegant writer, told them what was needed and asked what it would cost. The answer was almost instantaneous. Yes, we can do it and it will cost $20,000. Typically, they'd fixed a price that gave them a bare profit, if any, and a verbal agreement that was more reliable than a thrice-witnessed document. "You're on," I told them. "When do we start?"

The preparatory work began immediately. We asked the National Kidney Foundation for a list of points they'd like to see covered and invited the National Association for Gifted Children to piggyback on the movie so two films could be made at the same time. Peter Rosenstein, the association's executive director, agreed to take $4,500 from the money we'd sent them from Nicholas' college fund. Jack drew up an outline. It was just a page or two, widely spread out to look like more. But the main point was clear: there's no script and we don't know how we'll structure it, but we'll come up to Bodega Bay and you can talk. "This is our kind of plan," I said to Maggie, "free fall." Our full schedule held things up for a while, but one February day they arrived—Jack, Don Snell, the producer, and two cameramen. They left the next day and the two films were in the bag.

It was all delightfully simple. Jack asked questions to bring out the points we'd all agreed on, we talked—indoors mainly because of heavy rain—and they rolled the cameras. A few weeks later, we looked at the rough cuts and saw what a work of art it was. The raw material had been shaped into a story that captured a little life, while making the case for organ donations in the most telling way possible, from the heart. They called it *The Nicholas Effect*, added a haunting musical track, and invited Gigi Politoski, our chief contact at the Kidney

Foundation, to come to Los Angeles to preview it. "It's the best thing I've ever seen on the subject," she said without hesitation, disdaining the bureaucratic rule of not committing yourself until you have a consensus back at headquarters. It will go down with me as one of her finest moments. Her judgment was right too. We've taken it everywhere, and in those darkened rooms, people cry silently and come out converts. "I've seen it fifty times," one veteran healthcare executive in Texas confided, "and every time I bawl like a baby."

Our job now was to make sure it was seen. We set the selling price of each copy at the cost to us, and I started to write letters, and more letters, first to the main organ and tissue groups, then to hospitals, then to people I met on planes. I sent copies, unasked for, to schools, DMV offices, and television stations. We contacted *Booklist*, the Librarians' Association publication, which wrote a strongly approving review, and public libraries from Sno-Isle in Washington state to Ouachita Parish in Louisiana put it on their shelves. We sent it, in the hope that clips would be shown—and they were—to news and talk shows of all kinds, such as the Sally Jessy Raphael show, *Good Morning America,* and NBC Nightly News. Television stations in Japan and Poland, Germany and France, Britain and Australia all used excerpts, showing the real boy at the center of the drama.

Organ procurement groups from Guam to Alaska and Puerto Rico bought it, as did a laundry list of top hospitals: Mayo and Emory, Johns Hopkins and Loyola, Baylor, Barnes, and Rush. It is shown in healthcare settings as different as the Swedish American Hospital in Rockford, Illinois, Cedars-Sinai Medical Center in Los Angeles, and Southwest Texas Methodist Hospital in San Antonio. Eye banks and the American Red Cross, business and charitable clubs, drivers' education programs, surgeons and chaplains, undertakers and Scouts all use it. When we first thought about it, I'd have been satisfied if we'd sold three hundred copies. It's now three thousand and still growing.

As far as we know, it did its job with all these segments of society. "We've all seen it so often we know every word," the head of one of the most experienced organ procurement teams told me. "Every time the audience cries. And every time we cry too." "We've worn out our copies. Please send more," said another. More convincing still, organizations ordering one copy typically come back for more. TRIO, the recipients group, for example, has bought almost two hundred, and the Oklahoma Organ Sharing Network more than fifty.

I had no hesitation then when Dick suggested making a sequel focusing on the recipients. This came out as *Thank You, Nicholas*, with the same sure feel for deep but controlled emotion his company has always shown, and within a few months five hundred copies of it too were being used across the country.

Meanwhile, we had *The Nicholas Effect* dubbed into Spanish, splitting the cost with the office of George Ryan, then secretary of state for Illinois, now governor, and the Regional Organ Bank of Illinois. The response from organ procurement groups in centers with large Latino populations—San Diego, Miami, Chicago—was gratifying, and dozens of copies of this version were soon being shown. Watching it always comes as a surprise, however. I once saw John Wayne in a dubbed movie in Rome. *"Arrivederci,"* as he rode off into the sunset didn't seem right. I get the same sensation hearing Maggie talk about *"El legado de Nicholas."*

Is all this helping change minds? I don't doubt it. I've met literally dozens of people who have said they signed a donor card after watching one of the videos. At a meeting in the South, a member of the organ procurement team took me aside. "We show the movie all over the state," he said. "A few months ago, when I went to one of our hospitals, a woman came up to me. 'You won't remember me,' she said, 'but I was in the group here when you showed the video about those people in Italy. A few weeks later'—and she paused—'my son was killed in a road accident. I donated his organs and now I work here as a volunteer. I just want to say thank you. It helped.' "

I've never cottoned to standing ovations, feeling them to be a form of coercion by a committed minority, but we got them regularly. After it had happened a few times I began to see some value in them. I was less happy about the meetings that opened with a standing ovation and closed with polite applause, but soon I started not to mind those either. The most welcome were the opposite kind, routine clapping at the start, enthusiasm at the end. Yet, now I come to think of it, I liked them to stand at the beginning as well as the end. These talks often included evaluation sheets, and I began to like those too: these sympathetic audiences mark high. Once when we got a 9.7, I said to Maggie, "We're slipping. Gymnasts get more than this. Maybe we should open by Eleanor doing cartwheels across the stage."

I drew on lessons I'd picked up over the years. The best introduction I have ever heard was at a London theater by David Jacobs, a well-known raconteur. That evening his entire presentation went like this: "Ladies and gentlemen, Mr. Frank Sinatra." I don't know how much he was paid for that speech, but it was worth every penny. His self-denial gave us a whole extra song, and we loved him for it. Wanting to be loved too, I also opted for brevity.

I owe to Bruce Hasson—as so much else—an invitation to give a workshop at the Dalai Lama's glittering Peacemaking Conference in San Francisco in June 1997. Thousands of people were there, presided over by the avuncular gentleness of the Dalai Llama himself, described by one nonbeliever as exuding secular holiness. I was just a droplet in an enormous conference that covered everything from urban renewal and domestic violence to meditation and the power of Qi. But even as one of a vast audience, you felt he believed in you personally and tried to be very careful not let him down.

Bruce, a San Francisco sculptor, had been asked to discuss his most ambitious idea, a series of bells to be placed in key places around the world—among them, Jerusalem, Florence, and Manaus—to ring in the new millennium with a celebration of human achievement. He told the organizers he thought Nicholas' story would be perfect for the peacemaking theme, and I think it was. At any rate, at my presentation both the audience and I were more than usually moist.

Once my part was over, I could turn to some of the other workshops. "I've been wondering which of these to go to?" I said to Maggie, holding up the program. "Here's one that might be useful," I added, pointing to martial arts: "Marital Arts." "Go," she said, "it'll do you good." I looked again. "Even better," I told her, "there's an advanced course the following day. It's called Extra Marital Arts." From then on we gave the conference a slogan: "Make peace not love."

Every meeting contained a surprise. In Sacramento, a surgeon who has been transplanting hearts for ten years said he's still amazed that, when something looking like what you might see at the butcher's is put in a new body, it suddenly springs steadily and powerfully to life. At a seminar in Berkeley, a nun made an appeal for organ donation. "There's a widespread impression that nuns look forward to dying," she said. "It isn't so. Everyone wants a chance to go on living." When Eleanor had a temperature in Genoa, I said to one of the organizers that a conference of two hundred doctors was perhaps the best place to have it. "Maybe, but they're all surgeons and they'll want to operate. You'd better leave her to me," he said. "Oh, what do you do?" "I specialize in autopsies," he replied. I recently came across a note to myself about a speech at a park. It read: "If it's raining, don't use the quote about we're all standing in the mud."

The reactions at these meetings confound all notions that transplantation is a subject people don't want to hear about. Among dozens of others, Judy Ninman for the Circle of Life in Dallas commented, "The response has been overwhelming. Many have written or called to say their lives have been truly changed." "The story inspired me to revitalize our organ donor awareness efforts," said Virginia Beecher, New Hampshire's director of the motor vehicles department, and the innovative programs she introduced thereafter proved it. After one talk, a woman with a kindly face told me that when her three-and-a-half-year-old daughter had been killed in a car accident she was unable to donate the organs because of some mix-up. "And that hurts so much," she said, her eyes filling with tears. Now she attends meetings like this, working long and late as a volunteer, to repair an omission she feels is somehow her fault.

I'm still at a loss to understand the impact on people who know infinitely more about this subject than we do. But perhaps it comes from the simplicity of a human experience that is easily lost sight of in a busy hospital. Administrators can discuss endlessly when to ask for a family's consent, but their debate must surely be illuminated when Maggie says quietly, "What makes donation so difficult is that you have to say good-bye at the same time."

Normally she speaks first—it seemed important to establish this from the beginning so that in public at any rate she doesn't have the last word—and we always try to use these meetings as starting, rather than finishing, points. We offer to turn up at seminars people in the audience are planning, suggest an article for their newsletter, start planning a project together. Diane Donlon of Roche Laboratories' public policy department was at one of these meetings. A few weeks later, she phoned to say the company had brought out a new drug to reduce rejection in kidney transplants and asked me to speak at a meeting they were planning in Houston for doctors and sales representatives. It's easy to imagine what hopes lie in that little pill and others like it: an organ is donated, the fading hopes of a desperately ill patient are sent soaring, and the medical team puts its skills and emotions into saving a life that only a few hours before seemed over. And then, agonizingly, the body starts to reject the new organ. Anyone who can reverse that process has a magic wand in his hand.

The talk was at a dinner in the Houston Museum of Fine Arts, a setting to bring out the best in everyone: the gleaming floor, the snow-white tablecloths and glistening glassware, the huge windows looking out to a spectacular sunset, Monet and Renoir looking at us. I showed the video, during which there was the now-familiar mixture of rapt attention and discreet sniffling, and then talked about our experience.

There were about eighty people in the room, and most of them came over afterward to say those unreservedly personal things this subject seems to bring out. Many had been crying, some still were. One said, "You've changed my life." Another, a doctor, said he'd switched from pediatrics to transplants two years before and had been having doubts about having made the right decision. "Tonight helped convince me I did the right thing," he said. The next morning, I had confirmation that these comments were more than just passing fancies. At 6.30 a.m., waiting to go to the airport and with last night's emotion safely tucked away, one of the doctors walked across the hotel lobby and said, "That was the most moving experience of my life."

Viva Nicholas.

CHAPTER NINETEEN

THE CHILDREN'S BELL TOWER

The children's bell tower in Bodega Bay is a magical place. It stands on open ground, a thick growth of cypress trees on one side and green hills on the other. In the background are high dunes and a tantalizing glimpse of the ocean. The tower is 18 feet high, three tubular steel pyramids from which hang 140 bells: school bells, church bells, ships' bells, mining bells, cow bells. The centerpiece is a majestic bell, thirty inches high, from the Marinelli foundry in Italy, which has been making bells for the papacy for a thousand years. Nicholas' name and the names of the seven recipients are on it, and Pope John Paul II went to the foundry to bless it. Whenever the wind blows, as it often does on this exposed coast, the bells chime, sometimes a few at a time, emphasizing the solitude of the surroundings, sometimes an entire orchestra, sounding like happy children at play. Then the sound fades away, and the children are gone.

Although it was inspired by Nicholas' death, Maggie and I always wanted it to be a memorial accessible to everyone. It was to be a place too where children would feel at ease. Its delicacy reflects both the preciousness and fragility of young life. I imagine some families giving thanks there for their children, others finding a little solace for a loss, and all drawing closer to each other. When Bruce Hasson, a man of surpassing modesty, first suggested the idea, it took our breath away.

Even now, I am astonished at the elegance, originality, scope, and sheer humanity of it.

Our first encounter with Bruce was typical. Despite his 6'4" frame, he had managed to make himself completely invisible in the small space of the Italian-American Museum in San Francisco. He was just finishing a bell for the fiftieth anniversary of the United Nations, a project for peace made from melted-down firearms confiscated by the police. He and the Italian Cultural Institute director, Amedeo Pignatelli, he told us, were working on a plan to ask Italians to donate bells for a monument in Bodega Bay. It was another example of the power of this story that Bruce, a stranger until then, having only read about it in a newspaper, should have been so moved by our decision to donate and Italy's reaction to it, that he was prepared to give months of unpaid work to it, and that Amedeo, having no pressing reason to get involved at all, threw himself into the idea with incandescent enthusiasm.

The first part worked like a dream. We found the site—which by chance is overlooked by the preschool Nicholas attended, and is therefore a view he would have seen every schoolday for two years—and were given a sympathetic hearing by the county supervisors. The Italian press welcomed the idea, highlighting the concept of a bridge between the two countries. It is that, but I think of it more as a little piece of Italy's soul.

None of the three of us had any experience with fundraising—you could say we had negative experience, all of us finding asking someone else for money an uneasy business. But between us we drew up lists, wrote letters—I called them the bells lettres—and contacted the media. Giulio Prigioni, the kindhearted Italian consul general in San Francisco, promised his support, and the momentum picked up in Italy when *Oggi* magazine put its weight behind the idea, printing articles, inviting readers to send a bell, and making a much-needed contribution.

The reaction to the idea was beyond anything we had foreseen. As we walked along streets in Italy, people would thrust a bell in our hands. Storekeepers would rush out of their shops to give us a bell from their shelves. Some bells had been in families for generations, others were specially made. Some were inscribed in memory of a child or a friend who had died. Some gave thanks for a life saved. One woman told how she and her mother had each owned one of a pair of bells, a lifetime bond. Now her mother had died, and instead of holding on to both bells as she'd always planned, she thought the connection would be better kept up in the memorial. One bell used in the coal mines of Italy at the beginning of the twentieth century had been an immigrant family's link to their homeland; now it too found a more appropriate place in company with its countrymen. Andrea Scarabelli, a young man from Rome who had written several long letters expressing his closeness to our family, managed to unearth one from the Marinelli foundry after months of searching. Mariangela Contessi, whose son, Simone, had died in a climbing accident in the Dolomites, had a bell made with his name on it.

Money came in much more slowly. I contacted the telephone and electricity companies, among others, hearing they were a soft touch. There's iron inside that velvet glove, however, and no money. I wrote also to sports teams, including the San Francisco 49ers, who have a foundation that supports community projects. One day the phone rang. "It's George Seifert, Reg"—the coach himself!—"We'll be sending some money." A couple of sentences more of chitchat and that was all. What a pleasure to talk to a famous man who wasn't full of his own fame, didn't talk through a secretary, and even called you Reg. In time $1,500 arrived from the 49ers. The city of Bari—where Anna Maria, one of the recipients, lives—the warmhearted Wanda Ferragamo, and the Banco del Lavoro all made generous contributions. A hundred dollars came from a social group, including twenty-five dollars from the person who'd won that week's raffle; a retired woman from the south of Italy sent a thousand-lira bill, or sixty-five cents.

There was still a long, long way to go to the $50,000 we needed, but when we dug into our foundation, it was enough to start. Bodega Bay rallied round as always with quiet work, carried out without any charge, and generally without our having to ask. Then, gloriously, the government of Calabria, at the instigation of its president, Giuseppe Scopelliti, came through with $9,000. That too took our breath away.

The delivery was on an appropriately heroic scale, most of the bells coming in an Italian Air Force transport plane to Alameda naval air base, which was specially opened for the occasion. The captain told me the crew had recently been in Russia to bring back the remains of Italian soldiers who had died there in World War II. Taking them for relatives in Italy, he said, was one of the most affecting experiences of his life. I thought of those people, sons and daughters, brothers and sisters, perhaps even a mother or father, waiting more than fifty years for those pathetic bags. "Bringing in a cargo of bells must seem very bland after all that," I said. "No," he replied, "I have the same feeling of great love and great sorrow I did then."

When the Marinelli foundry first offered their big bell, I wondered if this was a common practice with them. No, we were told, the closest parallel they could think of was that when *glasnost* came to the Soviet Union, and with it a religious freedom unknown for more than sixty years, they had made a bell for Moscow. Somehow Bruce had managed to put his memorial on the same historical scale. All this time he was driving to foundries, designing and drawing, chipping and polishing, submitting and changing plans, substituting metal clappers with rubber for a more delicate sound, and neglecting his career. Then he placed the bells on the tower, one by one, as carefully as if each of them were his own child.

For weeks we talked about the stone for the semicircular wall that would set off the tower. Bruce saw all manner of quarries with prices ranging as high as $1,200 a ton. This was an important decision: we needed seven or eight tons. Why not try our local quarry, Maggie asked. He did and was told it would cost fifteen forty a ton. Too much, he told them, we can get something we like for $840. There seems to be a misunderstanding, they told him. It's not $1,540, it's $15.40. For a while, it was our front-runner. It did not have the angular structure Bruce wanted, however, and in the end we decided on a beautiful Montana stone, warm and strong, and Bruce and the masons we employed made what most of us connected with the project think is a second masterpiece.

On an empty stretch of the California coast, it is like one of those immemorial English stone walls. But he has also managed to keep it in harmony with its special purpose. An adult can sit on it comfortably, taking in the sight and listening to the tinkling orchestra. At the ends, however, it is low to the ground. "I want children to enjoy this too," Bruce told me. I was delighted to see that when Eleanor saw the monument for the first time she immediately sat on the low part of Bruce's enticing wall.

Once again the media sent the story round the world, and soon the letters were coming in. Here is one, from Elsa in Italy. "Have see in telebision set she to interview from an Italian journalist the died of our dear little great Nicholàs, then I have see the Mrs. Maggie Green, have called my mother have telled come to see there is the family green in television set, come at to see the childrens how are beautiful, my mother to cry for those what have to do to Nicholas. Then have to see the monument of little Nicholas with the bells what to come from Italy between in which the bell more great there to engrave the name of the people what to live thanks to dear Nicholas."

A local storekeeper gave us another perspective. "Visitors used to ask where *The Birds* was made," he said. "Now they ask where the bells are." I was a little sad for Hitchcock. Then I reflected that in its time the movie had wiped out virtually all memory of the Daphne du Maurier story that inspired it. To everything there is a season. Many callers tell us of the monument's healing power, like the woman who asked if she could hang a bell for her brother who had died many years ago. "It's just for a day, his birthday," she added. "My mother still can't let go." They had been there a few days before and hung a scarf to remember him. "I think it made my mother feel a little better," she said.

I hope that will be true of many others. Soon after Nicholas died, we had received a letter from an American nun in Rome, Susan Pieper, who had helped found an order, the Apostles of the Interior Life, young nuns whose aim is to help people develop their own spirituality. She invited us to tea when we were next in Rome, but we never had the chance to take her up on it. "If only you knew how much your story has touched the heart of Italy," she said at the time. We kept in touch and one day she telephoned from her parents' home in the Napa Valley where she was spending a vacation. She was calling, she said, about the tragic death of a local three-year-old girl. "Could you write something to comfort those parents?" she said. "Oh, no," I told her. "I know too well how little one can say." "God will guide your hand," she said firmly. "I know you don't believe that, but I do." So, with a heavy heart and slow pen, I started to write a few words. One after another I tore them up until suddenly I had an idea: I'd offer to have a bell made for the little girl and put on the tower. Having made the decision, the words came quickly. The parents replied immediately, saying they were very touched.

Bruce had a different reaction. "Where am I going to put it? It's full already. We can't take off any of the bells that are there now. I just don't see what I can do." He was right. I felt like such a dope. I should have talked to him first. There wasn't a single space. But the story was working on Bruce's soft heart and after a few minutes, he said, "You know, perhaps there is something we can do"—we!—and he sketched out a plan to make a space by putting one of the smaller bells inside another. Then he'd cast a new bell with the girl's name on it. It all worked out as planned and now her beautiful bell chimes along with the rest, watched over by the bigger bells around it. One day the girl's parents and brothers came on a visit. We sat on the wall and talked for a while, and I thought they had probably had enough for one day. But when I got up to go, they stayed. As I got into the car, I looked back at them across the field and saw all four of them sitting in silence, their faces turned to one spot on the tower. I called Susan before she returned to Rome. "What a lovely idea," she said out loud. And, to herself, no doubt, "There, I said God would guide your hand."

Nine months after the Marinelli family had offered its magnificent bell, a letter arrived from Paola Marinelli. We'd sent them a photograph of Nicholas and, thanking us, she sent back a photo of her exquisite child, Chiara, whose black tousled hair, large brown eyes, and gentle smile made you smile back. The letter went on, "Our little child unexpectedly left us last summer." My spirits, buoyed by this little glimpse of heaven, fell back to earth. "She was only twenty months and she never woke up after an operation." Reading the letter again, I grapple with a feeling of utter helplessness. These were the people who had instinctively asked themselves, "What can we do to help?" when they heard about Nicholas. Yet in all that time they had not said a word about their own breaking hearts.

One day, a year or two after we put up the tower, I telephoned Bruce. "Maggie and I think we should have a bell for Italy," I said. "Let's make one and send it to Calabria." Everywhere I went in Italy, people asked about the bell tower. We wanted them to have the chance to make it part of their lives too. "Let me think about it and I'll get back to you," Bruce said thoughtfully. I was disappointed. I'm all for thought, unless it gets in the way of action, but I'd expected him to jump at it. "Oh, and Bruce, I know it's difficult, but can you make it from melted-down firearms?" I heard his swift intake of breath. Maybe it wasn't such a good idea, after all.

A week or two later, a cardboard cylinder arrived by mail. In it were colored drawings of not one but seven bells. Each was crowned by a bird that seemed to soar upwards with it. All seven were suspended on wires from an elegant wooden frame and would sway gently as if in flight. And, yes, a note said they would be made from firearms. "Come and look," I said to Maggie. "It's beautiful," she said immediately and there were tears in her eyes. The symbolism is inescapable: a bell for each recipient, the birds rising above violence, and weapons of destruction turned into tokens of peace. We called it "The Birds," in the hope that it will conjure up an image of the place where Nicholas lived. We had the makings of a masterpiece.

Now we had to see if Calabria was interested. We were too impatient to write so Bruce telephoned Dr. Scopelliti's office and sent the drawings by Federal Express the next day. The response was all we'd hoped for: they loved the idea, loved the execution, loved the feeling of solidarity that went with it. "It can't be in the open, because the steel will rust," Bruce explained. "But we'd like it to be where many people will see it." "We've got just the place," he was told.

The most impressive development going up in Reggio di Calabria is the new assembly building, home of the regional government. It's modern, large, and handsome, and stands out strikingly in the center of the old city. Inside is a huge lobby, through which the crowds of people going into the building will pass. And here, we're told, the bells will be placed.

As I write this, the building isn't ready and something could change, but it was clear to us that the people we talked to in Calabria thought as highly of the sculpture as we do: in shining wood and steel it turned out to be as evocative as the first drawings suggested. We hope it will remind everyone who sees it how much good can come out of even the most heartbreaking tragedy.

CHAPTER TWENTY

WE GET BUSIER...AND BUSIER

Much of our life remains just as it was—toast or cereal at breakfast for us, waffles—always waffles—for Eleanor, bills that seem too big, phone calls at dinnertime from telephone companies. I was struck by how little the scaffolding of daily life had altered. We lived in the same rooms as before, ate at the same times. Housework, cooking, grocery shopping, getting out the newsletter were all much the same. Take them together and routine fills a lot of the day, enforcing a pattern of thoughts and emotions that helps keep you on track. I don't think the inner core has changed much either. I feel I am still the person who always preferred the less-traveled path, has never looked neat in his life, and blames the nail when it won't go in straight. So when I'm asked how much our lives have changed, I don't know how to answer. But certainly the externals did.

We have traveled a lot, all of us. The accommodation has varied from a hotel suite where Eleanor, Maggie, and I each had our own luxurious bathroom, to a place where, when I checked in during a snowstorm, the desk clerk handed me a roll of toilet paper to dry my glasses, the bedspread was dotted with what looked like bullet holes, but turned out to be cigarette burns, and the inside of the door was covered with penciled messages to Jesus. I spent one night in the stately Mount Washington Hotel in Bretton Woods—a manicured garden of

Eden—and another sitting upright in a chair at the Kansas City airport, wakened every time I dozed off by a tape which blared all night, "Smoking (or perhaps it was 'sleeping') is not permitted in the airport buildings."

Meals came in every possible form from sumptuous to nonexistent. With some people, we exchanged lavish hospitality. With others, the watchword was careful husbandry, like the ten healthcare workers who, after the waiter presented a combined bill, asked for separate checks, reminding him who had coffee at $1.25, who had tea ($1.00), and who had plain water. Some meetings ended with bratwurst and beer, others with slivers of nonfattening toast and sparkling water.

Language changed for us, both broadening and narrowing: "recipient" no longer means someone who receives something; "cadaver" means Nicholas. "Reinstitutionalize" means going back to hospital. An "in-room refreshment center" is a refrigerator in a hotel room with high-priced chocolate in it. I've conversed with a wider variety of answering machines than ever before, from the friendly one that answered, "We're having a great day in Memphis," to the one at the foreign newspaper that said, "We're on strike. If you must leave a message, do so now." I learned to loathe the one that said, "We appreciate your understanding," while I turned violet with a lack of it. Was it my imagination or did one hospital really say, "Thank you for your patients"? National Public Radio's Susan Stamberg tells a story of being able to play in her mind every note of a Dave Brubeck recording, which she did while waiting for subway trains in New York. Similarly, traveling by United Airlines, I've held the line so many times that, if their recording of "Rhapsody in Blue" is ever lost, I could do a note-perfect version and still throw in, "Your business is very important to us," every half minute.

The days were full and long. We got up with the chicken farmers and went to bed—figuratively—with the bartenders. Dawn over Europe became a common sight. The morning I met Lorenzo Minoli, the movie producer, I had three breakfasts: one at home, one on the 7:00 a.m. plane, the third—and by far the best—with him at the Peninsula Hotel in Beverly Hills. Some days I was on the phone to an Italian newspaper at 2:00 in the morning and to New York at 7:00.

At a peak of activity, this was what one day was like: Received phone call from the American Association of Motor Vehicles Administrators asking for a synopsis of my talk at their annual meeting.

Received call to say that the land we'd chosen for a memorial was not included in the lease we'd been counting on and we'd have to think of a new plan. Held phone discussion with the National Alliance for Excellence on the scholarships being set up in Nicholas' name. Made travel arrangements for talk in San Diego. Visited with Benedictine monk looking for information on Nicholas he could use in teaching. Signed twenty letters to people who'd sent a bell. Wrote letter to Scout troop in Maine wanting information for a jamboree. Wrote article for an Arizona organ procurement newsletter. Made calls to *Fortune, Business Week,* and *Investor's Business Daily* about emerging markets. Received second call to say the lease for the memorial was okay after all. This continuous splitting myself up to meet deadlines and work on new projects sent my mind searching for parallels. Dickens? Mozart? Sir Walter Scott? None was convincing. In the end, I settled for an amoeba.

All these meetings took some juggling with my real job. On trips I'd write articles on investing in the plane both coming and going and in odd moments between, in taxis, on envelopes, on the backs of programs. I'd seize on any interval in the schedule to start in on the round of calling money managers to find what they were doing with their portfolios, whether they thought high-yield bonds were vulnerable, whether small company stocks were likely to start catching up, and the other minutiae that make economics so boring to some people and so fascinating to others.

Losing some ingrained habits freed up some time. For the first year or so, I had no stomach for music: it always seemed too much or too little, too penetrating or too superficial. I was so emptied of musical sounds that a week after I'd been to the dentist I'd hear a tune from his Muzak tape running through my head. I couldn't recreate the enjoyment of going for long hikes either, and for the first time in my life just about stopped reading for pleasure. As for television, in that first year or so we were on more shows than we watched.

I also discovered there were more hours in the day than I ever knew. I started work earlier, which wasn't difficult, because almost every day seemed to bring faxes or phone calls from first light, went to bed much later, and treated weekends like any other day. Maggie said the only way she knew it was Sunday was if I was working in the living room instead of the office. Lois Perry, who became my secretary after Dee left, plowed on doggedly every morning, without coffee breaks, time off for chats, or any diversion from the continuous round of letters, phone calls, and email, and when she went home we took over.

In more than four years since Nicholas died, while we traveled long distances, here and overseas, and the projects we were working on multiplied instead of tailing off, I interviewed, wrote, edited, and got the finished stories to the printer. Nor did this seem just something I had to do for a living. It's work I've always felt is worthwhile, and I didn't want the standard to fall. My goal was that if, later on, anyone looked back, they wouldn't know anything unusual had happened.

It was useful too to be reminded that for the rest of the world things were going on as before. One winter's day, a phone call came while it was still dark, always a bad sign. What urgent news was there from Italy? I jumped out of bed and picked up the phone. It was from New York. "I'm looking at an investment prospectus," a voice said. "It says something about interest rate cycles. Do you know what it's talking about?" Doing this work at the computer where Nicholas had so often journeyed excitedly along "The Oregon Trail" wasn't easy, however. Recently I came across a note I sent to someone soon after Nicholas died, explaining a problem we were having sending out an article: "The humans are functioning, but the computer is too sad to work today."

The combination of no exercise and large Italian meals took its toll. When one clipping came in that called me an international figure, Maggie suggested they meant global. I also managed to give up doing almost any kind of housework for a few months. As I sat working in my comfortable chair, unseen—but not inaudible—hands would clear the dinner table and start to clean the kitchen. Like artists in garrets down the ages, I had the sensation that all these workaday tasks were beneath me. It was a relief while it lasted, but, for the record, I'm enslaved again and paying heavily for my bolt for freedom.

Eleanor adapted quickly too. On one of our early trips to Italy, I saw her sitting in the middle of the third row wearing a headset and listening intently to the simultaneous translation of a doctor's talk on kidney failure. On visits to Italian schools, I got used to seeing her disappear like a rugby ball into a scrum of children and emerge moments later holding an enormous fluffy animal. She coped well with this attention—more accurately, she basked in it—and it came from all sides. As she was going up a staircase one day, I saw a bishop coming down turn in amazement to look at her firefly sneakers flashing on and off. No doubt the upper clergy will soon be wearing them.

But many memories still seem unreal. As an English boy I'd watched American war heroes in the movies being honored for their unlikely exploits. The brightly colored scenery and lifestyle were on another planet from the drab blacked-out streets of wartime Britain. Now, standing on a stage, I heard the commander of the local U.S. paratroop base tell an excited crowd of Italians the Greens were "the embodiment of all America stands for." I felt like John Wayne. Maggie was not there that day, having things to attend to on the home front. When I called later, she'd just got back from sharing a speaking engagement with Robert Redford's son, James, a liver recipient who has become a vigorous crusader for increasing organ donations.

On the face of it, May 21, 1996, was not a day for surprises. I was at the place where, for the previous five years, I'd known I'd be. Although I find it impossible to forecast what I'll be doing next week, I do know the Investment Company Institute, the mutual fund association, invariably has its annual meeting in Washington in May and almost always at the Washington Hilton. I'd been going to those meetings for twenty-three straight years. It was my most faithful addiction.

This year was the second annual fundraising lunch for the Nicholas Green Scholarship Fund, and I was a speaker. Otherwise I might not have made it for the twenty-fourth time. At midnight the night before, I'd telephoned Maggie and been told, "Not yet. There's no need to catch the early flight back," and she had not called back during the night. But as soon as I went into the hotel that morning I was handed a message which read, "It's time. I'm leaving for the hospital now."

The staff of the institute's press room is under pressure at that time of day, attending to people like me who repeatedly lose their sets of conference papers or leave their badges in the pants pocket of the suit they wore yesterday. Now they dropped all that, calling airlines, checking reservations, and paging the hotel manager so that within minutes I was on my way to the Dulles airport in a hotel car with a fast driver and a faster-beating heart. The rush-hour traffic was thick, however, and I arrived to find the flight everyone had worked to get me on had left ten minutes before. I went to the telephone and called the hospital. Alicia, Maggie's mother, answered. "You have two beautiful new children," she said. "And Maggie's fine."

I suppose the idea of having another child must have come into our minds quite soon after Nicholas died. The emptiness of the house was a constant reminder of what we'd lost. But it was far too painful to think about it seriously. As time wore on, and we began to talk about it, we could see the problems. How would Eleanor react? How would we react seeing someone growing in Nicholas' place? Did we really want a child, or were we simply filling a gap? And at my age, wasn't it foolish to think of becoming a father again?

Eleanor was a fundamental consideration. She was coping heroically with the change in her life, but any suggestion that we were transferring our affections could have been disastrous. But, as we thought about it, the arguments began to run strongly the other way. She had lost companionship and was having to look for what had previously come naturally. She drew closer to Maggie and to friends. There was no harm in it, but it seemed a response to deprivation. As for my age, it had worked wonderfully with her and Nicholas a few years earlier: being mistaken for their grandfather only added to the magic. I think we also knew enough about ourselves to feel we'd treat any newcomer as a separate person, not a substitute. Another thought influenced me. At some stage I too would be leaving this household, and Eleanor and Maggie alone seemed a poor alternative to the full set of relationships we'd had at one time. In the end, the prospect of the house filling up again with gurgles and water splashing out of the bath carried the day.

There is no history of twins in either of our families, but these were IVF, in vitro-fertilized children, what Italian journalists and I still call test-tube babies. This is a high-tech, low-fun way to make a baby and frequently produces more than one. It had been our best chance of success, however, and at sixty-seven I had become father of a girl, five pounds five ounces, and a boy, six pounds six ounces. At a stroke, the population of Bodega Bay expanded 0.2 percent and the average age of our household dropped 40 percent.

I had the same headiness I'd had each time this had happened before, that mixture of relief that everyone was safe after a hazardous journey and of awe that something which wasn't there yesterday had just become the most dominant fact of life. I'd never been able to banish entirely the worry that a larger family might somehow change my relationship with Nicholas, dim the memory, or push him into a corner of my mind. But what I found that day, and to this day too, is that there was ample room for all the children. Perhaps the room simply expands.

I landed in San Francisco, got to the parking lot—not long now—and found my battery was dead. By the time I was on my way, I was in the San Francisco evening equivalent of that morning's Washington, D.C., rush hour. Time was passing. "These kids are going to be in college before I arrive," I thought. Then finally I was climbing the hospital stairs, no time to wait for the elevator, and into a room that was like an environmentalist's vision of the global population explosion. Two nurses, a radiant mother-in-law, a glowing wife, and a small girl, who had recently been in the front row of the stalls for not one but two of life's greatest dramas, were crowded together. Oh, yes, and two featherweight bundles, each containing a very old, wrinkled person.

We had the kind of excited conversation families have in these conditions, everyone with a story to tell, piling on extra details as they remembered them. The contractions had started at 4:00 in the morning, strong and rapidly strengthening. Alicia, driving Maggie and Eleanor along the pitch-black road, had so little time to spare that when the traffic light in the middle of Sebastopol was red she wondered if they'd make it in time. Laura came twenty minutes after they arrived. The labor coach arrived ten minutes later, just in time to shout "push" once before Martin was born. Eleanor, who had been practicing giving birth for weeks, screwing up her face as though she was on the toilet, found the reality less glamorous and a little frightening. But she was determined to be there and watched throughout.

Humiliatingly, on their first day, I was the last visitor, and the reporters and photographers had already done most of their work. Weeks before, we'd had a series of inquiries from the media about special arrangements, like the paper whose note read, "We are prepared to make a VERY SUBSTANTIAL offer for the exclusive rights." In Italy, *Oggi* magazine was equally keen to have the first pictures. They'd been very good to us—sending money to the foundation we'd set up in Nicholas' name and writing a series of stories—but this was not possible. This story belongs to everyone, we pointed out. "Well, what would you agree to?" they had asked and we entered into a headache-producing series of discussions in which we all finally agreed on a media pooling arrangement to give everyone the first pictures at the same time, while *Oggi* would have the first rights after the babies arrived home. It all worked out as planned. The first photographs were taken within a few hours of the births—Pat, a friend in Australia, saw the television pictures before I saw the babies—no one was mad at us, and *Oggi* made another generous contribution to the foundation. Still, my daddy-come-lately behavior added an item for the quick press conference they held now that I was finally there. "With the whole world watching," I was able to say, "I had to be late."

Someone handed me some phone numbers and a few names, two of which were for the next day's morning shows. "They wanted to talk to Maggie, but this will be in the small hours of the morning. Can you do them?" I was asked. So, as usual, in the even smaller hours, the television crews arrived, the furniture was rearranged, and I tried to find the words to say what it feels like to have new life coming back into a house still aching from lost life. I think I said my only regret was that Nicholas was not there to see it. I should have added that, if he had been, he would probably have said, "This is the best day of my life."

Picking the names had given us some problems. We like sturdy names that have borne a lot of weight over the years. Every parent goes through it, of course, but two names raise the problems to a higher level and a seven-year-old daughter, with 33 percent of the vote and hence veto power, raises it still more. We ransacked our memories, looked on every twig of our family trees, and combed the *10,000 Baby Names* book.

In the end, Laura was easier. I had just finished plowing my way with Eleanor through *The Little House on the Prairie* books, in which Laura Ingalls Wilder does herself a few good turns in portraying her own childhood. Eleanor was entranced by the story of this kind, brave, selfless person and enthusiastically endorsed the name. It also had a satisfying Italian connotation: Petrarch's Laura came to mind. We had to look around more widely for a boy's name, but the combination of a Roman god and the award by the St. Martin's Institute carried the day. There were some unexpected results. I conceived the idea of collecting every recording of the song "Laura" and quickly bought several, including Charlie Parker and Gerry Mulligan. Naturally, I already had Frank Sinatra. One day in a record store, I decided to find out how many I still had to go. I looked it up on the electronic screen and found the answer: 249. I gave up the idea without further thought.

Italy was as bountiful as ever. Enza, a stranger from Sicily, wrote that when she heard Maggie was pregnant her eyes "were filled with tears and I almost could not sleep that whole night." Elisabetta, from Parma, made two exquisite hand-embroidered baby gowns, saying simply, "I know what is life after sorrow." The dozens of letters that came in shared our happiness to the full, but most of them included a note that said: we know they will never take Nicholas' place. As always, they had not just dashed off a pro forma congratulations card. They had felt first and written second.

Those comfortable relationships are still there, and it is always easy to tell when the phone calls about the twins come from Italy. "How is L-au-ra?" they ask and, "And Martino, how is he?" To which, for the first two years, I was able to reply routinely, "Well, he's never a dry Martino." No doubt their personalities are being subtly molded by the names we chose, and it's lucky, I suppose, I wasn't still reading the *Wizard of Oz* books to Eleanor when they were born. Introducing strangers to little Dorothy and Toto would have produced some awkward moments.

Most school afternoons at 3:00 the front door slams, the house shakes, and I hear Eleanor shouting, "Laura! Martin! Where are you?" A moment passes and I hear feet scuffling toward the front door, followed quickly by sounds of tickling, whooping, and laughter. She's like a mother coming home from work, who has been thinking about her children all day, and the reunion is explosive. Whatever doubts we had about her reaction have proved groundless. She dotes on the twins. It had seemed likely from the moment we told her Maggie was pregnant.

We sat her down on the sofa and let her into the secret before anyone else, so it would be a complete surprise. The response was exuberant. It was better, she said, than having a new kitten.

At that time there were still long months to go, and we couldn't be certain how she'd take it when these creatures of the imagination became real. In fact, however, she has been delighted throughout. From the beginning I saw Maggie taking time out of the relentless toil two new alimentary canals bring to a household to pay some special attention to Eleanor and involve her in simple tasks for the babies. From the first days, she has helped look after them, and I watched in wonder as this elfin creature changed diapers with an assurance that makes a mockery of my pathetic fumblings. Happily too, she does not treat them like props for a dolls' house, to be dressed and paraded for the houseowner's pleasure, but as little people with their own desires and wishes.

The house no longer seems empty. Baby clothes are everywhere. Mr. Rogers, whom I had never expected to see again, is back. They have brought a savor to life nothing else could have done and, though sharing some characteristics with Nicholas, are both quite different from him and from each other.

One day too they will come to realize that, if he had not died, they would probably never have been born. I hope they will see that twist of fortune in a way that magnifies life rather than death. At present they are too young to know about their older brother, and when they do, I expect for years it will be like a fairy tale. Keeping the face in the newspapers separate from the real boy will not be easy, and we will need to be on our guard not to sanctify him. But I don't dread it. On the contrary, I look forward to recreating him for them so that, like some famous ancestor they will never meet, they will take from our memories a keener sense of how precious life is and how much it has to offer those who enter most fully into it.

CHAPTER TWENTY-ONE

THE STORY ON FILM

After the press conference at the San Francisco airport, when we first came back from Italy, the representative of a Hollywood producer introduced herself. "We'd like to make a movie of your story," she said. It might have been shocking—Nicholas still unburied and our minds filled by the thought of the rest of our lives stretching ahead without him—but it wasn't. We'd seen from the start that his story had the seeds for saving lives and what more direct way to tell it than on film?

As it happens, we didn't follow up on that approach. But in the following weeks executives of other studios, including Warner Brothers, came to see us and, flatteringly, a television actor who said he wanted to play me. I had a memory that tipped the scales—Nicholas emerging from the television room after a long session with Bugs Bunny and announcing, "I love those Warner Brothers shows." They seemed keen too, and the famous David Wolper agreed to be the executive director. In the end, that didn't materialize either. We never knew exactly why, but we were given to understand it had something to do with the story happening in a foreign country, that the death of a child was a difficult subject to deal with, that it was dated, and so on. Others apparently agreed, and months passed with only occasional eruptions of interest from filmmakers or agents.

Then one day Marc Bruno from San Francisco, who wanted to make a documentary about organ donation, introduced us to Lorenzo Minoli, an Italian living in the United States, who had produced a visually stunning series of biblical films for Turner Broadcasting—among them, *Joseph* (which won an Emmy), *Moses*, and *David*. Lorenzo had shown himself able to attract teams of a far higher caliber than is usual in television movies, and when he said, "I want to make a beautiful picture," I was sure he meant it. We took a deep breath and signed the sort of contract Hollywood has perfected that allows them to say with impunity whatever they want to about you.

Lorenzo and his team—Russ Kagan and Judd Parkin—moved quickly. They chose as director Robert Markowitz, an Emmy award-winning veteran, whose long list of titles included *Tuskegee Airmen*, a television movie about the first African-American squadron in World War II, which won a coveted Peabody award. Christine Berardo, a top writer for the *Dr. Quinn* series and, incidentally, Robert's wife, would write the script. The film would be titled *Nicholas' Gift*, and all the filming would be done in Italy. We were encouraged to learn that the top management of CBS was giving their personal support to the project, including Christine's daring idea of a Greek myth—Persephone fleeing from the king of the underworld—as its opening sequence.

But it was only when Lorenzo telephoned with the names of the leading players that we saw how far their commitment had taken them. Jamie Lee Curtis as Maggie, Alan Bates as me. "Wow," we said. It turned out that both had an involvement beyond acting. Jamie had helped raise money for a girl who needed a new heart and had then kept close to her for years through the operation, the emotional ups and downs of rejection, a second transplant, and finally her death. The hopes and fears of transplantation had clearly made a deep impression on her.

Delightfully informal, she hit it off with Maggie from the start and within a couple of hours of our first meeting insisted on changing Laura's diaper. In all our meetings since then, she has been the same warm unaffected person, taking a beaming Eleanor off to the nearest Gap store to buy clothes, or phoning and leaving terse, affectionate messages on the answering machine. Yet on the screen her performance was unwavering and, to my mind, riveting. Not Maggie exactly, but the mother, wife, companion, and moral force Maggie's generous nature embodies. At any rate, she was deservedly nominated for an

Emmy. She didn't get it, being up against some stiff competition, but I like to think that, besides her acting, the nomination was a recognition that the subject of transplants is no longer considered marginal, but squarely in the mainstream of public discourse.

Alan Bates, whose performances on the stage and in movies such as *Zorba the Greek* and *An Englishman Abroad* still gladden the heart, has had a tragedy like ours: he too lost a son, nineteen-year-old Tristan, one of twins. Every conversation we had, however it started, seemed to wind up with us talking about our children. It was clear that, although we all respond to death differently, in his thoughtful and sensitive way he was bringing to the part a deep intensity. His wife had died also, and his remaining son must feel fearfully the loss of his twin. Playing this part didn't give him much opportunity for that impish humor which has always been one of his hallmarks. But the skills were there, and it was a thrill to see the script come to life in his hands. Two delightful children, Gene Wexler and Hallie Eisenberg, played Nicholas and Eleanor.

The air date—during the "sweeps," when the networks traditionally put on their best programs to increase audience ratings, and immediately following the two highest-rated of all CBS programs, *Sixty Minutes* and *Touched by an Angel*—was to us the clinching indication that the network was treating this project, in the words of one of the producers, as a "jewel."

We gave Christine every item of information we could think of to keep the script as authentic as possible, including hours of conversation about why we did it, what we believe in, what the recipients were like, what we've learned. We provided copies of newspapers and television interviews, which recorded the exact words used at the time, articles we'd written, the videos we'd made. We took her on one of Nicholas' favorite hikes, showed her his school, put her in touch with his teacher. When the scene designers wanted to know what Nicholas' life was like, we sent them his toys, his clothes, his books. They offered to have mock-ups made from photographs, but we thought handling the real Robin Hood books that we read and his own fragment of sheepskin would give everyone an extra layer of reality. Maggie made drawings of the cemetery. Even the gold medal, which is shown in the movie, is the real thing.

Christine traveled to Italy to see the places for herself, and we gave her the names and phone numbers of everybody we could think of who met us on those first crucial days, including the police inspector who took our first statement within an hour or two of the shooting, the doctors at the Policlinico in Messina, and journalists who covered the story. All these people were shocked out of their professional detachment by the killing and were eager to tell their stories.

Now Christine and Robert and the rest of the crew had to shape that mass of information into a tale able to hold the attention of a prime-time audience without straining for effect, poignant but not sentimental, accurate but not pedantic, and where the central character is no longer there after the first few scenes. For us there were risks too: the web of relationships that make up our life would be compressed into ninety minutes of film time, divided rigidly into seven acts, demanding six cliffhangers and a conclusion, with all the dangers of simplification, invention, and overdramatization.

But I thought too of the imaginative horizons the movie would open: a tale that would show tens of millions of people, in the most vivid way, the power of a simple decision. Our hope was that viewers all over the world would find themselves thinking: donating isn't horrifying, isn't deflating, isn't disrespectful, but is quite simply the natural thing to do.

It also gave us $100,000 for the rights to the story, and for the first time in its life the Nicholas Green Foundation was well off.

A few months later, we were invited to Anzio, near Rome, to watch three days of filming. No one, us included, wanted it to be longer. We were a potential distraction in an intense schedule. As we arrived on our first morning, however, we were surprised to see a cluster of camerapeople and reporters there too, waiting outside a small hotel, where a scene was about to be filmed. We knew plans for the movie were making an impact—we'd seen the fulsome press articles—but for a country renowned for filmmakers, this put it on a higher level than anything we'd expected.

As we watched, a police car swung fast into the hotel parking lot, the press converged on it in a rush, the doors were flung open, and Alan and Jamie, holding Hallie, got out. "Cut," a loud voice said and everyone relaxed. The press were actors, doing the scene of one of our days in Messina, and we had fallen straight into filmmaking's mixture of painstaking accuracy and illusion.

For the rest of the time we were there, we were suspended in that disturbing limbo. It took many forms. Intrigued by bright sunlight peeping around the blinds of the hotel windows, I stepped outside into a black winter's night, only then seeing a battery of lights simulating daylight. We did without coffee, unwilling to ask a waiter for fear he was an extra, and when I heard actors say the exact words we'd used ourselves in some of the most important moments of our lives, they seemed as disconnected from us as quotations learned from a book.

One day we went to see Mr. Rutelli, the mayor of Rome, at his splendid office at the Campidoglio, where one of the scenes was being filmed. He looked much the same as I remembered him on that day more than three years before when everything we saw had a crystal clarity. He apparently thought of it in the same way, remarking how "*civis Romanus sum*" had fitted Nicholas so well. "We will always think of you two as Romans also," he added. As he talked I could see behind him two enormous centurions from the Rome of 2,000 years ago preparing for the upcoming scene.

There was one gap even a willing imagination couldn't leap, however. Soon after we arrived, Gene was pointed out to us on the beach. I watched him for a minute or two, comparing this flesh-and-blood boy with a memory of another boy almost as clear in my mind. Looking up, he half ran, a bright eager face that looked straight at you. Almost his first words were, "Am I like Nicholas?" "Yes, he is like Nicholas," I thought, the same slim build, the same love of life, the same frank and open countenance. They could have been best friends, perhaps. I didn't think of him as Nicholas, however, even for a moment.

Even those who have spent their lives in show business apparently felt the same uncomfortable intersection of reality and make-believe. "When we did the cemetery scene yesterday," Alan Bates told us, "those tears were real," and, as anyone could see, Jamie often found it excruciating to go on. She was also laboring with a problem unusual in her acting career. "I hope I don't let you down," she said to Maggie more than once. It was a touching thought coming from such a professional, another revelation that she wasn't just playing a role, but making her way sensitively through a real life. The unreality persisted. Months later at the preview in Rome, I recognized a distinguished face among some of Italy's most prominent transplant surgeons. As I was on the point of asking him which hospital I'd met him in, I remembered he was the actor who played the chief neurologist.

So many people in Italy wanted to work on this film, we were told, that only the best qualified of their kind, from camerapeople and scene setters to the composer of the musical score, were picked. One, who had worked with Fellini, was dealing with a formidable variety of production problems, but his most visible job (if that's the word I want) was to shout for silence at the beginning of every take, and he did it with such fearful authority that for weeks afterward I could even get Eleanor to pay attention by a single word, *"Silenzio."*

Isabella Ferrari, whom no less an authority than Jamie Lee Curtis called "unfairly beautiful," and who played Alessandra, the doctor who befriended Eleanor, is a star in Italy. Here she was in a part so small that her agent had advised her not to take it, but which she wanted badly enough to have gone to see the real Alessandra so as to portray her as true to life as possible, and all for a role that lasted perhaps two minutes. Despite all this experience, some of the crew on the set said things like, "Did you see the man on the lights? There were tears in his eyes during that last scene." Then a pause. "Mine too."

Even minute differences in detail in scenes that stayed true to most of the essential aspects of the story added another element of fiction. No, the clothes Maggie wore in that car ride weren't like that—much too well looked after—and the meeting with the heart recipient didn't happen that way. When, at one point in the movie, Jamie says "Oh, come on, Reg," it was a shock. Nowadays no one in movies is called Reg. "She's talking about me," I thought with surprise.

And so, watching the most searing parts of the movie, both Maggie and I have wept, but only as we would at any sad story. By contrast, I suppose I've watched our own video, *The Nicholas Effect*, a hundred times or more at meetings where I'm the speaker, and its pictures of the real Nicholas, doing things I remember him doing, often bring on a bleakness I have to fight when I stand up to go to the podium.

The audience reaction, however, confirms the power of those scenes in *Nicholas' Gift*, a tribute to the way all the elements—controlled direction, sensitive writing, imaginative casting, and good lighting—had come together. Both friends and strangers have told us they couldn't bear to sit through the movie at one sitting. The sounds and sights too were often disturbingly real. When the camera first focused on the gravestone, it seemed so exact that, for a moment, I thought they must have sent a crew to Bodega, until I saw the face on it was not Nicholas' but Gene's.

They did something else that pleased me greatly. In the original screenplay, the bagpiper at the burial played "Amazing Grace," as Maggie's stepfather did that day. But "The Minstrel Boy" still haunted my memory, and I asked if they could include that instead. There was some technical problem and, like other details, it was only when we watched the preview in Rome that I saw they had made the change. That night I told the musical director how glad I was, and he said, "Yes, Mr. Markowitz was very insistent that I should include it." It's just a snatch of the tune and perhaps only I—and Robert—in the whole world care about it. But each time I see the movie, I sense Nicholas mustering in the ranks of history.

The movie played to large audiences everywhere—an estimated thirty million or more in the United States, five million in Italy out of a total population of fifty-seven million, four million in Germany. It has been translated into Spanish and Portuguese for Latin American audiences, French, and Japanese. In time, the producers expect it to be seen in more than fifty countries. Al and Tipper Gore were impressed enough to make a public service announcement for organ donation to go along with the screening.

Following the showing, organ procurement groups around the United States and overseas reported a sharp increase in requests for information. Among many others, LifeGift in Fort Worth said it had an "amazing" number of calls from people wanting donor cards and asking for speakers for their organizations, Tennessee Donor Services in Knoxville spoke of an "astounding effect" on awareness, and SAT1, the German network, said the showing there brought "tens of thousands" of phone calls. Months later, donor networks were still receiving phone calls, web site hits, and letters mentioning the film.

There was one other thing we wanted to show, the joy and sorrow inseparable from being a parent—and, in the end, of all the messages, that, I feel, was the one that touched most hearts.

CHAPTER TWENTY-TWO

TRIAL FOR MURDER

"Will you hire a lawyer to represent you?" The first time a journalist asked this, we realized how little we knew about the rules governing the upcoming trial of the two men accused of killing Nicholas. He told us we had the right to have one if we wished. Suddenly everyone was asking, and we had no idea what the answer should be. A lawyer from Calabria sent a message that he would act without charging a fee. I consulted the obvious people. But, although everyone wanted to be helpful, these conversations contained so much of on the one hand this, and on the other hand that, only an octopus could have weighed them. The advice can be summed up as follows: the state will prosecute, but you have the right to appoint your own attorney, although you are not obliged to do so. We'd known that from the first phone call.

We inferred that you appointed a lawyer if you wanted to ask for damages or beef up a prosecutor you had doubts about. To this day, I'm not sure about any of this, but neither of us liked the sound of it. I'd mentioned our ignorance to a number of people, and some time before the trial began we received a letter from one of them, an interpreter whose father was a lawyer. His opinion was given in one sentence. "If I felt deeply that they have to get the punishment the worst as possible, I would stay in the trial giving strength to the prosecutor; if I, on the contrary, would leave only the court deciding, I wouldn't enter the trial." It seemed the most we'd get, and without further discussion we decided against it.

It was a decision that caused some consternation in the Italian press, some of whom asked, "Are you serious about prosecuting these people?" For a while we wondered if we'd misunderstood the whole thing, and who knows what difference it would have made? But we weren't after damages, of course. What amount of money can make up a lost life? We didn't want the harshest punishment, but only what was customary. We did have confidence in the prosecutor's ability, and we didn't want an attorney having to justify his part in the proceedings by pandering to emotion. Patiently going through all this with the reporters who covered the trial, we eventually made the point we wanted to make: the trial was about justice, not revenge, and in the end I think that was generally accepted.

I'm pleased that it was. Anyone who applauded the concept of vengeance before the trial began must have had his beliefs severely strained. The trial revealed an underworld where double-crossing and betrayal, suspicion and fear, cruelty and deception were the rule. Friends played on each other's trust and turned on each other without regrets. In the peculiar intimacy of prison, cellmates manipulated each other to worm out secrets they could reveal in return for leniency for themselves. Lovers turned out to be informers. And when they were finally caught, killers, who had so little regard for other people's lives that they got rid of them as part of the day's work, ratted on whomever they could to save their own skins. It was a miserable life that greed and vendetta had created. Can anyone believe vengeance is a serious alternative to the conventional legal process?

This threadbare world contrasted vividly with the seriousness of the proceedings. I can't remember what I expected an Italian court to be like—rowdy probably, like the British House of Commons at question time, free-flowing certainly, plenty of latitude to all concerned and a great deal of emotion. There was scarcely any of that.

The prosecutor's office, headed by Alfredo Laudonio, was admirably correct. They took our depositions without a hint of the answers they wanted. There was no prompting, no indiscretions to point the way. "A light-colored car, probably white, you said on the night of the incident. Are you sure? You said you heard more than one shot. Can you be certain? What did the gun look like? What speed were you doing?" They asked each question as though it was equally important, and only much later, during the trial, did it become clear which were the critical ones.

One morning in February 1996, we got a telephone call from Italy telling us the trial was going to start soon. "How soon?" "In two weeks," came the reply. It was an absurdly short time to get ready—somehow an earlier message had gone astray—but it was clear we had to go. On our side, we had always kept at arm's length from the investigators, not wanting them to feel under pressure either to make an arrest or to move quickly to prosecute. We hadn't asked for details of the people they'd arrested, what evidence they'd found, or what their strategy in court was going to be. All these things would be revealed in time. The more deliberately they worked, without us peering over their shoulders, the more likely the right people would be caught and convicted. We'd always had an impression that the prosecution had done its job effectively. Now we would find out.

The courtroom was in the provincial capital of Catanzaro, in the big, forbidding-looking justice building, stern but fraying. Witnesses waited, and we waited for two days, in a chilling bare room as legal points were argued out. We were rigorously screened from the proceedings so as not to benefit from anyone else's testimony. For most of the two days we huddled in our coats, Maggie almost six months pregnant and Eleanor, six years old, all of us just waiting for time to pass. The police escort who were with us at all times did what they could, buying coffee and cakes and refusing all payment, and letting Eleanor win at tic-tac-toe. We read, talked in a desultory manner, walked into the cold corridor and back, and closed our minds to speculation.

When at last I was called, I went into a huge room, with an ornate ceiling and tiled floor, bare of floor or wall coverings, a place of little comfort for either the guilty or the innocent. At the head of the room the jury sat, men and women ranging in age, probably, from the late thirties to the sixties. They looked like dependable, solid citizens, most of them parents, I'd guess, and on the days I attended I never saw their attention wander. They seemed to follow every word, their eyes fixed on the attorney or witness who was speaking. They didn't talk or fidget or look about, even with sessions in that cold room lasting up to four hours. There were two other jury members, both professional magistrates, and I gathered they would have a considerable influence on the outcome. They made notes carefully. It was workmanlike and serious.

Along one side of the courtroom was a cage, and in it was a young man. The bars were half an inch thick. It was about thirty feet long and twelve feet high. This was Francesco Mesiano's place in court, but why exactly he was there I was never able to find out. I looked around for the other defendant, but for a long time couldn't see him. Only when I took the stand did I find myself staring into the face of the man who had admitted to killing four people, but denied killing Nicholas. He was sitting, but standing in a semicircle around him were half a dozen *carabinieri*, the special police force, screening him from, again, who knows what? This was twenty-nine-year-old Michele Iannello, said to be a small-time Mafia operator, who was "cooperating" with the police, providing information on other criminals and unsolved cases.

I liked the public prosecutor, Maurizio Salustro, from the start: an unassuming, honest, thoughtful man who, even when examining us in the privacy of his office, carried a sense of genuinely wanting to get at the truth rather than obtaining a conviction. In court he frequently wore sneakers. He carried the entire burden of the prosecution alone. The defense attorneys were a whole team, six or seven of them, expensively suited, well-groomed, and, when not cross-examining, affable. A couple of them were well-known throughout Italy.

Twenty-three-year-old Ignazio Carbone had been assigned as our interpreter for the trial. He was straight from university—he'd been at this job, his first, just one day when we arrived—but with the prosecution and defense ready to pounce on any error in translation, he was steady under fire. We got on well and sometimes, as we ate dinner together or chatted easily about our lives, it was hard to imagine that what had brought us together was the murder of my son.

When the clerk read out the charge, I heard my own name with surprise. In the focus we'd all put on Nicholas' death I'd almost forgotten the shot to the driver's window. The bullet that narrowly missed me, and then Maggie, was plainly murderous, indifferent at those speeds to the lives of any of us in the car. The name of the victim came as a surprise too: Nicholas William Green. It sounded too big for the small boy trustingly asleep with his sheepskin on the back seat of the car.

The prosecutor took me through the various statements we had made to the police. As I heard them, I was pleased to have confirmed what I'd always thought, that Maggie and I were both controlled and observant enough that first night to have told a story that remained the same through all the retelling.

Although it had been talked about in the press since the earliest days after the arrest, the prosecution's explanation for the baffling attack on a private car now emerged officially: their evidence indicated that the thieves had received information that a small car carrying jewels would be making a delivery to southern Italy. Our rental car, with its Rome license plates, happened to fit the description, and I wondered again how the rest of us can defend ourselves against blunders of that magnitude, made by people who act with such violent disregard for the results that no recompense anyone can make afterward can repair the damage they do. The cross-examination was rough, four defense attorneys, jumping up and down on my simple story, looking for a contradiction here, an uncertainty there. Except perhaps in a detail or two, it remained intact, however, as the truth does, and as far as I know was never seriously questioned by the defense thereafter.

Maggie, who had spent all this time in the witness room, was on next. I went quickly to Eleanor, asked her to wait just a bit longer, and went back in the courtroom. Maggie was already on the stand in the black dress she'd bought to conceal, rather than show off, her pregnancy. In simple sentences, strong but unemotional, intelligently understood and expressed, she described what she saw of the attackers' car, the masks they were wearing, and, to the evident surprise of some of the men in court, the difference between a pistol and a revolver. It was an account with no discernible difference from what she said in the police station in Polistena, as Nicholas in a coma was being carried away from us by ambulance through the night. She had shown then the moral strength that comes naturally to her, and she was doing it now. I don't think I've ever felt so proud of anyone. Against this obvious clarity and honesty, the defense had little to say and after a few perfunctory questions let her stand down. Every minute she was up there was doing their clients a lot of harm.

We went back to where Eleanor had been waiting with a group of men, strangers who spoke scarcely any English, and knowing we were going through some kind of ordeal in the adjoining room. There she was, letting time pass with a mature self-control that made my heart ache. "They seemed to give you a much harder time than me," Maggie said later. "Yes," I said. "I was wishing I was pregnant." We caught the plane home the next day in the early morning light, and our police escort fought back tears. I think our family always looked incomplete in those days, not able to pair off as we used to do, too heavily weighted on one side or the other, and they seemed to sense it.

For months afterward, the trial moved along a couple of days at a time, then a break for a week or so, and a long summer vacation. Dozens of witnesses were called by both sides, including a professor from Wales, described as a world authority on the Calabrian dialect, who gave evidence on the sensational wiretaps that were presented in court. All this time we stayed away from Italy. We told the organ donation groups there we didn't want to come back to hold public meetings or give interviews that might include questions about the trial while it was still on. We wanted to avoid any suggestion that we were trying to influence the jury's views. In retrospect, it was probably unnecessary: the court was very professional. Still, it was best to leave no doubt.

Most weeks passed without our hearing anything at all. Then one day the phone rang, and an Italian journalist wanted to know what we thought about Iannello being released. Released, are you sure? That's what it says in this story from Italy, he said. I asked him to fax the copy, and things became a little clearer. It wasn't release, but some form of police custody. As the day went on, a steady stream of calls came in from both American and Italian papers, and we were able to piece the facts together. Iannello had been declared a *pentito*—a repenter—by a special court. This meant he would be released from his present confinement and given twenty-four-hour-a-day police protection in return for providing evidence about other crimes. He would continue to stand trial for Nicholas' murder, however, and if convicted face a jail sentence.

The whole *pentito* program is highly controversial in Italy—what isn't?—and answering the insistent questions about whether this was good or bad was almost impossible. A version of no comment would have been sufficient, but I've always thought of that as a cop-out. In the end, our answer went like this: everyone must have mixed feelings about a system in which hardened criminals worm their way out of the consequences of their actions. But if the information these people give genuinely weakens the criminal element, it makes everyone a little safer. Clearly it depends on each individual case—how useful the information is, how genuine the cooperation, how serious the crimes. Only the courts know such things, and we were content to leave it to them. As a comment, it wasn't very illuminating, but it did reflect our views. We have no idea how important the evidence was that Iannello was said to be providing about bigger crime figures than himself. Mesiano, by contrast, was released from confinement pending the verdict.

I returned in January for the closing days of the trial to hear the summing up by both sides and to wait for the verdict. The courtroom was as cold as it had been eleven months earlier, the jury, the defense attorneys, the aged clerk of the court all the same. The defendants, however, had changed. Iannello I mistook at first for one of his legal team. He and Mesiano, who was no longer in his cage, were clean-shaven, smartly dressed, and well scrubbed. This time they looked like a couple of clean-living young men with whom you might have discussed the football scores if you met them casually.

But as I looked at Iannello and reflected that here was a man who admits to four murders, it seemed even more reprehensible that he should appear to be so normal. It gave deceit an extra dimension. Mesiano was now living at home and looked better on his mother's cooking, though still pop-eyed and full of nervous energy, as was natural in a young man facing a possible twenty-three-year sentence.

Dr. Salustro summed up the case: among other points, that Iannello owned a car like the one that attacked us; the car was usually dirty, but a few days after the crime had disappeared and came back cleaned and scrubbed; traces of gunpowder were found by the front passenger window; the pistol used was of a rare type, and a witness said Iannello owned one; and the wiretaps had a series of incriminating statements, including one allegedly by Iannello that appeared to say, "The fact is I killed him." The summing up took four hours and was done without a hint of an appeal to emotion.

The defense had its own version of each of these points: the car was never positively identified; cleaning a car isn't a crime; the gunpowder could have been deposited there at another time; the pistol, which disappeared, wasn't positively identified either; and the wiretaps in thick Calabrese voices, including the comment about killing, could be interpreted in quite different ways.

The jury was out for five hours while we sat and made conversation. I didn't hear anyone in our group speculating on the outcome. When the prosecutor's cellular phone beeped to say they were coming back, we were at lunch and I was answering a series of his questions about the American political scene. When we went back, the courtroom was fuller than it had been all week. The attorneys, the defendants, friends, and relatives were there, as before, but now instead of three reporters, there were twenty or more. The bell rang calling the court into session and for the last time in this trial we all stood. We remained standing while a brief statement was read: both defendants were acquitted. One of Mesiano's female lawyers put her arm around his waist and squeezed joyfully. I saw no other demonstration of emotion—no cheering, no shouts, no fists pumping the air.

As the jury left, a tidal wave of reporters pressed in on me. What's your state of mind? What do you think of Italian justice? What will you tell your wife? I answered as best as I could, in essence, that the trial was fair, but did not answer conclusively whether these two had done it or not. As I took to saying in innumerable interviews, courts are required to be fair, but they are not omniscient. Our opinion about guilt or innocence was of little value, I pointed out. Victims are not good judges. That's why we have courts. I added that Maggie and I had always regarded the killers as bit players in a drama much bigger than themselves. From the start I had wanted those who did it brought to justice. I believe people should be accountable for their actions and in a terrible crime should incur severe punishment. But, compared with the way Nicholas' death brought people all over the world closer, and the thousands of lives it had saved, the trial was to us a secondary issue. As for closure, I'm not sure I'll ever have it, but I am sure that Iannello and Mesiano serving twenty-three years in prison wouldn't produce it.

The reporters moved on, and I found Mesiano's father standing next to me. Tears were reddening his eyes, and his hand was extended. I shook it, of course. Almost immediately Mesiano himself came up and held out his hand. He said he was sorry for what happened, but he didn't do it. I thanked him for his words about Nicholas, but made no comment on his denial. Still, he had gone through a long ordeal, the court had just found insufficient evidence to convict, and, still in his early twenties, he is young enough to have the chance of making a new start in life. In the circumstances, I couldn't rebuff him, and I shook his hand too. But then his mother was at the father's side, a tiny woman in black, tears streaming down her face. "I've suffered so much," she said. My heart went out to her, and I put my arms around her. It was all over in a moment, but editors around the world saw it as a symbol of the pain that parents everywhere share.

Back at the hotel, the rows of pigeonholes behind the reception desk were empty, as usual. Except one—room 416's was overflowing. I flipped through them in the elevator. Urgent. Very Important. Second time we've called. Among others, CNN in Atlanta, NBC in London, CBS in New York, the *San Francisco Examiner*. In two hours, the news had gone round the world and back again.

The telephone was ringing as I turned the key in the door. It was a reporter in London. "Can it wait? I asked. "I've just come in, and there's a stack of messages already here." "We'd better do it now. We might never get you again," he said. That seemed to sum it up, and I did the first interview. As I put the phone down to look up the number where Maggie was staying, it rang again and I did interview number two. As soon as it ended, I found her number and called. Busy. I started to look through the messages to see which were the most urgent, Italy first because their deadlines were closer, then New York, then the West Coast. Before I could start the sequence, the phone rang again. It was an American network. "We'd like to interview you in half an hour." "You might not get through," I told them. "I'll call you in a few minutes." This time I put down and picked up the phone in one motion, and called one marked, "Very Urgent" and "Call Collect."

And so the night wore on, put down, pick up, how did I feel, were we bitter, what about Italian justice? After every two or three calls, I phoned Maggie. Each time, it was busy. Every few minutes one of the desk clerks, unable to phone the room, would knock on the door and deliver a new batch of phone numbers. Ignazio, the interpreter, sat on the edge of the bed, translating the Italian messages.

One call was from Stephen Weeke, of NBC in Rome. We'd talked a few days earlier, and he'd planned to come to Catanzaro for the verdict. That had fallen through when he'd been put on the Arab-Israeli peace talks, and I'd agreed instead that whenever the verdict came I'd to go to Rome for an evening show on the fledgling cable program. Now he wanted to change the plan.

"Can you come to Rome tomorrow morning to do the *Today Show?*" he asked. I reminded him that only a few hours before I'd changed my ticket to be there in the evening. "I know, Reg. But this is Katie Couric, zillions of people," he replied. "And Reg, we'll have a car waiting for you at the airport, a Mercedes, with NBC's best driver." "All right, I'll do it." "Gee, that's great, Reg. Now, one other thing. Can you do the nightly news? It's around midnight your time." "Midnight when?" "Tonight, of course." "You're kidding." "No, I'm not, it's Brokaw, Reg. It goes to zillions of people. I know it's a lot to ask, but we'll book a hotel for you in Rome tomorrow morning so you can rest up before doing *Today*."

"Are you getting a local crew down here for tonight's program?" I asked. "No, that's another thing. We can't get one there. I'll have to ask you to go to the studio." "Where's that?" "Catanzaro." For a moment I thought it was a joke. "Catanzaro? I've just come back from there. That's where the trial was. It's almost an hour each way." "Yes, it's too bad but"—I knew what was coming—"it's Brokaw, Reg. You know how many people watch him? I'll arrange a taxi and everything. Just be ready at ten."

My next call was to ABC, which had left two messages, saying, "We want you for an interview. Urgent." When I got through, however, and told them about the *Today Show*, they said sorry, that was too much of a conflict. I put in a quick call to Maggie's number. Still busy. Then to *Inside Edition* in Los Angeles, whose message read "Very Urgent." I'd been impressed before by their speed and now they didn't waste time either. They did the interview by phone there and then, early enough to be on the air that evening.

As soon as that interview ended, Steve Weeke was back on the line. "Everything's arranged. We've got a taxi that will come to the hotel, take you to the studio, wait while you do the interview, and bring you back." I couldn't complain: he'd done well, I thought, finding a local taxi service and tying up the details from Rome. "Where are you calling from?" I asked him. I expected him to say "the office" or "home." "Tel Aviv," he said.

Instead of the tempo slowing, this new timetable quickened it. One question that cropped up frequently was, "What did you tell your wife?" "I haven't been able to get through to her," I'd answer. Then suddenly the problem cleared. A West Coast television interviewer said casually, "By the way, one of my colleagues is interviewing your wife." "Now?" "As we speak." It was quickly arranged. On a signal, both interviews ended simultaneously, I dialed California, and there she was. And so was the explanation for the busy signals. "When Lois went into the office this morning there were seventeen messages on the answering machine, all media. I've been working my way through the ones we can decipher," she said. So, while I'd been doing my "Very Urgents," she'd been doing hers, from Vatican Radio to all three television networks and a range of radio stations.

As these reporters had supplied her with all the details of the trial, I had scarcely anything to tell her. We talked instead about what they'd been doing in the last few days, including Eleanor's high spot, the visit to Disneyland. It was typical family talk, but for a few minutes I was back in the safe harbor that gives meaning to the long and lonely journeys we make away from home. Before I hung up, I said it was a pity I couldn't do ABC. "It's okay," she replied, "They called me instead." And at 3:00 a.m. next morning they picked her and the twins up and took them to the studio in Los Angeles.

At 10:00 p.m., accompanied by the ever-faithful Ignazio, I drove back to Catanzaro on the road we'd taken a few hours earlier from the court. For once, the location of the studio matched the directions, and we entered a cavernous hall like a basketball stadium. I sat on the single hard chair, staring at the camera, unable to tell if Tom Brokaw or anyone else was behind it. The technician in charge pelted up and down the stairs between the playing field and the upper tiers, shouting orders to his two or three helpers. Evidently something was coming unstuck, and there was no time to put it right. With just seconds to go, he hurtled down the last flight of stairs, three at a time, signaling desperately that it was a go and bellowing for quiet. But then for a few minutes the satellites smiled down on us, and Fort Lee, New Jersey; Burbank, California; Catanzaro; and Tel Aviv were in alignment by a technological miracle I could only guess at.

When we arrived back at the hotel, a few more messages had arrived and, amazingly, there was still time to reach the West Coast and a couple of more interviews. I lay in bed for a few moments before falling asleep and pondered what had been done. All that activity. Had it accomplished anything? You can't be sure, of course, and you have only experience to go on. But my sense was that having watched us going through an ordeal in the most public way, those who were interested in the story would want to know how we felt at one of the key turning points. If it provided some pieces of information to help them make up their minds on what society should do about crimes that have such calamitous results, I thought it was worthwhile.

Ignazio arrived at five in the morning, and in a police car we drove yet again over most of last night's route, this time to the airport. As I walked out to board the plane, a calm dawn was just coming up over the valley, but the villages in the folds of the hills were still in darkness, lights twinkling like necklaces around the foot of every peak. To the right, along the Mediterranean coast, I could see where the road stretched south to the scene of the worst moments of my life. The books call this a beautiful, tragic land. For us, another chapter in its story was just closing.

Alfredo, "NBC's best driver," was at the airport in Rome as promised and we sped into the city. All that day the phone calls continued, and just about all the American ones included the same question, "What do Italians think of the verdict?" The only Italian unconnected with the trial I'd spoken to was Alfredo, however, and he had considerately avoided mentioning it at all. We had talked instead about how he had started to speak English. "From my father's Frank Sinatra records," he said. "I love that man, Mr. Green, I love him." So I told him a story about Nicholas who, when he was six, came into the room while I was watching a rerun of one of Sinatra's concerts. "You know I'm really a saloon singer," Frank was saying. "What's a saloon, Daddy?" Nicholas asked. Well, I told him, it's a place that sells food and drink. "Remember when you went to the Statue of Liberty and we had breakfast at McDonald's? That was Hoboken, right where Frank

Sinatra was born. He probably sang there when he was just starting." Nicholas said nothing, but smiled his happy smile and wandered off. I like to think that to his dying day somewhere in that innocent little head he had a vision of a bow-tied Frank moving among the Big Macs singing "High Hopes."

When I finished the tale, Alfredo was silent for a while. Then he said, "Mr. Green, when Mr. Sinatra came to Rome some years ago and did some work with NBC, I had the great privilege of meeting him. Now I have the great privilege of meeting Nicholas' father." He looked away quickly, but not before I saw the tears. So when interviewers in America wanted to know, "What do Italians think about the trial?" I could only say, "I just don't know." I was able to add, however, "But I do know they still mourn the loss of Nicholas as though he were one of their own."

That wasn't the end of the legal procedures, however. As soon as the trial ended the prosecution said it would appeal, as under Italian law it is permitted to do, and a fresh stage began under a new prosecutor, Salvatore Murone. More than a year went by, then early one morning the telephone rang. "The appeals court has found the two men accused of killing your son guilty," a voice said. Iannello had been sentenced to life imprisonment and Mesiano to twenty years. I sat propped up in bed trying to absorb the news. "Do you know why?" I asked. There seemed to be no special reason, simply that a new jury had reviewed the evidence—the car, the gun, the wiretaps, and the rest—and concluded that, after all, it went beyond a reasonable doubt.

Neither of us felt any elation nor that sense of closure I've heard about, but never really understood. Two young men's lives were ruined and their families thrown into despair. It just reawakened the futility of the whole episode. Nor was it really an end. They still had the right to appeal to the Italian supreme court and, as of this writing, that appeal is pending.

A few weeks later, we received an emotional handwritten letter from Mesiano, protesting his innocence and saying he had been singled out because "the appeals court wanted to find someone to blame at all costs." The letter took a long time to reach us and, when I started to reply, I telephoned a contact in Italy to find a fax number to save time. "I want to send it privately, however," I said. "The letter that came to us was personal." "But we know about that letter," I was told. "It was published in the newspaper, the *Gazzetta del Sud.*" Despite its apparent privacy, Mesiano's letter had become a public document. "There's something else you should know," my contact added. "At the appeals hearing, one of their attorneys said that, when you shook hands with him, it showed you thought he wasn't guilty."

On the spot I made a decision. I faxed a letter to Mesiano, so it would reach him first, but I sent it to *Gazzetta del Sud* a few days later also and I included a few words about what I'd just learned. It read as follows, "Although you wrote your letter early in June, Maggie and I received it only at the end of last week. We are sending this reply by fax so you will have it as soon as possible. The incident on the Salerno-Reggio autostrada has brought grief to many people. We think we understand how your family feels. The legal process must go on, however. It's the only way any of us can hope for justice.

"I've been told that one of your attorneys said that, when I comforted your mother at the end of the first trial and shook your hand, it showed I believed you and Mr. Iannello were not guilty. That is not the case: they were simply gestures of common humanity. I did not express any opinion about your guilt or innocence. These are matters for the courts to decide by weighing the evidence objectively, not by the emotions of either the victims or the accused. On your side, you have a team of highly skilled attorneys. I'm sure they will give you all the help they possibly can."

I felt its inadequacy then as I still do. One day, perhaps, we will learn what happened that night, and I will see more clearly what I should have said. But, for now, it's the best I can do.

Chapter Twenty-Three

Life Without Nicholas

An Italian journalist, filming an interview in St. Peter's Square, suddenly said, "Tell me—and I want the truth now—don't you feel any anger?" It would have taken a brazen man to look a million Italians, and the founder of the Catholic Church himself, in the eye and lie. And when I said "no" I meant it. Why? I don't know the real answer, of course. These things lie too deep. But I think that, at one level, the loss of Nicholas has filled my mind—and I believe Maggie's too—with so much hurt as to relegate all other emotions to the sidelines. The finality is so absolute. Never again to run my fingers through his hair or tickle him or hear him say, "Good night, Daddy."

I read once that Einstein said that after he evolved his theory of relativity it never left him, not for a minute. "That's it," I thought. "It colors everything." I haven't had a single moment of exultation since Nicholas died, although previously I had them frequently enough to regard them as a natural ingredient of life. No joy is pure any more. Monday mornings are a little gloomier, Friday evenings less liberating.

Remembering has always been a great satisfaction to me. I can conjure up scenes ten, twenty years ago, calling up almost the exact words and feeling the mood vividly enough to experience it all again. These are treacherous trails now. My thoughts, whatever the setting, seem to find their way back to him. Even when there is no logical progression from one subject to another, the way through the maze goes there. He's always seven and I want to hug him, feel him in my lap for a book at bedtime.

I no longer have the bounce a good piece of news used to bring: a job that turns out well, perhaps, or the car coming back from servicing without needing new brakes. Now I think, "Well, this is okay, it's much better than it might have been." But it's a tepid version of the charge I used to get. The house is often busy and noisy again, but at every meal I always know there is an empty place at the table. Sadness comes in waves, sometimes strong enough to make me feel physically sick. While doing some everyday job, a picture will suddenly come into my mind and I'll say his name out loud. For a few moments, life is as empty as I imagine it gets. It passes, and I pick up where I left off.

All my life I've been able to anticipate the end of an unhappy period, warming myself on the feeling of what it would be like when everything came right again. Meantime, I'd find solace in a book or going for a walk and often discover that, even at its worst, the problem wasn't as bad as I'd expected. Even just allowing time to pass was a cure, since nothing lasts forever. But this time it does last forever, or at least for a lifetime, with no way of repairing the damage or even finding a second-best solution, no cure except forgetting—and what kind of cure is that?

Instead, I want to remember everything. Photographs generally help, bringing back whole periods in one image, like the hike on Point Reyes when we found the deer's antlers or splashing in the bathtub with Eleanor. I can think of only one where he looks unhappy: the day I took him out on a boat to see the whales. He is resting a pale, seasick face in his hand, puzzled by a world that can cause such pain.

Time will dull the pain of separation, I expect, but what won't go away, and what seems to me the worst part of this whole story, is that Nicholas has been denied forever the chance to live out his potential. I think of all those books he'll miss, all those sunsets, all those friendships. I remember my childhood or someone I met who said something funny, and the surge of pleasure comes with a trailing cloud of sadness, knowing he won't know any of those things. Some people, wanting to ease the pain of young death, say a work of art can be beautiful and complete even though it is quite short. I see that and rejoice in Nicholas' triumph as a human being. It's difficult for me to believe, however, that a prelude has the same weight as a concerto. Life goes on, it's true. But not for him.

C. S. Lewis' description of the death of his wife goes to the heart of it for me. "I look up in the night sky. Is anything more certain than that in all those vast times and spaces, if I were allowed to search them, I should nowhere find her face, her voice, her touch?" Whatever eternity has in store, I know I will never again hold Nicholas' hand as we set off on a hike.

I recently visited Rob Kiener, who wrote the poignant article for *Reader's Digest*, at his house high in the mountains of Vermont. It was the sort of occasion I used to immerse myself in, enjoying it at every layer, the views, the companionship, swapping journalists' stories. But now I remembered those witty and perceptive friends of my parents, not unlike Rob Kiener, who had fired my imagination when I was growing up. What a depressing deprivation that Nicholas cannot meet people like that who would have confirmed to him that the magic in life is not just for little boys. Nor do we have the prospect of smiling in later years at fears that didn't materialize, the trees he didn't fall out of, or the sicknesses he recovered from. Now the fears are only a pale imitation of the reality.

We all joke about death from time to time, rightly, since it will have the last laugh. But I can't be wry about Nicholas' death. It's a deep, wrenching, daily pain that won't allow verbal conjuring tricks or self-deception. It isn't ironic or wistful or soothing. It isn't like a book or a movie you get caught up in. In the middle of some task, I still catch myself being surprised that his death isn't just a tale. I don't see Nicholas in a star or in the waving grass or among the heavenly host. To me, he has gone. The memory of him can provoke smiles, though rarely laughter, and we are a family that continues to find a good deal of fun in life. But death itself has no comfort in it.

The mind reaches for whatever consolation it can find, of course. One afternoon I suddenly thought, "This is the time Nicholas would be coming home from school." A sadness came over me as I began to relive those days. Then I remembered this was a school holiday and he wouldn't be coming home at this time anyway. Irrationally, I felt a surge of relief.

The year before he died, we'd been sad together thinking about the boy who outgrew his friend Puff, the Magic Dragon. Nicholas knew about aging and death, and I fancy he foresaw the day when I'd no longer be there. In his understanding way, I sensed he was trying to comfort me. Now the words have a cruel irony, "Dragons live forever, but not so little boys." I looked recently into a box that was going to Goodwill and saw with a shock it had some of Nicholas' best clothes in it—a shirt he used to wear with his blue blazer and the warm sweater that made him look so grown up. "Are we really letting these things go?" I thought. Then I reflected we'd given away his heart. But I still haven't been able to bring myself to part with his hiking boots. I can't find his blue striped shirt, which he liked to put on when I wore one like it: it looked so pitifully small when I saw it after he died. I still have mine, however, fraying at the cuffs and collar, but too full of memories to be thrown away yet.

Nostalgia comes in all forms. Eleanor and Nicholas shared tricks of speech: *hambugger, quastion, intersting*. In the car on the day he was shot, Nicholas asked as he often did, "If we be good can we have an ice cream?" They got their ice cream and the phrase outlived him. When Eleanor, in another room, said something like it the other day, I thought for a moment I heard his voice. A reference to 1987, when he was born, brings a warm feeling, 1994 a chill, even if it's about something as distant as an article on economics. Our dividing line is 1994. "That was before Nicholas died," we say of something that has no other connection with him. When I came across a mutual fund that was started on his birthday, the date in small print leaped out of the page. Eleanor still says wistfully from time to time, "Wouldn't Nicholas have enjoyed this?" or "Do you remember when Nicholas did that?"

Entries in the office calendar mark the Great Divide in our lives. Before September 1994 are the appointments of a busy working life, reminders to make phone calls, interviews scheduled with portfolio managers, and overnight airline reservations. There are weekend family trips and, as we approach the date of our Italian vacation, I feel a tremor, as I see the phone entries marking calls I made to airlines, car rental agencies, and railroads, trying persistently to make it possible for us to drive from Rome to Palermo instead of flying. A few days are blank, our time in Switzerland, then back home after the shooting to a blizzard of events: media interviews, funeral arrangements, articles to write. Had I been asked then, I would have said that following this initial flurry, interest would have died away, reviving now and again with developments in the trial or on anniversaries. But, no, they go on and on.

When the number of people who came into our lives because of Nicholas suddenly exploded, I decided to group them under the letter "N" in my filing system. From simple beginnings, it has expanded beyond all expectations, demanding more and more subdivision: N media, N media overseas, N media overseas U.K., N media overseas U.K. newspapers. It has worked tolerably well, but at a price: instead of looking up a doctor in Italy or a donor group in Illinois, I have to start with N and another reminder, just a split second, but enough to inject a little ice into the veins. Just now, as I typed this, I noticed for the first time that the "N" on the keyboard is almost rubbed away.

Looking ahead is ambivalent too as thoughts of Eleanor learning music or thinking about a career, those fancies that warm the cockles of a parent's heart, rarely come without a sense of loss. At first I thought I might need some things to remember him by more clearly— like the flag on his toy fort which I put at half staff—but they aren't necessary. Memories come unbidden every day. When I lock the door at night, I often have the feeling that not everyone is home safe and sound.

I'd looked forward to reading *Three Men in a Boat* to him—so much that by mistake I'd bought two copies—and the stacks and stacks of P. G. Wodehouse stories. He was much too young at seven, but I already had a glow of anticipation as I planned to try them out on him when he was about ten and perhaps give him the lifetime of remembered pleasure that reading them as a boy has given me. So far he knew only two and a half lines of Shakespeare and, although I suppose only partially understood, their packed imagery had opened up worlds for him:

"The game's afoot:
Follow your spirit; and upon this charge
Cry 'God for Harry! England and St. George.' "

Then upon that charge he'd spring into action and, against all odds, firmly but chivalrously, put the French army to flight one more time.

When he was four years old, I had to go into the hospital for a heart operation, a valve replacement. It's routine nowadays, I was told.

Well, maybe, but to be on the safe side I cleared out a few drawers and wrote a note to everyone. I still have them. This is the one for Nicholas:

My dear little boy,

Saying good-bye is the hardest thing I've ever had to do, but Mummy will have told you that I had to go. I didn't want to leave, however, without letting you know that you have given me some of the happiest times of my life. Times like our long walks together in the mountains and along the beaches, the books we read at bedtime, and the stories we told about Puffer, the magic engine.

You've been a super little pal, and I know you will grow up to be a fine, upright man. Take care of Mummy.

Your loving
Daddy

But in the end it was he who gave me a lifetime of memories. One late fall day at a checkout counter in Canada, a few months before he died, he pointed to a 99-cent plastic holder for a razor and said, "Look, Daddy, wouldn't that be a good thing for you to have when you go away?" Those are the sort of things I don't have the foresight to do, putting up with rummaging for loose blades in the bottom of my wash bag, but it having been pointed out, I bought it. It was a good choice, and coming home after a trip I told him how useful it had been. He smiled with pleasure. Now I take it with me whenever I travel and on some early mornings, as I start to shave in a hotel far from home, a picture of that checkout line, clear in every detail, with twilight coming on and snow in the air, brings on a shiver of loneliness.

St. Teresa's cemetery is in a narrow, steep-sided valley. It has no buildings or fine inscriptions, no springy turf, no water. A simple cross nailed to the wooden double gate is as near as it gets to art. But

Maggie and I have always loved its simplicity. It's a place where the contemplation of life and death comes easily, Thomas Gray's country churchyard set in the West. Not being Catholic, however, it never crossed my mind that I would become a pilgrim there.

Now, every few days in the long dry season, we carry water up the steep concrete path—two gallons in each hand in milk containers, 130 paces from the gate, past the Gleasons and the Furlongs and into the Italian quarter, breathing hard at the end. Sometimes I see someone has been there recently watering the flowers, Donna Walter, perhaps, who lost two sons, one of whom is buried here.

I like to go there in the calm evenings when one side of the valley is in shadow and the other still warm with bright sunlight. The nearby hills are mostly bare, but with thick clusters of trees on the tops and along the watercourses. There are scarcely any buildings in sight. It is always peaceful.

Nicholas' picture is on his headstone and a few lines from the poem Wordsworth wrote about the six-year-old son of his friend, Samuel Coleridge:

> "Thou art a dewdrop, which the morn brings forth,
> Ill fitted to sustain unkindly shocks,
> Or to be trailed along the soiling earth;
> A gem that glitters while it lives,
> And no forewarning gives;
> But, at the touch of wrong, without a strife
> Slips in a moment out of life."

Maggie chose it, one of those things that stirred in the memory, and however many times I see it I think, "Yes, that was Nicholas and that is exactly what happened to him."

As I splash water from the containers on the dry earth, I feel as though I'm taking part in an age-old ritual. Sometimes I wash the headstone, very gently as I get to his face. If I'm alone, I may say a few words to him. I know he isn't there, but it's hard to resist the impulse when I look at his smile. And then, before I leave, I often say how much I miss him, if I can get the words out.

From the beginning, people have left things there, small toys, letters, coins, or whatever they had in their pockets. John Cooley, father of the Bodega Bay family our children always felt closest to, made a beautiful redwood bench and someone has fastened a bell to it. Recently, more chimes have appeared and even in the gentlest breeze they tinkle a welcome, like a child's voice. A toy pistol has been there for some time, not an appropriate gift it seems at first sight, but no doubt some small boy felt it was just what another small boy would want. From time to time, we find affectionate letters in Italian. At Halloween a young friend who hadn't forgotten this was Nicholas' favorite night left a pumpkin, carved into a face, complete with candles. Sometimes in the winter when the pelting rain comes in, I find myself wondering if he'll catch cold on that chilly slope.

On what would have been his ninth birthday, Eleanor and I lit a candle at twilight and put it on the grave. After she'd gone to bed, I felt the urge to go back, almost certain it would have blown out. At the gate my heart gave a leap. Through the blackness, high on the hillside, I could see a tiny point of light. The fog had rolled in, there wasn't a star to be seen, and all the sounds were muffled. A small animal rustled in the grass. Everything else was still. I sat on the bench, watching the warm light playing on his face and the shiny leaves of the rose bushes Maggie had planted. For a long time, there was nothing else in the world.

I'd always thought Nicholas would respond to the eternal flame. We have a photo of him in Paris looking gravely at the one on the tomb of France's unknown warrior. Now it was my turn to try to see eternity in fleeting life. But sitting there, and looking at that mound of earth, all that would come was the sense of an irreparable loss. As I got back to the car, however, I looked up and there in the encircling darkness, scarcely quivering, was that one delicate reminder of the unending power of love.

Chapter Twenty-Four

The End of the Road

All my adult life, I've been an agnostic. Since Nicholas died, I've thought harder than ever about this. What a comfort it would be to feel that one day we would be together again in some way. Being agnostic means recognizing that it is a possibility. Many people have written to us to say they see Nicholas as an angel or in the arms of God, and I can agree thus far: if there is a heaven, Nicholas has surely earned a place in it.

Unconvinced, however, I have to make do with whatever consolations I can find on earth. There are many of them. To have had him at all was against all likelihood. At an age when I should have been filling the role of grandfather, I was crawling under furniture looking for pacifiers. But in return I got a little friend who for seven years brought sunshine into every day.

All I know of life tells me how little I know of it and so how tentative all judgments have to be. I've never been attracted to big theories that come and go, are dominant for a time, unquestioned even, then simply discarded and in time begin to seem ludicrous. Yet at one time, people just like us believed in them as passionately as we believe in today's theories. So now, when I'm faced with drawing conclusions from what happened to Nicholas, I don't seek the answers in theories, but in small pieces of evidence I can rely on: the kindness of strangers, the efficacy of modern medicine, the superiority of truth over lies.

It's not as though death is a surprise. As Colin Dexter says, we are all moving toward it at the same speed of twenty-four hours a day. The idea of railing against it or beating the air with puny fists is manifestly futile. We already know the world is a hazardous place and full of random accidents. We expect our children to outlive us, but we can't be sure. Who is free of fear when a child doesn't come home on time?

So, when death strikes, it isn't as though the world has lost the meaning it had yesterday. It's our place in it that has changed. If you are a believer, you can't throw God away because he has failed to protect you, and if you have never believed, you can't turn to a God who will give life an explanation it didn't have before. Our beliefs evolve, certainly, but deathbed repentance is suspect, even when it is someone else's deathbed.

I was pleased to read Maggie's comment in an interview that I'd been tenacious in retaining my agnosticism. I'm equally pleased to see how little this whole affair has altered her views. No doubt her beliefs too will continue to evolve. But, as far as I can tell, her faith is neither significantly stronger nor weaker than it was. It's the mark of principles held by conviction rather than habit.

I believe too that, after all is said, every man is an island. No one, I think, can truly share our moments of exultation or despair. The islands, however, can be set either in a warm and pleasant sea that encourages contact or in a cold and hostile ocean. The response to what happened to us has strengthened my conviction that the environment around these islands is a good deal friendlier than is widely supposed. Hundreds and hundreds of people have written to us, offering whatever help they can, their voices clear and uplifting. I think of it as a benign form of global warming.

The slaughter of an innocent reminded people all over the world of the fragility of life, and hence the importance of living up, rather than down, to it. At the time, I said I imagined parents who heard the story giving their children an extra hug before they went off to school in the morning or reading an extra chapter with them at bedtime. If Nicholas were asked what would be the very best thing that could come out of all this, I bet that would be it.

The awards given to us have put him in the company of Mother Teresa and Walt Disney, St. Valentine and Pope John XXIII, Raoul

Wallenberg and Lambchop. Obviously we never fooled ourselves into believing his stature was in their league—he was there representing the power of childhood to transform the world. Nevertheless, when the history of the world comes to be written, I like to think Nicholas will be a shining footnote.

When we were planning our vacation to Italy, we played a game. In it, he was a Roman soldier returning after years of service on the frontiers—the Scottish border, Gaul, the Alps, all places where he'd seen evidence of the Roman Empire. Back in Rome you'll be treated like a hero, we told him. People will write poems about you, you'll be given gold medals, children will cheer when your name is mentioned.

It was just a game, but it all came true. With this difference, however: that Nicholas conquered not by the force of arms, but by love—and that, of course, is much stronger.

An Invitation

Please remember, the Nicholas effect continues whenever you make a response.

ORGAN DONATION

A wide variety of organizations provide information on organ and tissue donations.

- The American Association of Tissue Banks, (703) 827-9582, *http://www.aatb.org.*

- The American Red Cross Tissue Services, (888) 4-TISSUE, *http://www.redcross.org/tissue.*

- The Association of Organ Procurement Organizations, (703) 573-2676, *http://www.aopo.org.*

- The Children's Liver Alliance, *http://www.livertx.org.*

- Coalition on Donation, (800) 355-SHARE, *http://www.shareyourlife.org/.* The broad-based Coalition on Donation offers a free brochure, which you can order by calling the number above. This is a recorded announcement, but the brochure you receive will have on it the phone number of an organization in your area to contact for more information.

- The Division of Transplantation at the Department of Health and Human Services, (301) 443-7577, *http://www.organdonor.gov* and *http://www.hrsa.gov/osp/dot.*

- The Eye Bank Association of America, (202) 775-4999, *http://www.restoresight.org,* email: *sightebaa@aol.com.*

- The James Redford Institute for Transplant Awareness, (310) 441-4906, *http://www.jrifilms.org.*

- National Kidney Foundation, (800) 622-9010, *http://www.kidney. org.*

- The North American Transplant Coordinators Organization, (913) 492-3600, *http://www.natco1.org.*

- Transplant News, (800) 689-4262, 10 Rollins Road, Suite 106, Millbrae, CA 94030.

- Transplant Recipients International Organization, (800) 874-6386, *http://www.trioweb.org.*

- TransWeb, *http://www.transweb.org.*

- The United Network for Organ Sharing, (800) 292-9547, *http:// www.unos.org.*

THE FAMILY PLEDGE

The First Family Pledge is managed by the American Society of Transplant Surgeons. Family members sign the pledge after discussion, to indicate to the rest of the family their intention to donate organs. A copy of the pledge is on the next page. You can get more information by calling the society toll-free at (800) 848-8836 or by visiting the web site at *http://www.familypledge.org.* You can also register your pledge online.

Every family hopes that if a loved one becomes seriously ill, medical science will be able to provide a miracle—and restore a husband or wife, son or daughter, brother or sister, mother or father, to a healthy and rewarding life.

Medical science has been able to do exactly that over the past decade for hundreds of thousands of families with loved ones suffering from disease and injuries that affect the heart, kidney, pancreas, lungs, liver, or tissues.

Transplantation of organs and tissues has become one of the most remarkable success stories in medicine, now giving tens of thousands of desperately ill Americans a new chance at life each year—and returning them to the love of their families.

But sadly, this medical miracle is not yet available to all in need. Waiting lists are growing more rapidly than the number of organs and tissues being donated.

Just as we would hope, in times of crisis, that the miracle of a gift that could save or greatly enhance the life of a loved one would be available to our family, we want to pledge to make this same miracle available to others.

Therefore, we hereby sign the First Family Pledge, agreeing to talk about the importance of organ and tissue donation with our loved ones, and pledge with them to make this gift available, if medically acceptable, in the event of a family member's death.

And in hopes of encouraging other families to join us in this affirmation of love and life, we hereby add our names to the public roster of those taking the First Family Pledge. Pledge signers will be listed on the Internet at *http://www.familypledge.org* as testament to the growing public support for donation. The pledge is not a legally binding document.

SIGNED _____   DATE _____

SIGNED _____   DATE _____

SIGNED _____   DATE _____

SIGNED _____   DATE _____

Copyright © 1999. Reprinted with permission of the American Society of Transplant Surgeons.